# EROS UNVEILED

# EROS UNVEILED

## Plato and the God of Love

CATHERINE OSBORNE

CLARENDON PRESS · OXFORD

1994

*Oxford University Press, Walton Street, Oxford* OX2 6DP
*Oxford New York*
*Athens Auckland Bangkok Bombay*
*Calcutta Cape Town Dar es Salaam Delhi*
*Florence Hong Kong Istanbul Karachi*
*Kuala Lumpur Madras Madrid Melbourne*
*Mexico City Nairobi Paris Singapore*
*Taipei Tokyo Toronto*
*and associated companies in*
*Berlin Ibadan*

*Oxford is a trade mark of Oxford University Press*

*Published in the United States*
*by Oxford University Press Inc., New York*

*British Library Cataloguing in Publication Data*
*Data available*

*Library of Congress Cataloging in Publication Data*
*Eros unveiled : Plato and the God of love / Catherine Osborne.*
*Includes bibliographical references and index.*
*1. Love. 2. Philosophy, Ancient. 3. Philosophy, Medieval.*
*I. Title.*
*BD436.082 1994 128'.4—dc20 94–15728*
*ISBN 0-19-826761-4*

1 3 5 7 9 10 8 6 4 2

*Typeset by Selwood Systems, Midsomer Norton*
*Printed in Great Britain on acid-free paper by*
*Bookcraft (Bath) Ltd., Midsomer Norton*

*For Michael and Margaret Rowett*

# PREFACE

It is fortunate, I suppose, that philosophy, as a subject, does not have any hesitation in treading on territory that belongs to a variety of different subjects, and claiming to be able to say something worth hearing. That fact seems to lend some credibility to my claim to have written a book on the subject of love, and that it falls into some recognizable field, despite its concern with a topic that respects no boundaries of disciplines. Philosophers, it seems, are entitled to reflect on the assumptions that we make in our talk of love over a whole variety of contexts, and to unravel the confusions that arise from misconstruing that talk, as we are occasionally wont to do. That is part of what I set out to do in this book, and as such it is a book that pretends to the title 'philosophy'.

There will be many who say, however, that this is not a philosopher's book. The texts that it chooses to look at are some of them examples of philosophy and some not; but that is unimportant. What I do with them is sometimes philosophical and frequently not; some of it (not much) is historical, some of it detailed literary analysis, and a lot of it is theology, in the broadest sense in which that can include reflection on discourse about the divine both within the Christian tradition and according to the norms accepted by Ancient Greek philosophical theology. So the result is a varied sort of agglomeration of things. If that is a complaint, which I hope it is not, it will be perfectly correct. The book reflects my enthusiasms of the past ten years, and during that time my interests and concerns have taken a variety of turns in response to the life of the scholarly communities I have found myself in, the books I have read, the papers I have heard. It would be surprising, perhaps, if that were not so. But I do not think it is necessary to apologize for the variety; I hope that the theological reflections will be better for the insights gained from philosophical material, and perhaps the reverse may occasionally prove true too.

The book is also, in one sense, incomplete. I have left out the thinkers before Plato. I have left out everyone after Aquinas, except for rather selective mentions of recent work. Between Plato and Aquinas there are huge gaps, and even some important texts of

Plato and Augustine are scarcely mentioned. Anyone looking for a history of a chronological sort should look elsewhere. My point here is to explore the questions and ideas that emerge for us in considering how some texts, the ones I have chosen as rich material for my theme, handle the notion of love. Some of them are responding to each other, and hence they show us the interplay of thinkers dealing with the same questions or different questions in relation to the same texts. But my point is not to trace who said what when, but why it makes sense to say one thing rather than another. For that purpose completeness is not achieved by a thorough historical survey but by a critical handling of some relevant texts, and that is what I aim to offer here.

# ACKNOWLEDGEMENTS

I have benefited from comments from many friends and fellow-scholars, debts which I have not recorded in detail in the individual chapters but which have made a great difference, sometimes to the accuracy of what I say, sometimes to the style in which I say it. The whole manuscript was read by John Dillon, who has helpfully sent me copies of his own work when relevant to my theme, and by another reader appointed by the Press. On Chapters 1 and 2 I received extensive comments from John Ackrill while he was overseeing my research when I was in Oxford. In connection with Chapter 2 I learnt about the characteristics of Hebrew and Aramaic languages from Sebastian Brock, Martin Goodman, and Richard Resnick. Chapter 3 is a revised version of a paper I gave some years ago to the Patristic seminar in Cambridge, when I first became interested in this topic. I owe some of my points to the contributions of Christopher Stead and John Procopé on that occasion, and some to Andrew Louth, who joined me in discussing the same topic at a meeting of the St Theosevia centre in Oxford.

The chapter on Plato's *Symposium* is based on papers I read to the Southern Association for Ancient Philosophy in 1989, and to the Warwick University Philosophy and Literature Society. I am grateful to C. C. W. Taylor, Andrew Barker, and Lucinda Coventry for comments and to John Dillon, who sent me a copy of his 1969 article.

Chapter 5 is based on a paper that I read to the Welsh Philosophical Society in 1991. Chapter 6 has been presented to three previous audiences: the Oxford Philological Society, the Philosophical Society at the University College of Swansea, and a seminar at Sheffield University department of philosophy. Chapter 8 was once a paper that I read to the Cambridge Patristic seminar, and subsequently to the Eastern Christian Studies seminar in Oxford. On each occasion there was an excellent discussion. I am aware that I have not done justice to these discussions in the final revision.

Two of the chapters include work that has been previously published as follows: Chapter 7 is a slightly revised version of 'Neoplatonism and the Love of God in Origen', *Origeniana Quinta*, R. Daly (ed.), Louvain, 1992, Peeters; and part of Chapter 9 is based on 'The *nexus amoris* in Augustine's Trinity', *Studia Patristica*, E. Livingstone (ed.), Louvain, 1990, Peeters. I am grateful to Peeters Publishers for permission to include this material again. The latter article also appeared in a Spanish translation in *Augustinus*. I must also thank H. Pietras for sending me his book, and many at the Origen colloquium whom I have not thanked individually for their contributions to my argument in Chapter 7. The other parts of Chapter 9 are based on a paper that I read to the history of philosophy seminar at the Warburg Institute in London.

Academic research can be a rather solitary pursuit, but the greatest joy is in sharing the task with others. During the writing of this book I have moved from one academic community to another, but in each I have most appreciated the chance to share my ideas and to learn from friends and colleagues. Rowan and Jane Williams were in Cambridge when I started this work; they were in Oxford when I was in Oxford, and Priory house was the place where most of the central chapters of this book came to birth; and they joined me in Wales shortly after I took up my post in Swansea. Many other colleagues have also been a source of inspiration and criticism during this time. I must mention in particular Christopher Stead, Geoffrey Lloyd, M. M. McCabe, Anthony Grayling, Andrew Louth, Sarah Coakley, Ian Tipton, Ieuan Williams, Ossie Hanfling, and Dick Beardsmore. I should like to thank all these friends, and others whom I have not mentioned who will no doubt find their influence traceable somewhere between these covers.

The practical side of my studies have been supported during the last nine years by a Research Fellowship at New Hall in Cambridge, a British Academy Post-Doctoral Fellowship, a Senior Research Fellowship at St Anne's College in Oxford, and my present post at the University College of Swansea in the University of Wales. Most of all, though, life is made possible by my husband Robin, and my patient and long-suffering children, Elizabeth and Anna-Magdalena. The fact that I have written a book on this subject is something to do with who I am; and that I owe first to my parents and to a home-life full of love and beauty and the finest aspirations; so it is to my parents that I dedicate the book.

CATHERINE OSBORNE

*Swansea*
*December 1993*

# CONTENTS

# ABBREVIATIONS

CCL            Corpus Christianorum, series latina

DK             H. Diels and W. Kranz, *Die Fragmente der Vorsokratiker*, sixth edition (Berlin, 1951)

GCS           Die Griechische Christlichen Schriftsteller der ersten Jahrhunderte (Akademie-Verlag, Berlin)

Long and Sedley    A. A. Long and D. N. Sedley, *The Hellenistic Philosophers*, vols. 1 and 2 (Cambridge, 1987)

SC             Sources Chrétiennes (Les Éditions du cerf, Paris)

SVF           H. von Arnim, *Stoicorum Veterum Fragmenta* (Stuttgart, 1903–5)

Works frequently cited in the notes are abbreviated as follows:

Origen:

| | |
|---|---|
| *CCels* | *Contra Celsum* |
| *ComCt* | *Commentary on the Song of Songs* |
| *ComJn* | *Commentary on John* |
| *ComMt* | *Commentary on Matthew* |
| *FragmMt* | *Fragments on Matthew* |
| *HomEzek* | *Homilies on Ezekiel* |
| *HomJr* | *Homilies on Jeremiah* |
| *PArch* | *On First Principles* |
| *PEuch* | *On Prayer* |

Gregory of Nyssa:

| | |
|---|---|
| *De an. et res.* | *De anima et resurrectione* |
| *HomCt* | *Homilies on the Song of Songs* |

Dionysius the Areopagite:

| | |
|---|---|
| *CH* | *Celestial Hierarchy* |
| *DN* | *Divine Names* |
| *EH* | *Ecclesiastical Hierarchy* |

Thomas Aquinas:

| | |
|---|---|
| *Summa Theol* | *Summa Theologiae* |
| *Summa CG* | *Summa Contra Gentes* |

Aristotle:

| | |
|---|---|
| *NE* | *Nicomachean Ethics* |

# NOTE ON EDITIONS AND TRANSLATIONS

Unless otherwise specified, all translations, other than biblical ones, are my own throughout. For biblical quotations I have generally followed the RSV in accordance with standard scholarly practice, but because the RSV tends to resolve the ambiguities in phrases I am discussing it has been necessary to alter it in some cases. I have indicated the reasons in the footnotes, and have generally inserted the equivalent phrase from the AV, which is a closer rendering of the Greek. The result is more cluttered but less archaic than if I had simply given the AV throughout.

Page references in Origen's *Commentary on the Song of Songs* are to the edition by W. A. Baehrens, OC, GCS, vol. 33 (Leipzig, 1925). Gregory of Nyssa's *Homilies on the Song of Songs* are cited according to the edition by H. Langerbeck, Gregorii Nysseni Opera vol. vi (Leiden, 1960), and references are given to pages of Migne, *Patrologia Graeca*. The page references to Anselm's *Monologion* are to vol. i of *S. Anselmi cantuarensis archiepiscopi opera omnia*, ed. F. S. Schmitt OSB (Edinburgh, 1946).

# I

# The Bow in the Clouds

## 1. INTRODUCTION: LOVE IN CHRISTIAN THOUGHT

Love, if thou dost direct thy darts in equal numbers to both sides,
then thou art a god;
but if thou art partial in thy shooting,
then art thou not a god.

Rufinus, Greek Anthology, 5. 97.

It has sometimes been suggested that Christianity has a special interest in love, and that the discourse of love takes on a new dimension in the formative years of earliest Christian thought. At this period, as never before, it might be claimed, love emerges as a way to describe the relationship between God and humanity. Furthermore, the significance of this paradigm-shift, if it is a paradigm-shift, can be seen to extend through the subsequent history of Christianity with more or less dramatic repercussions.

No one, however, could plausibly claim that love, as a phenomenon, has no history prior to its discovery by the founder, or founders, of Christianity; of course men, women, and gods loved and were loved before Christ, and so likewise the discourse by which they described or communicated their feelings not only pre-existed Christianity but was also subject to change and development over many centuries before Christianity inherited it. The Classical poets of Greece and Rome had been writing of love in its tragic and comic forms; mythology told of passionate affairs of gods and heroes; in Judaism likewise the scriptures included songs of love, and dwelt on the loving-kindness of God. And philosophy, from Plato or earlier, had used the terminology of love to describe our devotion to the search for wisdom: the philosopher was a lover (*philos*) of wisdom (*sophia*). For Plato this was not a dead metaphor.[1]

---

[1] The term *philosophos* was apparently used by Heraclitus (6th to 5th cent. BC), according to Clement of Alexandria, *Stromateis*, 5. 140. 5, Heraclitus, DK fr. B35. It is Plato who gives it its subsequent meaning, but it is clear that for Plato the love

What, then, is new about the love that makes its appearance in the New Testament? Not the words, for they had clearly been around for years. It is true that the term *agape* is prominent in the New Testament[2] whereas it had been employed only relatively rarely in Classical Greek literature;[3] but *agape* and the verb *agapao* were the words used for love in the Septuagint translation of the Old Testament, and naturally the New Testament writers would be influenced in their choice of vocabulary for writing in Greek by the vocabulary of the Greek version of the Hebrew Scriptures.

Thus the terminology of love was not new, but came steeped in tradition from the Jewish, and to a lesser extent from the pagan Greek, world.[4] Moreover it is not at all clear that the usage or context in which the terms turn up in the New Testament has dramatically changed: many of the occasions where love is mentioned, particularly in the Gospels, are direct quotations of the Old Testament. Doubtless Jesus too, along with his disciples and

implied by *philo-* was real. At *Republic* 475b he describes the philosopher as one with a passion for wisdom (*sophias epithumetes*).

[2] Anders Nygren, whose work on *Agape and Eros* is the classic treatment of the claim that Christian love is something dramatically different from all that had gone before, uses a technical terminology to specify the difference. For him the word *agape* stands for the authentic brand of love proper to Christianity, while *eros* is an intruder. He does not claim that the word '*agape*' had never been used before, nor that it carries its technical meaning at every occurrence, even in the NT. *Agape* serves as Nygren's *modern* term, and can translate a number of other terms in the Greek, such as *philia, philanthropia*. Nygren's thesis does not *depend* on the use of a new word in early Christianity, though in fact he does assign importance to the use of *agape* rather than *eros* in the New Testament, especially St Paul. See A. Nygren, *Agape and Eros*, English translation by Philip S. Watson of *Den kristna kärlekstanken*, 1930 (Chicago, 1953), esp. 33, 113–15.

[3] The claim that *agape* is rare in Classical Greek is only partially true. The noun (*agape*) is probably unknown before the third century AD outside Jewish and Christian contexts (see, for example, S. West, 'A Further Note on ΑΓΑΠΗ in P. Oxy. 1380', *Journal of Theological Studies*, 20 (1969), 228–30). Its appearance several times in the Septuagint is thus slightly peculiar. But the verb (*agapao*, I love) is not particularly uncommon in Classical literature, but is used from Homer onwards, in prose and verse, including several times in Plato. It is also pretty common in the Septuagint. In the New Testament the verb is marginally more common than the noun, but the Pauline Epistles are peculiar for having the noun more often than the verb. On this more below, Ch. 2, and see J. Barr, 'Words for Love in Biblical Greek', in L. D. Hurst and N. T. Wright (eds.), *The Glory of Christ in the New Testament* (Oxford, 1987), 3–18.

[4] I find it most plausible that the choice of *agape* and *agapao* words in the NT, rather than other love vocabulary, reflects the usage of the Septuagint. Others have argued that it is due neither to the LXX nor to theological concerns at all: see R. Joly, *Le Vocabulaire chrétien de l'amour: est-il original?* (Brussels, 1968); and C. C. Tarelli, 'ΑΓΑΠΗ', *Journal of Theological Studies*, NS 1 (1950), 64–7.

contemporaries, gained not only his vocabulary, but the categories and concepts that went with it, from his Jewish milieu. It seems naïve to the modern scholar, trained in anthropology or literary criticism, to suppose that Christianity sprang fully-fledged, wholly new and absolutely without ancestry, into a world both unsuspecting and unprepared, whether we mean by Christianity what Jesus himself said and did or what his followers wrote and taught.

Anders Nygren, when writing his famous study of Agape and Eros in 1930,[5] was able to assume the total discontinuity of the Christian notion of love with anything that went before; doubtless his work belonged to his time and the climate of scholarly opinion then, though the tendency, or even perhaps the desire, to underestimate the Jewish ancestry of the earliest themes in Christianity is nothing new. Nygren's project was to identify a pure and original Christian motif, unadulterated by influence from either Classical Greek thought or Hellenistic Judaism. The same project today would not expect to find things so clear cut: we should look for the novelty and dynamism of Christian thought on love not so much in discontinuity with earlier themes but in the redeployment or reworking of what was handed down in the tradition.

This is not to say that there was nothing new in Christianity. Christianity was not, in the New Testament period, and certainly is not now, identical with Judaism either then or now, just as it is not identical with Hellenistic or Classical Greek philosophy or religion. Paradigm-shifts, if there are paradigm-shifts, must perhaps be initiated at some time and place; or, if not initiated, then perhaps they may require a catalyst: someone with the vision to propose a new way of seeing an old problem. In this way we might find a role for Jesus (the historical figure of the first century AD) or St Paul as significant, or indeed indispensable, for the subsequent development and widespread adoption of a new outlook and value system. Nevertheless, even if we ascribe such a seminal role to Jesus and St Paul, we should still not expect that the revolution would be complete and perfect at its *first* appearance; rather experience suggests that the full implications will only emerge over time as subsequent thinkers take up the idea and put it to the test.

An analogy from the history of science may be helpful: this one happens to be familiar to me, but doubtless others would be equally

---

[5] Nygren, *Agape and Eros*.

relevant. Galileo and Newton might normally be identified as key figures in a scientific revolution that transformed medieval thought into what we now know as modern science. Certain specific doctrines can be attributed to them that changed the way people expected physical bodies to behave. However, we should be far from the truth if we claimed that modern physics was perfected by Newton; even what we might call Newtonian physics was not presented on a plate all in one go.

But equally it would be inaccurate to suppose that the ideas put forward by Newton and Galileo were wholly original and had no previous ancestry. Impetus-theory, for example, which becomes basic to Galileo's theory of dynamics, can be traced back to the work of Philoponus in the sixth century AD. Thus it is Philoponus' challenge to accepted Aristotelian doctrine that could be said to initiate a change in outlook that was fully worked out and influential only centuries later.[6]

Scientific revolutions may not be wholly comparable with religious ones;[7] but it is only on a very simple-minded view of Jesus's place in history and of the manner in which God would interact with the world at, during, and after the Incarnation, that we should suppose that authentic Christian teaching would reside only in the very earliest documents closest to Jesus himself (or indeed in some pure reconstruction of the 'true facts' behind those documents[8]) and that any subsequent development is bound to be corruption of the pure truth, a decline from the original insight. On the contrary we should expect the significance of a new outlook to be worked out only gradually with time, and that interpretation and reinterpretation would form an essential part of that process.

---

[6] On this subject see R. Sorabji (ed.), *Philoponus and the Rejection of Aristotelian Science* (London, 1987).

[7] Such comparisons easily become absurd, as when this or that development in Christianity is frequently said to amount to a 'Copernican Revolution' as though the analogy were helpful. In any case we need not suppose that the so-called Copernican Revolution really amounted to any significant paradigm-shift: see Peter Barker and Bernard R. Goldstein, 'The Rôle of Comets in the Copernican Revolution', *Studies in History and Philosophy of Science*, 19 (1988), 299–319.

[8] The project of reconstructing the historical facts has preoccupied theology for many years, and is neatly summed up in J. Bowden, *Jesus: The Unanswered Questions* (London, 1988); its bankruptcy does nothing to undermine the credentials of the New Testament and subsequent tradition as the basis of Christianity.

## 2. WORDS AND MEANINGS: AFTER THE NEW TESTAMENT

Of course it might be possible, unless we have a very firm trust in the infallibility of the Church, to argue that reinterpretation might result in retrograde steps as well as, or instead of, positive contributions. A reactionary thinker, meeting and attempting to assimilate an unfamiliar concept, may effectively transform it back into what she already knew and undermine its novelty. Thus Nygren might have a case if he were arguing that such a reversion took place when thinkers after the New Testament assimilated the notion of love adumbrated there; if his claim were that what they then offered as Christian doctrine was in all respects identical to Classical models, or effectively so, then we might agree that they had failed to take on board the novelty of what the New Testament had to say. But that claim would not wash, and it is not what Nygren actually demonstrates, even if it is what he would like to show. To support such a claim it is not sufficient to show that Classical ideas lie in the background, or that traces of them may be found in the way Patristic texts develop the theme; it would, after all, be remarkable if the influence of Classical culture did not show. What matters is whether the result is a positive contribution to the understanding of Christian doctrine, or merely a direct reversion to familiar pagan ways of thinking. It seems to me more plausible to argue that it is the fruitful juxtaposition of Greek and Hebrew traditions that leads to creative development, including, perhaps, the very first stages whereby the term *agape* achieves prominence in the New Testament writings.

Thus we need not suppose that the definitive account of the Christian idea of love must be the earliest one. Nor need it be the one that corresponds most closely to what Jesus himself said.[9]

The word used for love in the New Testament is not a new word, nor is it a word without a rich history. It follows that if we are to claim that something new is being said about love in the New Testament and later writings, what matters is not the word used but what it means and does. In exactly the same way in subsequent literature on the subject, when terms not found in the New Testament are introduced (such as *eros*, for example), again we must

[9] This is not quite the same thing as to say what Jesus himself *did*. But it should be clear that temporal proximity does not determine the degree to which any text (spoken, written, or lived) reflects the teaching or 'message' of Christ.

expect that they will be old words with a rich history, and that
they will therefore import implications that may differ from those
associated with the biblical terms.[10] This, however, is not sufficient
to condemn a term as inappropriate: what matters is not the word
used but what it means and what it does in the new context; and
what is more, it is not necessary to show that what it means and
does is effectively identical to what New Testament writers were
doing with *their* term. We should look rather for development of a
positive and creative nature, asking not whether a writer accurately
reproduces New Testament teaching, but whether he extends it in
a helpful and acceptable direction.

It will be clear by now why this study will not be concerned to
explore the concept of love, or different sorts of love, let alone to
develop a contrast between love as presented in Greek thought and
the love envisaged in Christianity.[11] My questions focus instead
on the role played by love in particular texts (no matter what
terminology they use): who is the lover, who the beloved, why they
love, and what that means about their relationship. For this we do
not require a notion of the 'pure Christian love' against which to
measure any particular example of love, and perhaps find it wanting.
On the contrary we might find the notion, or concept, of love was
identical in two cases but unsatisfactory or helpful depending on
how it was applied and to whom. I shall not be quick to dismiss a
text simply because it is out of line with the New Testament or
some other authority, without first pressing it for philosophical or
theological insights. Charity does not rejoice at wrong but rejoices
in the right: on the principle of charity I shall be concerned not to
identify failings in a writer's thought on love, but to locate its
strengths and acknowledge its value where it has value.

---

[10] Where the New Testament does not use a particular term (as *eros*) or uses it
only very rarely, it need not follow that it is avoiding it on purpose. Even if it were
avoided in the New Testament it would not follow that it could never be right to
use it in another text; indeed, to use a term previously avoided might be true to the
same spirit in another context.

[11] Vincent Brümmer, *The Model of Love* (Cambridge, 1993), though otherwise
sensitive to some of the inadequacies of previous work on the subject, still starts by
adopting and developing categories of love on the lines of C. S. Lewis's 'need-
love' and 'gift-love', which leave us stuck in the motivational contrasts Nygren so
disastrously proposed.

## 3. WHAT IS LOVE?

That is not love,
if one wants to possess the one with beautiful looks,
on the advice of sober eyes.
No, it's the one who sees someone unshapely, and loves dearly,
pierced through with arrows, burning from crazed wits,
this is love, this is the fire.
The beauties are equally delightful
to everyone capable of discerning good looks.

> Marcus Argentarius, Greek Anthology, 5.89.

In this is love, not that we loved God, but that he loved us and
sent his son to be the expiation for our sins.

> 1 John 4: 10.

The questions I shall be asking in this book can be summed up in
a simple formula: who loves whom, and for what? Asking these
questions will not be easy if we do not first clarify some areas of
our normal discourse on love that are either ambiguous or merely
vague. Our first task must therefore be to clarify the terms we shall
be using and explore the problem areas at a more general level.
This is not to imply that texts that use the terms ambiguously
should be tidied up to give a single sense, but rather to provide the
tools with which we may analyse the texts when we come to read
them.

### (i) *I and thou*

Love presupposes a relationship between two or more parties.[12] It
is conventional to analyse these in terms of lover and beloved. Even
though love may be reciprocated we may still analyse each side of
the relationship in terms of a loving subject relating to a beloved
object.

### *(a) Who loves whom?*

Does it matter who the lover and beloved are? Some might be

---

[12] See below Ch. 2, sect. (iii) (c).

inclined to answer no, on the grounds that love is no respecter of persons. Who it is that I love surely need not affect whether, or how, I love him, her, or it. But this answer may seem over-hasty, and indeed it is this question of who loves whom that will occupy us throughout this book; for however much we might doubt whether the status of the loving subject or the beloved object could determine the character of the love in question, the fact remains that the vast majority of writers on love have classified various types of love, and judged their worth, according to their subjects and objects. Thus for Aristotle there is a completely different class of relationship between those of unequal status such as God and man, ruler and subject, father and son, benefactor and beneficiary, and so on, as opposed to the type of relationship between equals, even though both count as kinds of friendship or *philia*.[13] Similarly for Nygren the fact that God is inherently desirable and attractive means that we cannot have agape for God, properly speaking; he can only be an object of desire;[14] and for C. S. Lewis we have 'Need-love', not 'Gift-love' for mothers and God.[15] The status of the object apparently determines the nature of the love, so that, in C. S. Lewis's analysis again, we will have one sort of love for the old gardener and another for a wealthy patron, one for the nanny who nursed us through babyhood and another for the tramp at the gate.[16]

This may seem like a caricature, and indeed it would probably be more fair to these writers, who classify love according to the beloved object, to take these objects as merely examples and illustrations, indicating the likely *motivation* of a particular relationship with a typical instance rather than some necessary implication of the relative status of lover and beloved; our love for a nanny who supplies our needs *illustrates*, they might say, a love motivated by needs, by giving a typical or familiar instance; thus the classification by object collapses into a classification by motivation, like that of

---

[13] e.g. Aristotle, *Eudemian Ethics*, 7. 1238b15–40. The sense in which Aristotle speaks of *philia* is not exactly that of love, nor is he concerned with emotions or feelings, but he is speaking of relationships that involve friendly behaviour. See Ch. 6.

[14] Nygren, *Agape and Eros*, 125–6, 213. Compare M. C. D'Arcy, *The Mind and Heart of Love* (London, 1945; 2nd edn. London, 1954); his analysis starts from language, rather than the objects of love. This is subsequently undercut, p. 48.

[15] C. S. Lewis, *The Four Loves* (London, 1960), 7–9.

[16] Ibid. 34–5.

Aristotle's types of friendship.[17] But it is easy to slip from illustrations and descriptions into generalization and prescription, by taking what are merely typical as necessary and universal. Clearly we must be careful: because a benefactor *might* be loved for the sake of the benefits she supplies, need it follow that that can be the only motivation for the beneficiary to love her? Need it even be a motive at all? Ultimately I want to suggest that such an analysis in terms of motives is misleading; although it has a place in Aristotle's analysis of friendship, that is because Aristotle's analysis is not an analysis of love.

However, it is plain that most thinkers have taken for granted the idea that love can be analysed and classified on the basis of the needs, desires, or motives that give rise to it. Even if that kind of analysis or classification is ill-founded, yet it is influential, and we shall have to look at what it has to offer. Can the claims about the classification of love stand up, even on their own terms? At present we shall be concerned with the relationship between God and humanity, as this appears to be a context in which theories of love frequently prescribe how God can, or must, love us and how we can, or must, love God.

## (b) God and humankind

If we try to place God and humanity in a relationship of love where one is lover and the other beloved we are likely to start by comparing the two in terms of superiority and inferiority or dependence and independence: the great and the splendid compared with the weak and the feeble:

| *God* | *humankind* |
|---|---|
| divine | human |
| immortal | mortal |
| great | insignificant |
| powerful | weak |

[17] The main division within Aristotle's analysis of *philia* is concerned with three kinds of friendship dependent on the motives (for pleasure, for profit, or for the good), a division which is to some degree independent of the kind of partner involved, though certain motives seem to be considered more common with certain kinds of partner, and the perfect kind of friendship is impossible with any but a good person. See Ch. 6.

| high | lowly |
| mighty | feeble |

The lists could go on and on. It appears that in all respects we are lacking where God is well-supplied. There is nothing that God really lacks where we are in a position to supply that lack; nor, perhaps, is there much that we lack that God could not supply. Thus, presented with a dichotomy of acquisitive versus generous love, we might find ourselves committed to the conclusion that, since God cannot reasonably look to gain, but only to give, by loving mankind, his love could only be generous, and conversely, since we cannot hope to give to God but can hope to gain, such love as we have for God must be acquisitive.

This, however, is inadequate for three reasons. First, it is insufficiently nuanced, in that it fails to take account of the Fall and Incarnation in altering the merit attributable to humanity. Secondly, it fails to consider whether the actual possibility of gaining benefit, or supplying real needs, is relevant to whether the motivation for love is the desire to gain such benefits or supply such needs, either as the dominant motive or even a motive at all. And thirdly, it overlooks the possibility that we are building in a demand for respectability on the part of God, which requires justification if it is to be adopted.

The second of these issues will come up again in more detail in a later chapter.[18] It is on the basis of human analogies that we shall be able to suggest that God *could* love his feeble creatures in the hope of a return that he could not in reality expect, and perhaps equally important, that those creatures do not have to love God merely for his benefits, even if God does happen to bestow benefits, but might equally love with a desire to give, or to serve, even if God has no need of such service.[19]

### (c)  The Fall and Redemption

The first issue outlined above is important. If the love between God and humankind is a relation, and the relations between God and humankind are subject to change in respect of the Fall and the Incarnation, are we to suppose that God's love for humankind changes, or our love for God, or both, or neither? If the relative

---

[18] See below, Ch. 3.
[19] Cf. Plato, *Euthyphro*, 12d–14b.

merit or status of the beloved substantially affects the character or type of love, it seems that God's love must differ according to whether we are considering humanity in its original prelapsarian state, or in its fallen nature. It is arguable that it is only in our fallen state that we would be wholly unlovely; so unlovely as to be the object of a love that *could* not be motivated by any beauty or attractiveness in the beloved, but must be purely generous. Consider the following scheme:

| Prelapsarian humanity | Fallen humanity | Humanity restored in Christ |
| --- | --- | --- |
| sinless | sinful | cleansed from sin |
| created good | goodness lost | goodness restored |
| worthy of life | worthy of death | worthy of life |
| in the image of God | distorted image | image restored |
| creatures | creatures | 'sons' |

Clearly humanity before the Fall, being a creature of God, does not surpass God in beauty: relative to God the creatures must be less beautiful; but we are not to suppose them by nature unlovely or distasteful to their creator. Thus, although God's love would be for something less good and lovely than himself, nevertheless he should find the beloved object good and lovely. Should this mean that his love for prelapsarian humanity must have been *less generous* than his love for fallen humanity? Of course it might seem harder to love, or to go on loving, what ceases to be beautiful and good; but that need not mean that the love for what was beautiful and lovely was selfish or motivated by acquisitive desire, or grasping or ungenerous, or less love than the love for the less lovely.[20] Evidently it cannot be the case that our sinful and weak nature is a necessary condition for God's love to be generous and full.

The same is even more true of God's love for humanity restored in Christ. Here humankind is not merely restored to the former loveliness of Adam and Eve before the Fall, but is incorporated into God's own Son himself, with a Grace that is no mere created beauty. Whereas Adam's loveliness was the goodness and beauty of a creature, in Christ humanity is raised to an unprecedented communion with God. If God finds humanity lovely then, it will be his own loveliness, the loveliness of his own beloved Son, that

---

[20] See below, sect. (ii), on quantifying love.

he finds there. So must God's love for humanity in the redeemed state actually be self-love? In some sense, yes.

### (d) Grace

If, on the one hand, we claim that God's love for a redeemed humanity is for an object that he finds both beautiful and good, it need not follow that his love is motivated by a desire to acquire that good. No such conclusion will follow for two reasons: first that we cannot infer the motives of the lover simply from the desirability of the beloved object; that one might desire such an object is clear; that any particular lover does desire it, or that he loves for no other reason than a desire to possess or acquire what good the object has to offer, does not follow. Secondly, the fact that the goodness and beauty that supposedly belongs to the beloved object in this case derives its origin from the lover himself affects the way in which such love could be considered acquisitive. Even supposing that we were inclined to consider that God's love might be motivated by his appreciation of and desire for humanity's new-found beauty, nevertheless that would need to be classified as acquisitive only in a reduced sense. Humanity gains that beauty by a gift of Grace, and that Grace is God's own gift to give. Thus he cannot be seeking to acquire something that he lacks, nor something that he never had before or would be otherwise unable to acquire.[21]

Thus for the first reason it does not follow that God's love need be acquisitive rather than generous; for the second reason it would not make sense to classify it as simply acquisitive, given that the beauty of the beloved was his own in the first place. On the other hand, while we may deny that God's love is motivated by a prospect of gaining something he lacks, we should not infer that he does not appreciate or enjoy the loveliness of his creatures. There seems to be a distinction between (a) perceiving an object as beautiful, (b) taking pleasure in the fact that it is beautiful, (c) loving an object that happens to be beautiful, (d) loving the object only because it is beautiful, and (e) loving the object only in order to possess its beauty. It is possible to deny that the last two would be a satisfactory account of God's love, and yet not deny that the first three are perfectly acceptable. Thus if the object of God's love is, in this case,

---

[21] Cf. Augustine, *Enarratio in Psalmos*, 144. 11: 'et ipsa tua merita illius dona sunt.'

beautiful, we need not infer that his love is acquisitive or less generous, nor need we suppose that he would prefer an object of less beauty, in order that his love might be more generous (or, indeed, in order that he might love at all, if, as with some thinkers, one were to say that love is only possible if directed towards the unfortunate).[22] It seems absurd to deny that God might seek or enjoy the beauty of his creation, but equally foolish to suggest that his 'motives' for doing so would be ungenerous or 'selfish'.

We are led, then, to recognize that simply counting the worth of the object of love will never be sufficient to enable us to classify its motivation or its aim. While it might seem that selfish love is impossible if there is nothing actually to be gained from the beloved object, the fact that the reverse is clearly not true—one may love a fine object without seeking to gain thereby—may lead us to question whether the former is true either. Clearly it is nonsense to say that there is a motivation for love that is determined by what the object is actually like. We might say, then, that the character of the love was influenced by what the lover *sees* in the beloved, but that immediately shows that it cannot indicate that the love is motivated by generous or selfish aims. One might idealize the beloved, or see in her good points that others might not see; but the fact that one sees her in that light is an attitude of love, and hence cannot be what originates or motivates the love. So far from indicating that a desire to possess those goods motivates that love in the first place, it seems to preclude such a motive. It may be *because* A loves B that she sees her as beautiful and lovely (when to another she does not seem so).

If the status of the object of love is taken to be significant, it should follow that it is important to clarify whether the object of God's love is humankind in its fallen state or not. Yet the question is rarely raised. It is not only recent or post-Reformation thinkers who start from the premiss that humanity is by nature entirely unlovely and rotten; the same tendency has sometimes been found in Augustine.[23] This assumption is justifiable on the basis that

---

[22] See F. Mora, 'Thank God for Evil', *Philosophy*, 58 (1983), 399–41; S. Lowe, 'No Love for God', *Philosophy*, 60 (1985), 263; Donald Mackinnon 'Evil and the Vulnerability of God', *Philosophy*, 62 (1987), 102.

[23] Nygren has some difficulty to explain how God's love can be directed to the righteous as well as the sinners (*Agape and Eros*, 77 ff.). In his view God's love never takes account of merit. For Augustine there is a sense in which God rewards merit, and there are plenty of passages that make it explicit that merit depends on Grace;

for the most part these thinkers are asking about God's love as exemplified in the Incarnation; thus by definition the subject matter is God's love towards those in a state of sin and weakness. Nevertheless, it is important to notice how far it would be inappropriate to generalize the conclusions reached on that basis, in such a way as to infer that the same holds true of God's relationship with mankind in general, or indeed creation in general, as opposed to just fallen humanity. Perhaps we also need to guard against the inference that the Incarnation was merely a response to sin, at odds with God's original plan for the world. Could God have loved Adam before the Fall with as great a love as that with which he loved him after the Fall, and with the sort of love that supplies the means of Redemption in the Incarnation? If not there seems to be a problem:

> *Blessed be the time that apple taken was:*
> *Therefore we moun singen Deo gratias!*

## (ii) *Quantifying love*

While we are on this subject, and before moving to the question of respectability, we may dismiss one other misconception, the temptation to quantify love in terms of the disparity between lover and beloved. This may not be a common failing, but it is one to guard against.

The idea is that love for a less lovable object will be a greater love, more in quantity, than love for a more attractive object. Most of us would concede that we love our nicest friends more than we love our most annoying neighbours or our least deserving beggars. If we met someone who loved them equally, doubtless we should be surprised and impressed. We should find such love and devotion to an unworthy object remarkable, and perhaps peculiarly generous. But the important feature to note is that we quantified the love as 'equal'. To have the same quantity of love towards different objects may mean we are more or less generous, but it does not mean we are more loving towards the more difficult object than towards the one we find it easier to love that much. That I might love my friends

hence there is implicit a distinction between humanity in its fallen state, which is wholly unlovely, and humanity in receipt of God's (free) Grace, which is a worthy object.

is easy; that I might love my enemies just as much is harder.[24] That God should lay down his life for sinful man is remarkable, and surprisingly generous; but it does not follow that it would be a greater love than the same act offered for a worthier object. When Christ says, 'Greater love hath no man than this, that a man lay down his life', he does not say 'for his enemies' but 'for his friends'.[25] God's love is great not because of sin but because of God.


## (iii) *Respectable love*

Our third issue was respectability, and this will surface more than once in this book. This is because, although it is not always invoked explicitly, the requirement that love be respectable sometimes lies just below the surface in the texts that we shall be concerned with. The same is doubtless also true of modern discussions. It is not so much that an unseemly or shameful type of love is first envisaged and then explicitly rejected, but rather that certain possibilities are never raised, or are ruled out from the start by considerations which, when examined, probably amount to the need for respectability.

Again the issue often arises in connection with the relative status of the beloved object, but it can work both ways, since various types of unseemliness can threaten. Let us consider three examples, all built on the assumption, which I intend to question, that the status of the beloved determines the kind of love or the motives for it.


### (a) *Love in bad taste*

Love that is thought not to be in good taste is most likely to involve a lover who is in some sense superior to, or better than, the beloved object. If the lover finds beauty in an object which educated or fashionable taste scorns, she is likely to be regarded as having a misplaced love. It might be considered 'not nice' for an eminent public figure to have an affair with someone of no class, or for God to consort with tax-gatherers and ex-prostitutes. The assumption, I take it, is that the love is motivated by a desire for, or approval of, the qualities displayed by the beloved, and hence reveals the poor taste of the lover in choosing and approving those qualities.

The idea that we disapprove of love of this sort is, I think, an

---

[24] Cf. e.g. Luke 15: 7, but also Luke 7: 47.
[25] John 15: 13.

inference made by those who analyse love as motivated by desire. In fact we are likely to disapprove of *desire* for certain kinds of low pleasure, but not to disapprove of *love* of the individual. If love were motivated by the presence of desired qualities in the individual, it would follow that we must disapprove of the love that gives evidence of such desires. The fact that we do not confirms the suggestion that we do not think of love as motivated in that way.

### (b) Excessive love

Closely related to love that is supposed to be in bad taste for taking an unsuitable object, is love that goes over the top for something that does not merit such devotion.[26] It might be reasonable to feel some affection for your old dog, but to mourn for her death for years would be unseemly. In that case it might be said that one had become sentimental.

How does this differ from the response of the Good Samaritan who stops to bind the wounds of the man fallen among thieves? Some might say that the love he shows, and the sacrifice he makes, are excessive, but we should hardly say they were sentimental. Nevertheless, there are ways in which following the example of the Good Samaritan is incompatible with what is usually regarded as a respectable lifestyle in terms of worldly success. To be a saint is usually to be unconventional at least, and often unacceptable to society. So love may be excessive and unseemly, not simply by being sentimental, but by refusing to recognize the conventional assessment of what is worthy of attention.

### (c) Love that is motivated

The third sort of love that is regarded as unseemly is that which arises, or seems to arise, for motives of personal gain.[27] What makes this unseemly? We might diagnose the impropriety in three possible ways:

　　1. The immediate object of my love is something valuable and

---

[26] This issue arises in discussions of 'ordered' and 'inordinate' love, e.g. Augustine, *De doctrina Christiana*, 1. 27. 28. The shame may derive from the error of judgement involved. Cf. Gregory of Nyssa, *De an. et res.* 92AB.

[27] Not all ulterior motives need necessarily seem shameful. If Augustine suggests that we should love things in the world for the sake of God, it is to suggest that loving them for their own sake would be shameful, whereas loving them for the sake of something more worthy is proper. Cf. *De doctrina Chr.* 1. 22. 20.

attractive to me; proper generous love is not concerned with objects valuable to oneself; hence my love is not a proper generous love, because it is directed towards an inappropriate object.

2. The real object of my love is not the immediate object but myself or some benefit (e.g. money) that I hope to gain; hence my love is directed to an object in bad taste, or insufficiently worthy.

3. The love is unseemly because of the motive, not because of the object, whether immediate or ultimate. What makes my love unseemly is not the fact that the beloved is wealthy (say) but that I love her because she is wealthy, for the sake of an unfitting goal.

The third of these explanations suggests that the unseemliness is not in fact a result of the disparity of lover and beloved. However, it might be thought that the shame derives not from the real motives (which may not be apparent to an observer) but from the way others would interpret the relationship. Thus, although the first explanation appears to depend on a fallacy, by supposing that love directed to what is valuable must be ungenerous, nevertheless it remains relevant because shame may accrue simply from the fact that the love is open to a shameful interpretation. We might want to say that such love only *seemed* shameful. If we are talking about what is regarded as unseemly in the conventions of ordinary society, we shall not need to be concerned with whether it is really shameful, but only whether it is so in the assessment of those who are ashamed or shocked.

Saying that love is unseemly if it is motivated by some further hope of gain implies that there is always some motive for love. This is precisely what I shall argue is a mistake. On the contrary we need to recognize that love *is* a motive, if you like, among other motives; where some other motive explains my action, the action is not motivated by love. If love is the motive, no further motive need be sought. So it makes nonsense to look for a motive for love, though it may make sense to ask for motives for action. If we see love as a kind of attitude, rather than a response provoked by some object of desire or concern, we shall be less likely to seek a 'motive' for the response.

## (d) God and the unseemly love of humankind

Of these three sorts of unseemly love, the first two are more likely to raise problems for God's love for us, though they can also be an issue in neighbourly love. The paradox of the Incarnation depends precisely on the conventional 'impropriety' of attributing to God an inordinate love of unworthy objects. The third type can be a problem for our love for God: how, we might ask, can we be commanded to love God, when to do so would appear shameful and selfish? But it can also be a problem for love for neighbours and for God's love for us, since it suggests that decent love must be primarily or solely directed to the unlovely who have nothing to offer in return. This leads to the conclusion that the righteous are not to be an object of love, and that generous love that seeks to add beauty to the beloved (as for example Grace or *agape* is said to do)[28] must cease when the beloved has received her fill and become beautiful.[29]

## (iv) *He and she*

Closely related to the issue of respectable and unseemly love is the matter of sex-stereotypes and gender-roles. The fact that human love frequently belongs in a sexual context means that it carries complicated conventions, for example about how a male lover behaves towards a female beloved, or even how he feels about her, what he looks for in her and what return he expects; and vice versa of a female lover in relation to a male beloved. These stereotypes and conventions may be culturally dependent and are likely to vary over time, but they will affect whether a particular sort of behaviour or a particular sort of love is considered seemly or unseemly at a particular time or in a particular society.

For example, we may take the conventions of chivalry and courtly love familiar from legend and literature. Whether this corresponds to the way things 'actually were' at any time in the past, is strictly speaking, irrelevant for now. Suffice it that the literature provides in itself a set of conventions and expectations about how things *ought* to be in an age when heroes and heroines did live up to ideals. Among the more general themes, such as the exaltation of unrequited love and the high value placed on the ill-starred, tragic,

---

[28] Cf. Nygren, *Agape and Eros*, 78.

[29] This problem is comparable with the problem sometimes raised for acquisitive love, that the love will cease when the desire is fulfilled. See Gregory of Nyssa, *De an. et res.* 93B–96A.

or unfortunate in love,[30] we may also notice an asymmetry in the expectations with regard to the male and female partners in love: whereas the man is devoted to the lady, she is unmoved; whereas he seeks a token of her favour, she will only reluctantly or in time consent to provide one, and will not show any inclination or desire for a similar token from him; whereas he will perform acts of heroism to win her, it is nothing that she *does* that wins his affection, but merely what she is, beautiful and desirable in herself. Although this may oversimplify the complexities of the conventions, the general impression is that the male partner takes the active role, while the woman takes a passive stance: she does not initiate the relationship or seek his love actively; rather he seeks her favours.

The conventions of courtship need not be confined to heterosexual love. Exactly the same type of expectations seem to have surrounded the pederastic love between adult men and adolescent boys in Classical Greece.[31] Here the boy was apparently not expected to initiate the relationship; rather the man was the lover, the boy conventionally the beloved.[32] Nor was the boy expected to respond in kind. He need feel nothing for his lover, or merely some

---

[30] For a spirited attack on the ideals of courtly love see D. de Rougemont, *Passion and Society*, trans. M. Belgian (London, 1962). But there are clearly problems with his association of these conventions with the breakdown of marriage and social disintegration. Arguably all love necessarily makes the lover vulnerable, and the stress on the tragic is only a recognition of the place of suffering in the lover's involvement with the fortunes of another person. To suppose that this risk is absent from the socially cohesive relationship of marriage, and present only in the socially disruptive relationships outside marriage, seems implausible; furthermore it does not seem likely that the ideals of courtly love, with its stress on the idea that love endures through all misfortunes, would contribute to the breakdown of relationships: rather the reverse. Similarly there seems little reason to suppose that the traditional tales (de Rougement takes Tristan and Isolde as his example) are conceived in opposition to the Church's motif of the love of Christ for the Church; on the contrary the twin ideals of love and death make good sense as an allegory of the Christian motif itself. Cf. also D'Arcy, *The Mind and Heart of Love*, for an attempt to make a strong contrast between courtly love and the Christian ideal.

[31] For detailed study of the evidence see K. J. Dover, *Greek Homosexuality* (London, 1978), and also David Halperin, *One Hundred Years of Homosexuality and Other Essays on Greek Love* (New York, 1990); John Winkler, *The Constraints of Desire: The Anthropology of Sex and Gender in Ancient Greece* (New York, 1990); Michel Foucault, *The History of Sexuality*, vols. 2 and 3 (Harmondsworth, 1987 and 1990); and the collection of essays in David M. Halperin, John J. Winkler, and Froma I. Zeitlin (eds.), *Before Sexuality: The Construction of Erotic Experience in the Ancient Greek World* (Princeton, NJ, 1989).

[32] *Eromenos*. It was not normal to refer to an older male as an *eromenos*; but cf. Plato, *Phaedrus*, 257b4 and 279b3, where it is philosophical maturity that counts.

regard or gratitude for the kindness shown to him. Here, then, the
adult is the active partner, the boy merely passive and perhaps not
fully masculine.

Given these conventions, we may easily see how attributing to
someone a love that contravenes the conventions may result in
unseemliness. Thus, for example, placing God in the passive role
conventionally assigned to women and boys, as the 'beloved', might
seem improper. Such scruples may well account for the fact that
some thinkers insist that human beings cannot have erotic love for
God;[33] what lies behind this might be an unspoken requirement
that God be masculine. The alternative responses (*a*) that God is
not masculine, (*b*) that human conventions are no guide in matters
of theology, and (*c*) that unseemliness is precisely what we expect
from an unconventional God, are all of them ruled out by the same
criteria of seemliness.

Nevertheless, we must not be too hasty to conclude that God can
be beloved only by taking on unseemliness, or by emptying himself
of his 'male-dominant' characteristics. For the convention that
supposes the beloved inferior and passive is only one half of a
paradox; exactly the same traditions, both of romantic love, where
the 'gentlemen' are devoted to the 'ladies', and of homosexuality,
where men are overwhelmed by the beauty of boys, also presuppose
that passion is the part of the masculine partner who finds himself
enslaved to the beloved; in this case it is *he* who is in the position
of weakness and *she* (or the boy) who has the power to 'conquer'
his heart, or to grant or refuse such favours as he desires.[34]

### 4. THE WEAKNESS OF GOD

Identifying the *beloved* as the one in a position of power has a long
and venerable history. It lies behind Aristotle's account of the
teleological structure of the world, and his analysis of the unmoved
mover (God) as one who moves others by being the object of their
love; in this way it becomes fundamental to subsequent theories of

---

[33] Thinkers who object to the use of *eros* motifs for love towards God include
D'Arcy, *The Mind and Heart of Love*, and Nygren, *Agape and Eros*.

[34] For a classic description of the weakness of the lover see Plato, *Phaedrus*, 230e6–
234c5.

motion as well as cosmology.[35] But it has its problems when it is applied to the relations between God and the world in the Christian tradition. Now it seems that God can manipulate the world from a position of power by *being loved*, the 'feminine' role, but cannot *love* without adopting a position of powerlessness and passion, the 'masculine' role. To put God in the position of lover is to make the supreme God mad and subject to passion.[36]

It will not take more than a moment's thought to see that this difficulty is no difficulty at all. It coincides very neatly with Christianity's stress on the humiliation undertaken by God in the self-emptying love of the Incarnation; God's love for us could very well be described as involving powerlessness and passion, even unseemliness. In the Incarnation God can step down from feminine power to masculine weakness. Thus we need not find it inappropriate to speak of God as lover, as well as beloved, in classical erotic terms.

There remain two problems, however. First, it is not clear that we should be content to classify *all* God's love as humiliating. We might wish to distinguish between the love manifested in the Incarnation (which does involve powerlessness) and the love manifested in creation which appears to be characterized by power rather than weakness. Short of suggesting that creation limits God's independence or implies a lack of self-sufficiency on his part, we should probably wish to preserve a distinction between creation, on the one hand, as ultimately respectable and a proper activity for the God who has everything and more besides, and on the other hand Incarnation, which is a surprising or shocking act for such a God. The extent to which either or both of these fit the conventional model of *eros* will be a question we shall consider further.

The second problem concerns God's perception of the beloved. It may be all very well to say that in the Incarnation God is enslaved with passion,[37] but enslaved to what? Enslaved apparently to the beauty and loveliness of the beloved creatures. This raises problems because it implies that those creatures are inherently beautiful and exercise a power of attraction over God who is desirous of favours

---

[35] See R. Sorabji, *Matter, Space and Motion* (London, 1988), ch. 13; and below, Ch. 5.

[36] Cf. the madness of the lover in Plato's *Phaedrus*, 244a–249e.

[37] Phil. 2: 7: perhaps a slightly tendentious rendering of μορφὴν δούλου λαβών.

from them. Nothing, it seems, could be further from the Christian evaluation of fallen creation.

### 5. ARROWS

It is at this point that we may see the importance of invoking the image of Eros as the figure whose arrows strike, if not at random, at least without regard to the real worth or beauty of the beloved.[38] It is this image that serves as an explanation, if any explanation is to be offered, of the very inexplicability of the love that takes as its object something that, in the cool light of reason, looks neither attractive nor valuable. Of course it is in reality no explanation at all; it merely personifies, as Cupid and his darts, what we might otherwise call wishful thinking, or 'beauty in the eye of the beholder'. But none of these are explanations of *why* the lover takes pleasure in this (unlikely) candidate rather than that (more likely) one. They are merely ways of observing that love, unlike *desire*, strikes without regard to any objectively observable beauty in the beloved.

This feature is far from unimportant. If we forget the role of Cupid and his darts we are likely to suppose that the classical model of *eros* presumes that there *is* beauty in the beloved and that the lover's regard for the beloved is a simple desire to possess that beauty (or whatever other favours might be envisaged). Taking Cupid's arrows as a fundamental feature of the model, we transform that desire into a willingness to see beauty in the most unlikely candidate, a wishful thinking that hopes to find loveliness where there is no real prospect of doing so, and a yearning to see that any capacity that the beloved might have for becoming beautiful is realized to the full. Thus there may be a sense in which this classical *eros* is a desire for beauty, but if so it is a desire to see beauty created and brought to perfection in the beloved, not a desire to possess it on the part of the lover. In this sense *eros* is a generous-spirited love, an attitude towards the beloved, not a mean and grasping desire.[39]

[38] See e.g. *Anth. Gr.* 5. 89.
[39] See below, Ch. 3, for further exploration of the relation between love and the real worth of the beloved.

On this model there need be no problem about casting God in the role of *erastes*, the classical lover, and in the form of a slave. The humiliation, enslavement, and devotion need not entail a corresponding real superiority on the part of the beloved. God's love for the world may be a devotion not so much to the goodness and beauty that the world already possesses as to the realization of his vision of what it might be. It reflects God's attitude towards the world he created, not some feature of the world that evokes that response.

The vision that God has for a perfect world may be idealistic and quite possibly mistaken.[40] This last feature may reassure us that the love is not a love of beauty in the abstract, since then it would make no sense to love those who would never achieve the desired perfection. It is part of the folly of devotion to individuals that the lover should hope against hope even where the hope seems vain. Here, then, is the explanation of why the actual possibility of gaining benefit, and the real worth of the beloved object, is irrelevant to deciding whether it is lovable and what the motivation for loving it might be.[41]

It is for these reasons that we shall be concerned to trace in Classical texts, and in the Fathers of the Church, certain particular features of the *eros* motif, and above all the presence of Cupid and his arrows, the notion that love is inexplicable when analysed in economic terms with regard to what the lover stands to gain or lose, and the question of *whose* perception attributes beauty to the beloved object, and why. Cupid, or Love (with the capital 'L'), is not merely an optional extra, a picturesque relic in poetry and art; he is an essential part of the structure of ancient theories of love.

[40] It may seem paradoxical to suggest that God could be 'mistaken' in his hopes. But this I mean not so much that God does not know that his vision might never be realized, as that he eternally hopes for what he knows probably never will, though it always might, come about. This is part of the 'foolishness' of God (1 Cor. 1: 18–29).

[41] See above, sect. 3(iii), and below, Ch. 3.

# 2

# God is Love: The Word *Agape* in the New Testament

I. HEBREW AND GREEK IN THE BACKGROUND TO THE NEW
TESTAMENT

In the Patristic period it is clear that the education and background
of the writers is reflected in their writings. The same is also true of
the New Testament, which was not written in a vacuum. The New
Testament writers were writing in Greek and clearly inherited with
their Greek language a certain amount of the prevailing Greek
culture; but they also came from a background more or less strongly
influenced by Semitic languages and styles of thought. Our
immediate concern now is not with the overall style or characteristics of the New Testament, but with one particular feature that
has been considered significant; that is the prominence of the noun
*agape* (love).

It seems at first slightly surprising that the New Testament
writings should employ this noun with any frequency. Abstract
nouns are not used in Greek so much as they are in English, and
many ideas that we should express with a noun would normally
come out better in Greek if we used a verb or a participle instead.
Why, then, should anyone writing in Greek favour the noun *agape*
when he could use the verb?

One line of enquiry would be the non-Greek background of the
New Testament writers: were they influenced by Hebrew styles of
thought? But this will hardly solve the problem, since Hebrew and
Aramaic share the preference for verbs rather than nouns that we
find in Greek, perhaps even to a greater extent.[1]

---

[1] There is some difference between Greek and Hebrew in so far as Hebrew gives
greater prominence to certain nouns referring to types of activity (mercy, kindness,
justice in the sense of the way one behaves). Abstract nouns in Greek are more often
related to adjectives describing a state. Aristotle's discussion of friendship in the
*Nicomachean Ethics* looks like an exception, given the high incidence of the noun

Thus we cannot conclude that the noun 'love' is prominent in the New Testament simply because the writers 'thought in Hebrew'; even if they did think in Hebrew, which is not particularly likely, it would not account for this particular feature of style. It might seem more plausible to argue that *agape* appeared in the New Testament because the writers were familiar with the Greek version of the Hebrew Scriptures, rather than the Hebrew, given that *agape* appears with some frequency in the Septuagint. But this also is insufficient to account for the facts. A quick survey of the Septuagint[2] can demonstrate that although the noun *agape* occurs more often than it does in Classical Greek[3] it is far less common than the corresponding verb *agapao*, and is extremely rare in the major books.[4] Where a noun is used, *agapesis* is more usual than *agape* in these books, but it is the preponderance of the verb over the noun that is important.

This preponderance of the verb *agapao* over the nouns *agape* or *agapesis* is also found in the New Testament, though the ratio is lower.[5] However, when we look more closely at the New Testament

Verbs and nouns for love in the Septuagint and New Testament

|  | Nouns | Verb |
|---|---|---|
| Septuagint | 28 | 271 |
| New Testament | 115 | 143 |

to determine the practice of individual writers we discover that the Gospels and 1 John are all much closer to the balance we expect

*philia* and the lower frequency of verbs. But the discussion is not really about loving or being friendly, but about the state of being or having friends: by far the most common term is the adjective/noun *philos* (dear/friend) and *philia* clearly names a state, not a way of behaving. On the characteristics of Hebrew language in comparison with Greek there is a discussion, somewhat oversimplified, in T. G. Boman, *Hebrew Thought compared with Greek* (London, 1960).

[2] My conclusions here were reached with the help of the Ibycus computer system (courtesy of the Lit. Hum. Faculty, Oxford) and Hatch and Redpath's concordance, but they correspond with Barr's authoritative analysis (Barr, 'Words for Love in Biblical Greek', 8–9).

[3] That, after all, would not be difficult. See above, Ch. 1 n. 3.

[4] Excluding, that is, the Song of Songs and Ecclesiastes, which Barr argues were significantly later translations: J. Barr, *Holy Scripture: Canon, Authority, Criticism* (Oxford, 1983), 62, and Barr, 'Words for Love in Biblical Greek', 8.

[5] The figures are all approximate because of variant readings in the text.

from the Septuagint, with more verbs than nouns; it is only in the
Pauline Epistles that the balance is actually reversed and the noun
*agape* becomes more common than the verb. Thus the problem of

Verbs and nouns for love in the main books of the New Testament

|               | Nouns | Verb |
| ------------- | ----- | ---- |
| Matthew       | 1     | 8    |
| Mark          | 0     | 5    |
| Luke          | 1     | 12   |
| John          | 7     | 35   |
| 1 John        | 17    | 28   |
| Romans        | 8     | 8    |
| 1 Corinthians | 13    | 2    |
| 2 Corinthians | 9     | 4    |
| Galatians     | 3     | 2    |
| Ephesians     | 10    | 10   |
| Philippians   | 4     | 0    |

where *agape* comes from and why it is prominent is a problem not
about the New Testament but about the Pauline Epistles.

While we need not assume that Paul made a deliberate decision
to give prominence to the noun *agape*, still it looks as though love
is treated as something special in these epistles;[6] the use of the noun
might be merely a quirk of style inherited from Paul's background
or training, but that in itself could affect the way he thinks.[7] In the
final analysis, however, Paul's own view of what he was doing is
clearly irrelevant to what subsequent readers made of the text.
Whether or not Paul thought so, there is little doubt that many
readers of Gentile origin accustomed to Classical Greek, as well as
those of Jewish origin perhaps, would find the prominence of the

[6] For reasons why there might be advantages in using the noun rather than a verb
see below, sect. 2(i).

[7] On Paul's Jewish background there is much recent work: E. P. Sanders, *Paul
and Palestinian Judaism* (London, 1977); F. Watson, *Paul, Judaism and the Gentiles*
(Cambridge, 1986). On the influence of the LXX see C. H. Dodd, *The Bible and
the Greeks* (London, 1935).

noun *agape* striking. It is usual in Greek to reify,[8] or perhaps even personify, the concepts expressed by abstract nouns where the normal expression would be a verb. Thus love, war, peace, death, and so on become forces, or gods, to be reckoned with.[9] It seems likely that Paul's texts, hitting the Gentile world, might provoke a response in subsequent thought that went beyond what Paul actually said; but it need not follow that such a response was a corruption, or an unwelcome development, of Paul's teaching. After all, the first move in this process comes in the New Testament itself; not only does the first epistle of John personify love when it says that God is love (1 John 4: 8, 16), but Paul himself in the famous personification of *agape* at 1 Corinthians 13: 4, 'Charity suffereth long and is kind ... ', makes a similar move. Few would go so far as to claim that these influential passages are a corruption of the pure Christian message, given that that message would have been considerably weaker without them.

## 2. WHAT WERE THE NEW TESTAMENT WRITERS TALKING ABOUT?

### (i) *The love of God*

'The love of God' is a phrase that appears both in the New Testament[10] and frequently in later writers. Its prominence in Augustine, for example, may account in part for the importance of love in Post-Reformation Western theology, though there are probably

---

[8] When we talk of reifying abstract concepts we might think particularly of Plato, but it is worth noting that his 'Forms' relate to adjectives rather than verbs: 'the good', 'the beautiful', and so on; the normal way of designating these is by *auto to* and the adjective (the 'beautiful itself'). Abstract nouns are also used (*kallos*, beauty; *dikaiosune*, justice) but these generally denote the qualities that correspond with the related adjective, rather than actions or feelings related to verbs. In the *Lysis* Plato investigates love and friendship using primarily adjectival forms: the subject is what is *philos* (friendly or lovely), why someone is beloved (*eromenos* or *philoumenos*), but not what it is to love. Again Plato reifies 'the lovely' (*to philon*) rather than love (*philia*). In the *Phaedrus* by contrast Socrates turns the discussion to 'love' (*eros*) and *personifies* it.

[9] This tendency also appears in the hierarchies of powers characteristic of Gnosticism. Hence it may not be peculiar to Greek thought.

[10] Cf. e.g. Luke 11: 42; John 5: 42; Rom. 5: 5, 8: 39; 2 Cor. 13: 14; 2 Thess. 3: 5; 1 John 2: 5, 3: 17, 4: 9, 5: 3.

other reasons why the loving attitude of God has been stressed in the twentieth century particularly.[11]

However, the phrase 'the love of God', along with its Greek and Latin equivalents,[12] is, of course, systematically ambiguous. It is not necessarily immediately obvious who is loving whom when this phrase is used; if the ambiguity is to be resolved it must be resolved from the context, not from the phrase itself. Clearly the fact that the phrase occurs eleven or more times in the New Testament is not in itself sufficient to show that New Testament writers were interested in God's loving attitude towards his people; on some few occasions that seems to be what is meant,[13] but in other cases it remains wholly unclear whether God is the lover, beloved, or neither.

It will be helpful to distinguish three distinct but equally acceptable uses of the phrase 'the love of God'.[14] We may render them in English with different prepositions for the purpose of analysing the ambiguity. The phrase 'the love of God' can mean (a) the love that you or I or anyone might have for God, (b) the love that God might have towards you or me or anything else, and (c) the love given by God, with which you or I or anyone might love me or you or anyone else. These three meanings we may distinguish as (a) love for God, (b) love by God, and (c) love from God.[15] I am not suggesting that these three uses of the phrase should be taken to be three 'types' of love, nor ought we to be troubled by the idea that the same phrase

---

[11] See below, Ch. 8.

[12] ἡ ἀγάπη τοῦ θεοῦ, amor dei.

[13] Perhaps the most convincing examples are Rom. 8: 39 and 1 John 4: 9.

[14] The ambiguity of this phrase is sometimes discussed by commentators of the Patristic and Scholastic periods: see particularly Thomas Aquinas, *Super Epistolas S. Pauli*: Ad Rom. ch. 5, lectio 1. 392; Augustine, *Tract. in Joh.* 82. 3. In the majority of instances they suggest that there are only two possible meanings: (a) our love for God and (b) God's love for us (i.e. objective and subjective genitive respectively). However in practice they also recognize the third sense, love that is divine or 'from God' regardless of subject and object (qualitative genitive) which may often also actually have God as subject or object. See, for example, Thomas Aquinas (*Super Epistolas S. Pauli*: Ad Rom. ch. 8, lectio 7. 722 and 733; also ibid., 2 Cor. ch. 13, lectio 3. 544–5 on the distinction between things attributed essentially or causally to the Persons, where love is attributed causally to God the Father because love is 'from God'. In R. E. Brown, *The Epistles of St John*, The Anchor Bible (New York, 1982), 255–7, five possible interpretations of the 'love of God' are suggested, but effectively they amount to the same three as I suggest: he proposes (a) love for God (objective genitive); (b) God's love for us (subjectival genitive); (c) both these; (d) divine love (i.e. a qualitative genitive); (e) love of God—a non-committal translation.

[15] See, for example, for (a) 2 Thess. 3: 5, for (b) 1 John 4: 9; for (c) 1 John 4: 12.

does duty for all three, since they are clearly related and, as we shall see in due course, the ambiguity is essential to the meaning of some passages; indeed, it could be said to be theologically important that this phrase, so frequently used where other expressions could have been chosen, is ambiguous as to who loves whom.

In most of the passages in the New Testament where 'the love of God' occurs, it appears that the love in question might equally well have been expressed in phrases involving verbs (I love, you love, God loves, or whatever); then the ambiguity would normally be resolved: the verb specifies who loves, and usually also the object of love. There are indeed many passages in the New Testament in which love for or by God is mentioned in a way that employs verbs.[16] The verb is, as we have already observed, relatively common in the Gospels and 1 John;[17] but it is in the Pauline Epistles that the noun *agape* comes into its own. Paul was concerned not only with God's love for us (love by God) but also the love that we show to our fellow men as a result of following Christ. It is for this latter use (the love that is *from* God) that the noun does duty more adequately than the verb: what matters is not that I love you, but that the love that I have for you is inspired or given by God. By using the noun Paul can make clear the connection between love by God and love from God.[18]

These claims about the ambiguity of 'the love of God' and the theological importance of the plurality of its meanings need to be supported by means of a close analysis of the relevant passages in the New Testament. How far can we distinguish one meaning as correct to the exclusion of others? Is there reason to believe that the text would make better sense if we went beyond the single most obvious meaning of the phrase?

---

[16] Love for God especially in quotations of the commandment 'Thou shalt love the Lord thy God . . .' (e.g. Matt. 22: 37; Mark 12: 30; Luke 10: 27) but also in other contexts (1 Cor. 8: 3; 1 John 4: 20). Love of God for man in John 3: 16, 14: 21 and 23; Eph. 5: 2; 1 John 4: 10, 19, and 21.

[17] Not only ἀγαπᾶν but also φιλεῖν which occurs relatively often in the Fourth Gospel. See Barr, 'Words for Love in Biblical Greek', 14.

[18] The conclusion applies to the use of the noun 'love' in general, not only in the phrase 'the love of God'. The same applies to 1 John 4. Nygren recognizes the close connection between love by God and love from God in the New Testament (*Agape and Eros*, 129 and 140) and the use of *agape* to make this connection, but he underestimates the extent to which love for God is also implied. That love *from* God might be love *for* God is something that Nygren's dichotomy of *agape* and *eros* misses.

*(a)  The Gospels*

The phrase 'the love of God' occurs twice only in the Gospels, once
in Luke (11: 42) and once in John (5: 42). In addition, however, we
should look at the passage in John where Christ speaks of 'my love'
and 'his love' (John 15: 9–10).


1. *Luke 11: 42*
But woe to you Pharisees! For you tithe mint and rue and every herb, and
neglect justice and *the love of God.*

The context concerns Christ's rejection of the preoccupation on
the part of the Pharisees with external details rather than internal
attitudes. Their obedience to the letter of the law, such as the
requirement to pay tithes on every herb as mentioned here, can
lead to neglect of what Christ considers equally important, namely
justice and 'the love of God'—though it should be noted that these
are not to be a substitute for literal obedience to the law, since he
continues: 'these you ought to have done [sc. justice and love],
without neglecting the others [sc. tithing your herbs].' What is it
that the Pharisees are neglecting? First justice (*krisis*, the distinction
between right and wrong) and secondly the love of God (*he agape
tou theou*). From the context we are disposed to interpret these as
an attitude of mind, the internal purity that goes along with the
external purity of adherence to the practical requirements of the
Law. Nevertheless, it remains unclear whether this attitude is expressed in relations with other people, in which case the failure
of justice would be a failure to act and think with justice towards
others and the failure of love would be a failure to love others
(neighbours) with the love that is of God because required by God
and essential to the divine Law. The alternative interpretation
would see the relationship that the Pharisees lack as being a proper
relationship with God, expressed in right judgement and the love
towards God that is required by the first commandment. Christ's
criticism makes sense on either interpretation: if the Pharisees
neglect to love others with the love that is from God (attending
only to the visible details of the Law) or if they neglect to love God
(preoccupied with the practical details of the Law) we may still
see the contrast between external practices and internal attitudes.
Probably we should see both interpretations in play since both are
intimately tied up together: love for God and love for neighbour go

hand in hand and are part and parcel of the same attitude of mind expressed as 'the love of God'. In this passage it seems that love for God and love from God both enter appropriately into the sense, but love by God is not relevant.

## 2. *John 5: 42*

[39] You search the scriptures, because you think that in them you have eternal life: and it is they that bear witness to me; [40] yet you refuse to come to me that you may have life. [41] I do not receive glory from men. [42] But I know that you have not *the love of God* within you. [43] I have come in my Father's name, and you do not receive me.

Jesus is addressing the Jews in response to their hostility to his behaviour. Their objection had been not only to his breaking of the Sabbath (5: 16) but also to his calling God his own father (5: 18). The context is thus similar to that in Luke, since Jesus is again portrayed as criticizing the Jews for their failures; this time it is their failure to use the scriptures with understanding. Their refusal to accept Jesus amounts to a refusal to believe what Moses wrote (5: 45–6). Thus when Jesus complains that they 'have not the love of God' the reference seems to be to their failure to love God: because they do not have love for God they cannot accept Jesus and they cannot read the scriptures in the right spirit that would enable them to see Jesus in them. To read the scriptures in that way might also reveal God himself as loving, but it is not evident that we should read that sense into this mention of the love of God.

## 3. *John 15: 9–10*

[9] As the Father has loved me, so have I loved you; abide in *my love*. [10] If you keep my commandments, you will abide in *my love*, just as I have kept my Father's commandments and abide in *his love*.

In his speech to his disciples before his betrayal Christ warns them of the troubles to come and instructs them in what their role is to be. Love plays an important part in this discourse;[19] it is in this context that Christ gives his disciples his 'new commandment':

---

[19] Words derived from ἀγάπη or ἀγαπάω occur 28 times in John chapters 13–17, that is two-thirds of the total occurrence of such words in the Fourth Gospel as a whole.

that you love one another; even as I have loved you, that you also love one another (13: 34). Christ's love for his followers (love by God) is here closely bound up with their love for each other (love from God). The commandment to love is repeated at 15: 12 and 17. Thus, when Christ, at 15: 9–10, emphasizes that the disciples will remain in *his* love if they keep his commandments,[20] it is clear that those commandments are summed up in the commandment[21] to love, and that Christ's obedience to his Father's commandments (15: 10) is also obedience to a commandment of love. 'My love' in verse 10 is clearly Christ's love for his friends (15: 13), but in verse 9 where Christ says 'abide in my love',[22] the phrase takes the form of a commandment, and it might be profitable to take it as ambiguous as between 'continue to abide in the love that I have for you' (love by God), 'continue in the love of the brethren, which is the love that I demand, my love' (love from God), and perhaps, in as much as keeping the commandment amounts to loving Christ, 'continue in the love that you have for me, i.e. by keeping my commandment' (love for God). Thus we can see that it may be no accident that the writer chooses the phrase 'my love' which conveys all three aspects of Christ's instructions and is richly ambiguous in this context.[23] Precisely the same ambiguity applies to Christ's reference in verse 10 to the Father's love ('his love'), which may mean both the Father's love for Christ and Christ's love for the Father as well as the love towards humanity that is the Father's commandment to Christ.

---

[20] τὰς ἐντολάς μου, 15: 10.

[21] ἡ ἐντολὴ ἡ ἐμή, 15: 12.

[22] μείνατε ἐν τῇ ἀγάπῃ τῇ ἐμῇ.

[23] Augustine discusses this passage at *Tract. in Joh.* 82. 2–4. Initially he assumes that 'my love' at verse 9–10 must mean 'your love for me' and explains 'if you keep my commandments you will abide in my love' on this basis (section 3). But he goes on (CCL, vol. 36, p. 533, line 16) to raise the problems of the ambiguity of the phrase, and then opts for the interpretation that takes 'my love' as 'the love I have for you', avoiding the unacceptable implications of making God's love conditional on keeping of the commandments by explaining it in terms of grace and reading the sense as 'unless he loves us we cannot keep his commandments'. In section 4 Augustine concludes that the meaning is unquestionably Christ's love for you ('illa procul dubio qua dilexi vos'). Thomas Aquinas, by contrast, starts by adopting the meaning 'my love for you', following Augustine's explanation in terms of enabling Grace (*Super Ev. S. Joannis*, 15: 2.II. 2000) but subsequently observes the ambiguity and advocates adopting both senses: 'observatio enim mandatorum est effectus divinae dilectionis, non solum eius qua nos diligimus, sed eius qua ipse diligit nos' (15: 2. III. 2002).

## (b) The Epistles

It has sometimes been claimed that in St Paul the phrase 'the love of God' always refers to God's love for us (love by God), or at least that there is no example where such an interpretation is impossible. The two claims are actually rather different, since there may be occasions on which the phrase can, in theory, bear the interpretation 'love by God', but where a more interesting interpretation follows from taking the phrase another way as well or instead. Here we can look briefly at the examples in Romans, 2 Corinthians, and Ephesians,[24] before turning to the First Epistle of St John.

## A. The Pauline Epistles

There are two examples in these Epistles where it seems clear that the love referred to as the love of God is the love that God has towards us (love by God).

### 1. Ephesians 2: 4–5

In this first case the meaning is made explicit by the use of the *verb* with cognate accusative, and it is worth noticing that it is the use of the verb[25] that clarifies who is subject and who is object of the love:

But God, who is rich in mercy, out of *his* great *love* with which he loved us[26] even when we were dead through our trespasses, made us alive together with Christ.

### 2. Romans 8: 35 and 38–9

This second example is marginally less clear: the phrase is repeated (almost) twice in the eighth chapter of Romans, and while the first occurrence (v. 35) could be read ambiguously as between our love

---

[24] There are no examples of this type of phrase in 1 Cor., Gal., or Phil.

[25] ἠγάπησεν.

[26] διὰ τὴν πολλὴν ἀγάπην αὐτοῦ ἣν ἠγάπησεν ἡμᾶς. I have altered the RSV ('*the* great love') to '*his* great love' which is a more accurate rendering of the Greek.

for God or his love for us, the second occurrence (v. 39) implies that God's love for us is meant:[27]

[35] Who shall separate us from the *love of Christ?* ...    [38] For I am sure that neither death nor life ...    [39] nor anything else in all creation will be able to separate us from the *love of God* in Christ Jesus our Lord.

Clearly we may read the clarity of the second phrase, 'the love of God in Christ Jesus', back into the first phrase, 'the love of Christ', and see there primarily a reference to the love that Christ has for us, which cannot be removed by external circumstances. Nevertheless, we should not use verse 39 to force a closure on our reading of verse 35, where we may gain from asking, if only briefly, whether the same claims of endurance through adversity could be made of *our* love for Christ.[28] Thus it might be a better reading to take the first phrase as openly ambiguous, leaving us briefly in suspense as to who loves whom, until the issue is resolved (if it is resolved) in verse 39.

In the four remaining examples in these epistles the phrase is ambiguous again and no clear resolution is provided by the context.

## 3. *Romans 5: 5*

And hope does not disappoint us, because *the love of God* has been poured into our hearts through the Holy Spirit which has been given to us.[29]

The preceding verses, from the beginning of chapter 5, refer to our own feelings and experiences: faith, tribulation, patience, and hope. Adding love leads us to read this as a love that we have, whether for God or for others (from God); however, verse 6 proceeds with a reference to Christ who died for the ungodly, which leads us to revise our reading of 'the love of God' in verse 5, taking it to refer instead, or as well, to the love God had for us, manifested in his

---

[27] On the other hand even the second example (v. 39) is still actually ambiguous. Aquinas takes it as our love *for* God without question in one context (Ad Rom. ch. 5, lectio 1. 392) and as love *from* God (including both our love for Christ and our love for others) in another context (Ad Rom. ch. 8, lectio 7. 722 and 733). It is 'in Christ Jesus our Lord' because *given* by him (Ad Rom. ch. 8, lectio 7. 733).

[28] To the question of how Paul might be certain that our love *for* Christ was enduring in this way Aquinas offers a solution at Ad Rom. ch. 8, lectio 7. 734.

[29] The RSV reads 'because *God's love* has been poured...'. I have substituted *the love of God* which leaves the ambiguity of the Greek phrase open.

death for us in our weakness. Thus the ambiguity in verse 5 is heightened rather than resolved by the context surrounding it.

### 4. *2 Corinthians 5: 13–14*

If we are in our right mind, it is for you. For the *love of Christ* controls us, because we are convinced, that one has died for all; therefore all have died.

Exactly as in the last example, 'the love of Christ' is used as a go-between in moving from talk of the attitude of Paul and his fellow-ministers ('us') to talk of Christ's death on our behalf. It is thus an open question whether we read 'the love of Christ' as the love which Paul and his fellow ministers have for Christ (love for God), or the love which they have for the brethren to whom they are writing when they say 'it is for you' (love from God), or the love which Christ had for us, as revealed in his death for all (love by God), and it seems likely that the phrase serves its go-between role precisely because it can mean all three.[30]

### 5. *2 Corinthians 13: 14*

The grace of the Lord Jesus Christ and the *love of God* and the fellowship of the Holy Spirit be with you all.

This closing formula is relatively independent of its context, which will not help with interpreting the precise meaning of the phrases. Clearly 'grace' and 'fellowship' can profitably be taken as gifts from God reflected in the relationship of the brethren to each other, and this might prompt us to take 'love' similarly as the love given by God whereby they love each other.[31] However, this is not the only possible reading, as love by God or love for God would also make sense.

---

[30] Verse 15 continues with the reasoning that Christ's death implies that his followers should live not for themselves but for Christ. Here it seems clear that a connection is being made between Christ's self-giving love, and the imitation of that love by his followers; both can be expressed as the love of Christ.

[31] Thomas Aquinas (*Super Ep. S. Pauli* 2 Cor. ch. 13, lectio 3) favours the view that it is love *caused by* God that is implied, though he takes it that the love caused by God is, in fact, our love for God.

## 6. *Ephesians 3: 17–19*

[17] That you, being rooted and grounded in love,  [18] may have power
to comprehend with all the saints what is the breadth and length and
height and depth,  [19] and to know the *love of Christ*, which surpasses
knowledge . . .

The sense we give to 'the love of Christ' here probably depends in
part on the sense we give to 'love' in 'rooted and grounded in love'
(v. 17). However, the content of that love seems to be left entirely
open. Nor will the claim that the love of Christ 'surpasses knowledge'[32] clarify who is lover and who beloved in the love in question:
it is not obvious whether the reason that it 'surpasses knowledge'
is that our love for Christ is *better than* any form of knowledge (e.g.
of Christ or anything else), and surpasses knowledge in that sense,
or that Christ's love for us is so great that it is beyond our comprehension, surpassing knowledge as an object that cannot be
known.[33]

On either interpretation of 'surpasses knowledge' a similar reading
would also be possible that took the love in question as the love that
we have as a gift from Christ.

### B. *The First Epistle of St John*

1 John uses the terminology of love more densely than any other
section of the New Testament.[34] Here, although we find that, as in
the Gospels, the verb is significantly more common than the noun,
nevertheless the noun *agape* is used relatively frequently, and again
it seems that the noun is particularly prominent where its ambiguity
as to who loves whom is productive and furthers the writer's
concern with how the brethren's common love for each other
derives from the prior love that God showed to them in Christ and
which is brought to completion in their love.

---

[32] ὑπερβάλλουσαν τῆς γνώσεως.

[33] Note that the ambiguity of this phrase is due to the abstract noun (*gnosis*) where
a verbal form might have resolved the issue.

[34] In the five chapters of this Epistle the noun (*agape*) occurs 17 times, the verb
28 times and the adjective (*agapetos*, beloved) 6 times. Compare this total of 51
occurrences in five chapters with the total for chapters 13–17 of the Fourth Gospel,
28 occurrences in five chapters. See n. 19 above.

Only one of the six examples of 'the love of God' in 1 John is wholly unambiguous, and this example has to mean love by God.

## 1. *1 John 4: 9*

In this *the love of God* was made manifest among us,[35] that God sent his only son into the world, so that we might live through him.

The English translation already eliminates part of the ambiguity of the Greek phrase, but although the construction remains ambiguous in the Greek, the context makes it abundantly clear that it can only refer to the love that God has for us, since only on this reading is the reference to the Incarnation relevant. Of course there are other ways in which the writer might make it explicit that he was referring to love by God, as he does for example in verse 16 of the same chapter where he mentions 'the love God has for us'.[36]

The remaining five examples of phrases of the 'love of God' type are all to some extent ambiguous, though in most cases it seems that love by God is the least satisfactory or appropriate of the three senses.

Two of the examples use the notion that the love of God is 'perfected' in us:[37]

## 2. *1 John 2: 5*

But whoever keeps his word, in him truly *the love of God* is perfected.[38]

---

[35] ἡ ἀγάπη τοῦ θεοῦ ἐν ἡμῖν. The Greek is ambiguous. It is unclear whether ἐν ἡμῖν should be taken with ἐφανερώθη as in the RSV translation given ('was made manifest among us') or with ἡ ἀγάπη as in the AV ('the love of God towards us'). The following clause indicates that the love in question must be love *by* God *for* us manifested in the Incarnation.

[36] τὴν ἀγάπην ἣν ἔχει ὁ θεὸς ἐν ἡμῖν. Note that ἐν ἡμῖν is used here to express the object of the love, as in the AV translation of v. 9 (see n. 35 above).

[37] On this idea see V. P. Furnish, *The Love Command in the New Testament* (London, 1973), 155–6.

[38] The RSV translation reads, 'in him truly *love for God* is perfected'. I have retained the ambiguity of the Greek.

### 3. *1 John 4: 12*

If we love one another God abides in us, and *his love* is perfected in us.

A careful reading of these passages, both of which concern the keeping of Christ's commandment to love and the fulfilment of that commandment in love towards one another, might see here the claim that God's love towards humanity is fulfilled and completed in the love that the brethren have for others, as if their love were incorporated into God's own love for humanity. In this sense to say that the 'love of God' is perfected is to say both that God's own love for mankind is perfected and that the love which the brethren have one to another (love given by God, God's love) is perfected.[39]

Nevertheless, this is not the only possibility; two other options are obvious: (*a*) the 'love of God' means love for God, and the reference is to how well we love God as evidenced by our keeping of his word and our love toward each other; (*b*) the 'love of God' means love by God and the implication is that God loves us fully if and only if we keep his word and love one another. This latter option seems less promising given the theological difficulties it might entail, though it is not clear that these difficulties would have occurred to the writer in this context or that they would be perceived as difficulties given the circumstances for which he is writing.[40]

### 4. *1 John 2: 15*

If any one loves the world, *the love of the Father*[41] is not in him.

Here the juxtaposition of 'loving the world' and 'the love of the Father' suggests that the Father is the object of the love in question, just as the world is the object of love of the world. On the other hand it might equally be tempting to explain the change from the

---

[39] Augustine takes it in the latter sense (we have perfect love if we love our enemies fully), *In Ep. Joann. ad Parth.* I. 9 (*PL* 35. 1984–5).

[40] Note that the phrase ἐν ἡμῖν appears again. If we take this to specify the object of love as in v. 16, and possibly v. 9, of the same chapter (see nn. 35 and 36) option (*b*) would be the only possible one. The theological implications of option (*b*) are closely parallel to those raised by John 15: 9–10 (see above, sect. 3 and n. 23).

[41] The RSV translation offers 'If any one loves the world, *love for the Father* is not in him.' I have retained the ambiguity of the Greek phrase.

construction with a *verb* ('if any one *loves* the world') to a construction with a *noun* ('the *love* of the Father is not in him') as implying a change of meaning: whereas the world is the object of love in the construction with the verb, the Father is not the object of love in the noun-construction. On this view we should then have two options: either (*a*) to take the Father as subject of the love in question, so that the Father's love is not directed towards that person;[42] or (*b*) to take the Father as cause or originator of the love in question of which the man is subject: because he loves the world he does not have a God-given love in him but his love derives from some other source. The implication on this last interpretation would be that if he loved with the love that is of and from the Father he would love the things of the Father and not the things of the world. This would then take advantage of the ambiguity of the 'love of the Father', since the love that is from the Father clearly emerges as a love that is for the Father.

## 5. *1 John 3: 17*

But if anyone has the world's goods, and sees his brother in need, yet closes his heart against him, how does *the love of God* abide in him?[43]

The love of God is here closely associated with acts of compassion and love towards one's brother, which makes it initially plausible that the phrase refers to the love that comes from God with which his followers love one another: someone who fails to act lovingly towards one he supposedly loves (with the love that is from God) does not in fact have that love in him.

On the other hand a comparison with 1 John 4: 20–1 will suggest a different conclusion; there it says,

If any one says, 'I love God,' and hates his brother, he is a liar; for he who does not love his brother whom he has seen, cannot love God whom he has not seen And this commandment we have from him, that he who loves God should love his brother also.

---

[42] Notice that ἐν αὐτῷ is parallel with the ἐν ἡμῖν of 1 John 4: 9, 12 and 16. In 4: 16 at least ἐν ἡμῖν defines the object of love. See nn. 35, 36 and 40. Compare ἐν τούτῳ in 1 John 2: 5.

[43] The RSV reads, 'how does God's love abide in him?' I have retained the ambiguity of the Greek phrase.

Here the constructions are all done with verbs and it is entirely clear that it is our love for God that is lacking if we fail to love our brother. On an analogy with these verses the point at 3: 17 would be that the man who fails to act lovingly towards his brother does not have love for God abiding in him. But was the writer making exactly the same point at 3: 17 as he was at 4:20–1?[44]

## 6. *1 John 5: 2–3*

By this we know that we love the children of God, when we love God and obey his commandments. For this is *the love of God*, that we keep his commandments.

Here the best and most natural way to take 'the love of God' seems to be as our love for God, since it follows immediately on the suggestion that 'we love God'. Nevertheless, the whole phrase is supposed to express how we 'love the children of God'; thus although we might see verse 3 as saying that the two aspects mentioned in verse 2 are the same thing (for to love God is, quite simply, to keep his commandments) it could also be taken to refer further back to the love for the children of God: the reason why loving God and keeping his commandments amounts to love for the children of God is because loving the children of God (that is loving with the love that is from God, the love of God) is keeping God's commandments, namely, of course, the commandment to love. The commandments to love include both love toward God and love toward others, but for the writer of this Epistle it is clear that the commandment to love one another is supremely prominent.

It is clear from this brief survey that although the verb *agapao* is more frequent in 1 John, nevertheless the noun *agape*, and particularly phrases of the 'love of God' type, do have a role to play as they do in the Pauline Epistles. As in the earlier examples, we find that the ambiguity of these phrases with regard to who loves whom is used to explore the connection between the love that God has for us (principally revealed in the Incarnation for 1 John, and in death

---

[44] Again we have ἐν αὐτῷ in 3: 17, but here it can hardly express the object of love, since it follows μένει and must specify the subject in whom the love abides, not the object to which it is directed. Compare 3: 24. The only alternative would be to take μένει to mean not 'dwell' but 'last' ('how can God continue to have love toward that person?')

on the Cross for Paul) and the love with which we respond in loving one another and in our love for God. The ambiguity of the noun is exploited in this way for theological ends. But while we should recognize the importance of this function of the noun *agape*, we should also note that its significance has nothing to do with any special meaning that *agape* has for the New Testament writers or any distinction between *agape* and other possible words for love: any word for love would serve exactly the same purpose and have exactly the same ambiguity as regards who loves whom; we might equally have spoken of the *philia* of God or the *eros* of God and still not known who was subject and who was object of the love in question.

Furthermore, the noun serves to connect ideas that are also regularly expressed by verbs, and a study of the discourse of love will need to do more than focus merely on the noun *agape*: the verbs employed so frequently by the Gospel writers and I John are as good a way to speak of loving and being loved as are the nouns preferred by the Pauline Epistles.

## (ii) *God is love*

Both occasions on which it is claimed that God is love occur in I John 4.[45] The passage is well known and has always been influential. But what does it actually mean?

To judge by modern discussions it seems that in English (and some other European languages too) the phrase 'God is love' is usually taken to imply that God himself is the one who loves. To say that God is love is to say that God is loving, only rather more strongly.[46] In Greek, by contrast, the phrase 'God is love' (ὁ θεὸς ἀγάπη ἐστίν) does not so obviously imply that God is loving; it is usual for the Patristic commentators, both Greek and Latin, to take it in a different sense, namely to refer to God as the source or origin from which all other lovers derive their love.[47] It is apparently a straightforward reading of the Greek to understand it in this way,

---

[45] I John 4: 8 and 16.

[46] See the classic comments of C. H. Dodd, *The Johannine Epistles*, Moffatt New Testament Commentary (London, 1946), 106–10.

[47] See, for example, Origen, *ComCt* 71–2; Gregory of Nyssa, *HomCt* 369–70; Also Augustine, *In Ep. Joann. ad Parth.* VII. 5 (*PL* 35. 2031) and *De Trinitate*, 8. 8. 12.

no less natural and perhaps more natural than to take it as meaning that God loves.

We shall be looking more closely in later chapters at Patristic texts which take the phrase to mean that God is the source of love. But we may also ask whether this reading makes good sense in the New Testament, within the context of the Epistle in which it first occurs. When 1 John says 'God is love (or Love[48])' should it mean (a) that God loves, or (b) that God causes, gives, or inspires love in others?

The claim that God is love occurs twice in the fourth chapter of 1 John, at verses 8 and 16. The context concerns both *our* duty to love the Christian brethren[49] and the love that God has towards us. According to this chapter our duty to love one another follows from a number of truths that we know about God. Thus we are told (a) that love is from God,[50] (b) that God loved us,[51] and (c) that God is love.[52] It is clear that the argument hangs on (c) as well as (b): it would not be sufficient to say that God loved us, although that is, of course, one factor that contributes to our understanding of why we should also love each other; but to say that God *is* love is to say more than that God loved us: (c) is not merely a repetition of (b) but adds something more.

What exactly is it that (c) adds to the argument? Most modern commentators, following and citing C. H. Dodd as their authority,[53] take it that (c) differs from (b) in specifying that love is not merely *one* of the activities of God, so that God might act in some cases lovingly and in other cases in other ways, perhaps with anger, jealousy, or indifference, but rather that love is *the* essential activity of God. On this view the point is that every activity of God is loving activity, and all his relations with men are characterized by love on

---

[48] 'Love' with a capital 'L' is ruled out by Neil Alexander, *The Epistles of John* (London, 1962), 107 as a rendering of 1 John 4: 8; what he means is unclear. Does this exclude sense (b) or only a personification of sense (b)? Or is Alexander thinking of some other meaning of 'Love'? Cf. also Dodd, *The Johannine Epistles*, 108. On the personification of Love see below, sect. (iii) (d) and Ch. 3.

[49] The preoccupation with love of the *brethren* in this Epistle need not worry us at present. It has been a subject of scholarly argument for centuries: see Augustine, *In Ep. Joann. ad Parth* VIII. 4 (*PL* 35. 2037–42).

[50] ἡ ἀγάπη ἐκ τοῦ θεοῦ ἐστιν, verse 7.

[51] ὁ θεὸς ἠγάπησεν ἡμᾶς, verses 11 and 19.

[52] ὁ θεὸς ἀγάπη ἐστιν, verses 8 and 16.

[53] Cf. Dodd, *The Johannine Epistles*, 106–10. More recently see, for example, Alexander, *The Epistles of John*, 107; Furnish, *The Love Command*, 154.

his part. Hence on this interpretation the claim that God *is* love adds to the claim that God *has* loved the clarification that that loving activity is essential to his nature and characteristic.

The claim that all God's activities are loving activities might indeed be true, and in its own right that might be a helpful observation, but it does not obviously belong in the argument as we have it in 1 John 4.[54] What we need for that argument, and what the claim that God is love in verse 8 is clearly supposed to be, is a premiss that relates the nature of God as we know him with our behaviour towards one another and particularly our duty to love one another:

He who does not love does not know God; for God is love.[55]

The claim that God is love is not merely a reinforced repetition of the assertion that God loved us; indeed God's love for us has not yet been mentioned in this chapter when we meet 'God is love' in verse 8. Rather it follows immediately on the claim that love is *from* God in verse 7, and leads *into* the reflection on God's own loving activity towards us introduced in verse 9.

Beloved, let us love one another: for love is of God; and he who loves is born of God and knows God. He who does not love does not know God; for God is love. In this the love of God was made manifest among us, that God sent his only Son into the world, so that we might live through him.[56]

The important point that the chapter is stressing is that love, our love for our fellow human beings, comes from God and derives from our relationship with God. Augustine was surely right, therefore, to see a vital connection between the claim (*a*) that love is *from* God in verse 7 and the claim (*c*) that God *is* love in verse 8.[57] What (*c*) adds is the point that God is *the* source of love in our lives, and that his very being is constituted in the effect he has on the way we live

---

[54] Of course this claim might not seem wholly inappropriate: the more we recognize God's love the more we might feel obliged to respond in kind. On the other hand it is not necessary: the chapter proceeds to emphasize that the full extent of God's love is manifested in the Incarnation; that in itself would be sufficient to demand a response regardless of whether love was an essential and consistent characteristic of God (vv. 9–11).

[55] 1 John 4: 8.

[56] 1 John 4: 7–9.

[57] Augustine, *In Ep. Joann. ad Parth* VII. 5 (*PL* 35. 2031).

and love. This is why it is nonsense to claim that we know God if the effect of his influence is not apparent in a life in love. Thus the claim (*c*) that God is love, is directly related to (*a*), that love is from God, but puts it in stronger terms. Love is not just one of a number of alternative effects that God might have on our lives (say love, joy, peace ...) any one of which might demonstrate that we knew (or dwelt in) God; rather love, unlike those others, is both a necessary and sufficient condition for the truth of the claim that one knows God, because God is essentially (the cause of) love.[58]

This gives us a clear connection between points (*a*) and (*c*), both of which are directly related to the concern with the love that the brethren should have to one another, which is the subject of the chapter. The effect is to leave it unclear how point (*b*) fits in: why is it relevant to mention that God loved us and revealed his love in sending his Son, and what does the observation contribute to the argument? It is apparent from verses 9–11 that it serves two purposes. First, the Incarnation is presented in verse 9 as evidence: 'In this the love of God was made manifest ...'[59] This is evidence primarily of God's loving activity, but the structure of the argument suggests that it is serving here in a more general capacity as evidence that God's nature is intimately bound up with love and that he is source and cause of love. Love, we are told, derives from God: in support of that claim the writer cites God's own love in sending his Son. Clearly this does not amount to a rigorous demonstration that God himself is the source of that or other such love, let alone the only source of such love, but the point is suggestive rather than conclusive.

Secondly, we should probably take verses 9 to 11 as a subsidiary argument in their own right in which God's own unmotivated love for us is cited as a model for our own practice, and a moral obligation is derived from the fact that we have been beneficiaries of such a love: 'In this is love, not that we loved God but that he loved us, and sent his Son to be the expiation for our sins. Beloved, if God so loved us, we also ought to love one another.'[60] This moral argument stands in its own right, independently of the argument in verses 7–

[58] For knowledge of God love is both a necessary condition (verse 8: he who does not love does not know God) and a sufficient condition (verse 7: he who loves is born of God and knows God; or verse 16: he who abides in love abides in God).

[59] I John 4: 9.

[60] I John 4: 10–11.

8 that we must love because love is from God and because God is
(the cause of) love. The two arguments are then brought together
in verse 16 where our *knowledge* of the love that God has shown to
us and our knowledge of God (that God is love) result in our
'abiding in love', 'abiding in God' and God's abiding in us. Clearly
there is a close connection between 'knowing God' (vv. 7–8) and
'knowing the love that God has for us' (v. 16). It appears, then, that
it makes reasonable sense in the context of this Epistle to take the
phrase 'God is love' to mean that God is the source of love; such a
reading coheres well with the concerns of the passage, and its
emphasis on the love that the brethren should show to one another
and that derives from God. The fact that this was how it was taken
by many Patristic writers lends support to the idea that it is the
most obvious way to take the text, as well as being much better as
an interpretation of the argument presented by the writer of the
Epistle.

### (iii)  *Four definitions of love*

The main reason why we have particular difficulty with handling
the New Testament claim that God is love is that it is not clear
what is the reference of the word 'love'. The same difficulty obscures
many other passages of the New Testament where 'love' is mentioned; to say that someone loves his brother may be tolerably clear,
but problems arise when we say love is, or does, certain things.
What is love? A thing? An abstract concept? A funny feeling? A
relationship? A person? This sort of hesitation in locating the
referent of the term 'love' leads to defensive interpretations of such
claims in the New Testament as 'God is love'. In their concern to
avoid making God an abstraction[61] or a funny feeling[62] most modern
commentators hasten to the conclusion that what is meant is loving
activity or behaviour[63] since this alone, in their view, preserves
the personal nature of God so characteristic of New Testament
Christianity. Thus, they suggest, 'God is love' implies that God
loves, and furthermore it implies that 'all his activity is loving
activity'.[64]

---

[61] See, for example, Dodd *The Johannine Epistles*, 107–8.
[62] Emotion is, of course, a normal definition of love in other contexts: see below.
[63] An exception must be made for those who follow Augustine (e.g. *De Trinitate*, 9) in seeing love as a relation.
[64] Dodd, *The Johannine Epistles*, 108. See above, pp. 42–3.

Before we buy this conclusion we must question whether it is correct to say that this is the only definition that preserves a personal God, and indeed whether it does preserve a personal God, or only one programmed to act in a loving manner. We shall clearly benefit from examining a number of alternative interpretations of what 'love' might mean in various contexts, since it seems clear that it does not always refer to the same sort of thing.

### (a) Love as an emotion or feeling

This seems to be a popular definition of what we should be talking about when we talk of love. Love is either the feeling that the lover has with regard to the beloved (whether of desire or warmth or benevolence or whatever) or simply a tendency or impulse analysed in terms of the object rather than in terms of the feelings involved, as for example a love of oranges might be an appetite or tendency to choose oranges.[65] This would be to reduce love to the minimum appetitive desire.

More common is the idea that love involves more than mere impulse or appetite, since it includes a feeling towards the beloved object, or a particular emotional response. Love would be distinguished from desire on the basis of the feelings, perhaps on the basis that love, unlike desire, presupposes that the lover feels concern or benevolence for the beloved or at least seeks to preserve rather than devour the beloved. Thus, while love is still defined by the feelings involved, it becomes clear that those feelings can only occur within a particular relationship: whereas I might have a desire for any old orange, I can only have love for a particular individual or individuals.[66]

### (b) Love as a type of behaviour or action

On the view that love is first of all an emotion, it could only be in a derivative sense that we should call an action 'love'. Even if we held

---

[65] But note that the majority of thinkers would distinguish liking for *things* (oranges) from love proper which must have a personal object (human or super-human, or perhaps in certain circumstances a non-human animal). See Lewis, *The Four Loves*, ch. 2.

[66] For this view see, for example, Paul Tillich, *Love, Power and Justice* (London, 1954), 3. Against love as merely a feeling, D. Van de Vate, *Romantic Love* (University Park, Pa., 1981), 5–18. Of course in practice I might be choosy about my oranges. How does liking a particular orange better than another one differ from having a relationship with an individual?

that emotions could only be defined by the behaviour they lead to, it would still be the emotion and not the action that was properly speaking the love in question. On this view a loving act would be so described merely because it is the sort of action characteristic of one who loves.

This view recommends itself when we have to deal with actions that are commonly associated with love but need not imply love. When Judas kissed Jesus did he love Jesus? To answer this question it seems we need more than just the action; we need to know what his feelings or emotions or attitude were.

On the other hand, many would disagree. Love without action, it might be said, is not worthy of the name, and just as you cannot love but act as if you did not, so it would be impossible to act consistently in a loving manner yet have no love. In some sense the action is love, then, and it might be held that, in certain contexts at least, what we mean by the term 'love' is primarily the outward behaviour, not the inward disposition. In the case of Judas we should not only expect to take his actions into account, but we might even consider them the only relevant criterion for deciding whether he loved: loving behaviour is both a necessary and a sufficient condition for demonstrating an example of love. On the other hand, this will not mean that that is all we mean when we say he loves; rather we should probably in most cases mean that we understand from the behaviour that the corresponding emotion or attitude lies behind it. But while it is normal to consider both the appropriate actions and the appropriate feelings as essentially connected, it seems that the term 'love' can sometimes be used with reference to one or the other independently. Hence on this definition love is a way of behaving, and can become both a habit and a duty.[67]

## (c) Love as a relationship or bond

While it makes good sense to define love as behaviour or action when talking of situations in which we can choose to love, or be commanded or expected to love, it may seem less adequate for characterizing an individual action out of context. Even if we are not attempting to infer what the underlying emotions are, never-

---

[67] Cf. the command to love, in the Old and New Testaments; see Furnish, *The Love Command*. On the difficulty of taking the love command to apply to a feeling see ibid. 200–1; Tillich, *Love, Power and Justice*, 4. Also H. McCabe, *Law, Love and Language* (1968; 2nd edn. London, 1979), 14–17.

theless we shall not feel ready to classify one kiss on the part of Judas as love without a wider context. What we gain from viewing a wider context is, among other things, a sense of the relationship between two parties. For one thing, we expect that relationship to become apparent over time, even though some of the individual actions might be uncharacteristic. In classifying a relationship as love we should not be disturbed by brief departures from the characteristic behaviour, just as we should not be prepared to base a judgement on only one action. On the other hand, in some cases one action might be decisive (say in a moment of crisis or when a relationship is put to the test). In such a case, arguably what we conclude from the one decisive action is not so much that that one action was love, but that the relationship it evidenced was love. The fact that Piglet gave Eeyore a balloon demonstrates that Piglet loved Eeyore; but 'Piglet loved Eeyore' describes not an action but a relationship.

This is only one possible account of what it might mean to say that love is a relationship. Alternatively at the purely logical level it may simply mean that love involves two parties, A and B, lover and beloved. In the case of love there must be two parties and they must be related one to the other as lover and beloved. For instance, if it were right to suppose that love is merely an emotion it need not follow that any relation to a second party was involved. Some emotions are not directed at any specific object: I may feel afraid, without an identifiable object, either real or imaginary, of which I am afraid; one might feel sad, miserable, or depressed, but not for or about another person or thing. By contrast, love seems necessarily to be directed towards some object, or at least some class of potential objects. If I love I must love something (but not, however, 'about' something, as one is inclined to say with fear or sorrow). Hence love implies relation. Similarly, if we take the active aspect of love it will not be sufficient in its own right. Some sorts of action can be performed without a recipient to which or for which the act is done: it is not just that I can run or skip without doing that to anyone, but I can even act violently or nervously without an object to do it to. But it seems less plausible that I could act lovingly without implying some party whom I should be said to love, and for whom the loving act is done. To specify that love is a relation indicates that it is the sort of behaviour that requires an object.

To say that love is a relationship implies that there are two (or more) parties to the relationship.[68] To say that love is a *bond* implies something further. What more does it imply? There seem to be two alternatives. Either we may mean that the relationship is one of attachment, as opposed to other relations (e.g. independence) which are relations of detachment or some other sort. Thus it specifies more than that there are two parties, indicating also the *sort* of relation that holds between the two. Alternatively we may take it that a bond is not any attachment but a particular sort of attachment, for example an emotional attachment. Then the identification of love as a bond would serve as a combination of the first definition (an emotion) and the third (a relationship). Or alternatively 'bond' might imply not the emotion but the cohesiveness or enduring character of the relationship. In this sense love, to be a bond, must be lasting, whereas passing fancy, although also implying attachment of an emotional nature, would not be a bond.

### (d) Love as an external cause of loving relationships

In suggesting these various meanings of the term 'love' I am not intending that we should select one to the exclusion of the others as the correct one. The point is rather that on different occasions the word 'love' can imply any of these things, or sometimes more than one. The result is not to make the term strictly ambiguous since the meanings are all evidently related, and it is more satisfactory to analyse them as a case of 'family resemblance' or 'focal meaning'. In a case of 'focal meaning' a word bears a number of related senses that cluster round a single focus or primary meaning.[69] Nevertheless, in so far as philosophers have attempted any analysis of love, there is little agreement as to where the focus of the cluster lies:[70] do all the senses derive from the characteristic emotion, or

---

[68] We say two or more because it often seems that we may have a love directed to a plurality of objects: not only love of oranges but also, say, love of one's siblings or children. It is less usual to suppose that two subjects could share the same love, though there is a sense in which, say, siblings might 'share' a love of their mother.

[69] On focal meaning see G. E. L. Owen, 'Logic and Metaphysics in Some Earlier Works of Aristotle', in I. Düring and G. E. L. Owen (eds.), *Aristotle and Plato in the Mid Fourth Century* (Göteborg, 1960), 163–90. Aristotle applies focal meaning to friendship at *Eudemian Ethics*, 7. 1236a7–33.

[70] In addition to Aristotle see e.g. R. G. Hazo, *The Idea of Love* (New York, 1967). Works dealing with the theology of Christian love rarely stop to consider what love is; it is hard to give page references for the absence of discussion. On the question of how behaviour relates to inner feeling see McCabe, *Law, Love and Language*, 14–17.

from the relationship or the characteristic behaviour of one who loves?[71] It seems more appropriate to suggest that Wittgenstein's notion of family resemblance characterizes the situation better, since the meanings are all on an equal footing and none seems primary or more central than the rest.

It is worth making a distinction between the abstract concept 'love' that we think of when we argue about the meaning and uses of the word, and the other more traditional use of 'Love' (usually with capital 'L') for a god, a personified power who presides over the relationships for which he (or she) can be held responsible. This influential figure Love is clearly not identical either with the relationships or emotions he causes, or with our abstract concept 'love', that we can posit as an idea behind the varied everyday uses of the term. Confusion is likely to arise if we fail to distinguish between the concept 'love' and the god Love, confusion such as the doubtless well-motivated but misguided concern to deny that God could possibly be Love (with a capital 'L') because that would be to make God a mere abstraction, foreign to the whole Christian tradition.[72] So far from being an abstract generalization, the classic picture of Love is as a person,[73] an individual characterized as having responsibility for various manifestations of loving behaviour among mortals. To transfer this imagery to a Christian context is not to make God an impersonal or abstract being, but rather to make him personally responsible as the supreme cause of love. The notion that God gives the power and inclination to love, as well as being himself involved in love perhaps, is not only compatible with, but probably essential to the Christian tradition.

Thus it is in this sense that we are to consider the fourth possible meaning of 'love', as referring to an external cause: love, that causes me to feel affection for you, or you to act lovingly towards your brother. This is not to say, of course, that any time we meet the term 'love' we can take it to refer in this way to the source or cause of love; on the contrary, we can only take it this way in rather specialized contexts. Nor does it follow that everyone must be

---

[71] Aristotle distinguishes the senses of *philia* not in these terms but by the motivation: friendship for pleasure, usefulness, or virtue, *Eudemian Ethics*, 7. 1236a30 ff.

[72] Cf. Alexander, *The Epistles of John*, 107.

[73] Aphrodite (Venus) and Eros (Cupid) are the most obvious examples, but cf. *Philia*, one of two cosmic powers in Empedocles, and Love the aeon in various gnostic systems (e.g. *Apocryphon of John*, ii. 1. 8).

committed to the existence of such an external or supernatural being, Love, as a cause or explanation of some or all forms of love; clearly not. All that we must grant is that the word can be used (with or without the capital 'L') to refer to such a figure.[74]

I have suggested four possible ways of understanding the word 'love'. It may be that further possibilities could also be suggested, but four will be enough to be going on with. They are sufficient to suggest that there is not a single sense, but that we can use the word to mean somewhat different things in different contexts. This is quite independent of any attempt to classify different *types* of love, or to assign different names (such as *agape* and *eros*) to the various sorts of loving relationship that come under the English vocable 'love'.[75] The point is rather to observe that all those different types of love have this feature in common, that the word 'love' can be used to designate an emotion, a relationship, a certain sort of behaviour, or a person or power responsible for initiating those things. Exactly the same is true (for example) of the word 'charity', which is commonly used to specify one type of love. When we speak of charity we may refer to charitable behaviour, charitable feelings towards others, a charitable relationship between two parties, or Charity, a female person who presides over these things. There seems no reason why any of these meanings if applied to God should threaten his personal nature.

Observing that love has a number of related meanings in different contexts has nothing to do with identifying different kinds of love. What I want to emphasize is first that it is correct to use the term 'love' to name the cause or power responsible for loving relationships, and that that use is important in understanding the ancient and biblical texts; and secondly that we do not need to distinguish different kinds of love with different kinds of objects or different explanations, simply in virtue of seeing that the word can be used in different ways. All these ways cohere round the same kind of loving relationship.

---

[74] 'Love' can also be used personally to mean the beloved, as in 'I will give my love an apple'.

[75] It is important to distinguish my account of four definitions of love from possible classifications of four types of love, as for example in Lewis, *The Four Loves*, and indeed from the three types of love distinguished by Aristotle in terms of motivation in *Eudemian Ethics*, bk. 7.

# 3

# Arrows, *Eros*, *Agape*

In the prologue to the *Commentary on the Song of Songs*, Origen raises the question of how far and in what context we might be justified in using the language of *eros* to describe the relationship between God and humankind. While recognizing that the use of erotic imagery may be a source of moral error for some,[1] and hence allowing that scripture may deliberately prefer the language of 'charity', Origen is of the opinion that the two sets of terms are not importantly distinct; there is, in his view, no theological significance to the preference for the language of 'charity'. It would be perfectly correct and reasonable to substitute the terminology of *eros*.[2]

This justification of the use of the language of *eros* was one of the passages regarded by Anders Nygren as evidence of an attempt by Patristic thinkers to assimilate Platonic *Eros* and Christian *Agape*. Although Origen's views were not so influential as those of Augustine in the same area, the identification of the two traditions was, Nygren claims, already there in Origen. 'Thus in Origen, for the first time in the history of the Christian idea of love, we find a real synthesis between the Christian and the Hellenistic views of love.'[3] Nygren regards this as a damaging assimilation because, in his view, it is the Greek model that takes precedence and determines the character of the result, and it is axiomatic for him that the Greek model is in itself inappropriate to Christianity, and hence a corruption of the genuinely Christian motif of *Agape*.

Thinkers since Nygren have not always been wholly convinced by his opposition to Origen's project. J. M. Rist,[4] for example, argues that what we find in Origen is a non-appetitive type of *eros*, quite different from the selfish desire to possess that Nygren described and characterized as utterly opposed to the Christian

---

[1] Origen, *ComCt* 63.
[2] Ibid. 71.
[3] Anders Nygren, *Agape and Eros*, 391.
[4] J. M. Rist, *Eros and Psyche: Studies in Plato, Plotinus and Origen*, Phoenix supplementary vol. 6 (Toronto, 1964), esp. 204–7; cf. 79–80.

motif of *agape*. Origen, Rist suggests, describes a downward-flowing love that corresponds more closely to the Christian notion of *agape*, while yet being not alien to the Platonic tradition.

It seems plain to me that Rist is correct to interpret Origen in this way, and I propose in this chapter to take his basic insights for granted. It is apparent that Origen is not setting out to distort the Christian view of love so as to bring it into line with a form of Platonic desire, but rather that his analysis is formed first and foremost by an appreciation of the Christian tradition, and secondly by the recognition that certain features of the Platonic tradition can fruitfully be brought to enrich our understanding of the Christian ideal without corrupting it. Nevertheless, Rist's analysis depends on locating a downward-flowing love of the appropriate sort within the Platonic tradition, in order to demonstrate that Origen is justified in looking to Platonism and invoking *eros* at all as a suitable kind of discourse in this context. The task is not as easy as we might have hoped. Rist locates a suitable reference to such a downward-flowing love in Plotinus,[5] but it has to be admitted that this is not a prominent feature of Plotinus' thought; furthermore it is doubtful whether a reference in Plotinus will be sufficient, since it remains unclear whether Origen could have known the work of Plotinus.[6] However, Rist also argues that an outward-looking love of the appropriate sort can be traced in Plato himself, both in the *Symposium*[7] and in the *Phaedrus*[8] as well as in the concern of the demiurge in the *Timaeus*. Even if we take the words of Diotima in the *Symposium* and of Timaeus in the *Timaeus* as straight Platonic doctrine there is some scope to find there a notion of generous love.

---

[5] Ibid. 78–87. See particularly Plotinus, *Ennead* 6. 8. 15.

[6] It appears that both Origen and Plotinus may have studied at different times under Ammonius Saccas in Alexandria, and it seems that there may have been another Origen who was a pupil at the same time as Plotinus, whom Plotinus knew and respected. Alternatively it is possible that the Origen Plotinus knew was our Origen. Scholars are still not agreed on this issue (see e.g. Joseph Trigg, *Origen* (Atlanta, 1983, and London, 1985), 259–60; H. Crouzel, *Origen*, English translation by A. S. Warrall (Edinburgh, 1989), 10–11; Mark Edwards, 'Ammonius, Teacher of Origen', *Journal of Ecclesiastical History*, 44 (1993), 169–81). The evidence comes from Eusebius, *HE*, bk. 6, ch. 9, and Porphyry's *Life of Plotinus*. But our Origen certainly left Alexandria in 233, and since Plotinus was twenty years younger, it seems likely that most of Plotinus' thought dates from a period when Origen was not around. It is certainly possible that Plotinus knew something of Origen's work, and that both show the influence of Ammonius Saccas.

[7] 212a.

[8] 253a. Rist, *Eros and Psyche*, 33–7.

In this chapter I shall leave aside the relation between Origen's thought and that of Plotinus,[9] and focus on the issue of how far we should seek a new assessment of Plato's own position on acquisitive love; secondly I shall consider the terminology of lover and beloved, asking who loves whom, and for what; and thirdly I shall ask how far we may reverse those roles, and what theological implications emerge from placing God in the various available roles.

## I. PLATO

When the subject for discussion is love in Plato the attention of scholars naturally focuses first on the *Symposium*. The *Symposium* is a dialogue about *eros*, and it consists of a series of speeches in praise of the god of love. Its artistry builds on the tension between the conventions of the traditional discourse of love, and the unconventionality of Socrates both as lover and as thinker on love. This unconventionality is marked by his using a woman, the priestess Diotima, as his source of wisdom on erotic matters.[10]

If the speech of Socrates in the *Symposium* is taken as an exposition of *Platonic* doctrine, it is easy to assume that Plato's principal analysis of love is akin to what Nygren identified as *Eros*, a selfish desire to possess an inanimate good. It seems that for Plato love is primarily a desire for something that you lack and need and hope to gain.[11] This is the way that Nygren reads the *Symposium*, and indeed the myth in the *Phaedrus* too, while allowing that there is a background for both in the mystery religions and Orphism.[12] Although Rist argues for a modification of this interpretation in the sense that he finds in the Platonic texts *both* the acquisitive love that Nygren found *and* an other-regarding creative love, he too

[9] See below, Ch. 7 for thoughts on this theme.

[10] For more detailed analysis of the dramatic artistry involved in the *Symposium*, see Ch. 4.

[11] This interpretation is only partly accurate: for a detailed discussion of the kind of aspiration inspired by love, and the stress on the aspiration of the lover, rather than the beauty of the object, see below, Ch. 4.

[12] This is all part of the negative rhetoric of Nygren's case; he hints at three problems in Platonic teaching on *eros*: (1) it is egocentric, and hence unchristian; (2) it is pagan mystery religion and hence unchristian; (3) (despite 2) it is part and parcel of the 'doctrine of Ideas' and hence of a system that privileges the conceptual over the world of the senses, and thus is philosophical and unchristian. Nygren, *Agape and Eros*, 166–81.

starts from the same basic assumption that these texts, and within the *Symposium* Diotima's speech in particular, do include an account of acquisitive love, and do give us direct access to the doctrines Plato would affirm without question.

Starting from such a reading of the *Symposium,* Nygren was surely right to suggest that if such an acquisitive relationship occurs between God and humankind it can apply only to one thing, humanity's love for God, and in that context it would imply that one loves God because one needs God and desires to gain possession of him or of the benefits God can provide. It would be paradoxical to suggest that God could love mankind with a love based on need or lack. Thus 'Platonic Love' of this sort could be (and, according to Nygren, sometimes was) attributed to humankind in its love for God, but only with certain unattractive consequences. The implications of analysing mankind's love for God as a case of needy desire in accordance with such a reading of Diotima's speech are to make humanity's motives self-interested and grasping. It does not leave humanity morally the better for its devotion to God. If Nygren were right that this was the notion of love imported by the Fathers under the influence of Plato, we might fairly agree with him that the results would be unsatisfactory.

It is one thing to agree that the notion of acquisitive *eros* that Nygren found in Diotima's speech cannot be satisfactory as a motif in Christianity, but quite another to reject *eros* altogether. We must reject *eros* altogether only if that is the only available notion of *eros* to which early Christian writers might be appealing; but that is clearly not the case. As we have already seen, the idea that the Platonic tradition knows of no other kind of *eros* has been effectively challenged by Rist in his observation that even within Diotima's speech, and certainly within Plato and the Platonist tradition, there is an alternative model of *eros* at work. But he still assumes that the conventional reading of what Diotima says in the *Symposium* is at least part of Plato's doctrine of love.[13] What I shall be suggesting here is a more radical reassessment of Plato's position, to the effect

---

[13] 'This violent sense of need is what Plato primarily means by love, and to the casual reader his analysis of the nature of Ἔρως gives little trace of any non-appetitive ideal. However, when we come to consider the actions of the Gods and of those perfect mortals who have been able to follow the path of Ἔρως to its end, we find a considerably less egoistic, and as the future was to show, more fruiful notion, that of creation as a result of "Love perfected".' Rist, *Eros and Psyche,* 26.

that we need perhaps never suppose that the *Symposium* should be read in that way, and indeed that Plato himself suggests the reasons why it should not be taken as suggesting that love is motivated by self-interest, or explained by appeal to the desirable nature of the object of acquisitive love. If that was ever the teaching of the *Symposium,* which I would deny,[14] it cannot be seen as the unquestioned teaching of Plato on the subject of love, since in the *Lysis* he puts forward, or had already put forward, examples that undermine that teaching.[15]

There might be several reasons, in any case, for casting some doubt on the status of Diotima's speech in the *Symposium.* First, it is not safe to assume that the views put forward by Socrates or any other participant in a Platonic dialogue are those of Plato himself, and this is perhaps even more unjustified in the case of views that are presented in monologue than in passages where argument and discussion with an interlocutor suggest that a reasoned case is being presented, where we may assess the arguments Plato offers for a view and the seriousness with which he offers them. In the *Symposium* Diotima speaks the language of conviction but offers few arguments in support of her account. Her views are accepted almost without demur by Socrates and are not subject to criticism by his audience. How is the reader to respond to her testimony?

Secondly, there is a question of authority. Occasionally (for example in the *Republic*) Plato presents Socrates as speaking in his own person; but here in the *Symposium* Plato presents a Chinese box of nested narratives, at the innermost level of which Socrates

---

[14] See Ch. 4.

[15] In addition to the *Symposium* and the *Lysis,* to which I devote most attention in this book, there is also important material on love in the *Phaedrus,* which also counts against the acquisitive interpretation of the *Symposium.* I have included rather less than I would have liked on the *Phaedrus* in this book (see below, Ch. 4); there is clearly scope for further work in that area. Another dialogue that I have wholly neglected is the *Alcibiades,* where love is mentioned, somewhat inconsequentially, in a dialogue primarily about political expertise, responsibility, and self-knowledge. John Dillon has drawn my attention to the influence of this text in later Greek thought on erotic matters (John Dillon, 'A Platonist Ars Amatoria', *Classical Quarterly,* forthcoming). Perhaps most interesting is the fact that the *Alcibiades* leaves hanging an apparent contradiction between the need for justice, involving each citizen keeping to his own business, and the need for *philia* in a city, which is not acquired in respect of the citizens' knowledge of their own individual branch of technical expertise, yet is somehow connected with justice, *Alcibiades,* 126b–127d.

resigns his authority to the woman of Mantinea, Diotima.[16] It seems that we should need to explore the significance of this move, before we could determine the status of Diotima's account. There is, after all, no clear reason to suppose that more authority should be accorded to Socrates' speech (quoting Diotima) than to any other speech in the dialogue. Why has it generally been supposed that Socrates' speech is the one that does the work?[17] It seems fairly clear that this conventional assumption rests on the expectation that what Socrates says is what Plato means us to believe. But this expectation will need to be defended, particularly for a dialogue such as the *Symposium* in which the major part consists of speeches by others besides Socrates.

The third and most important reason for questioning whether the conventional reading of the *Symposium* is acceptable is the fact that Plato wrote the *Lysis*; and the *Lysis*, which contrasts with the *Symposium* in that it is composed of *arguments*, effectively undermines the notion of love that Nygren and many others have found in Diotima's speech. Indeed, the last argument in the *Lysis*, immediately before the dialogue ends in disarray, considers a notion of love so closely reminiscent of the *Symposium* that the reader cannot fail to notice that the impasse at the end, the failure to give any satisfactory account of love, effectively leaves such a reading of the *Symposium* in tatters. That is to say, it prevents us from reading into the *Symposium* an acquisitive theory of love such as Nygren found there, since Plato himself shows that that is unsatisfactory in the *Lysis*.[18] It will be worthwhile considering the implications of the *Lysis* for our assessment of Plato's views on love.

---

[16] On the significance of the nested narratives, see below, Ch. 4.

[17] This assumption does not always go unquestioned now. Nussbaum, for example, diagnoses the problem that lies behind Vlastos's assessment of Plato on love as a failure to read the dialogue as a whole; she herself takes the speech of Alcibiades as an important acknowledgement that Plato saw more than one side of the picture. Martha Nussbaum, *The Fragility of Goodness* (Cambridge, 1986), 165–99; cf. Gregory Vlastos, 'The Individual as Object of Love in Plato', in G. Vlastos, *Platonic Studies* (Princeton, NJ, 1981), 1–34.

[18] I do not think that it rules out the more subtle reading of the *Symposium* story, as an account of human aspirations, with its focus on the idea that our aspirations are inspired by the effect of Eros within ourselves, and not by the beauty of the object of desire itself. This interpretation is the subject of Ch. 4.

## 2. PLATO'S *LYSIS*

It is an open question where the *Lysis* occurs in the sequence of Plato's writings.[19] But the date at which Plato himself wrote it may not have much significance as regards the order in which the reader was expected to encounter the dialogues. It remains unclear, therefore, whether a reader would be expected to approach the *Lysis* having the *Symposium* in mind, or to approach the *Symposium* having already read the *Lysis*. Either way it has to be admitted that the two dialogues play off against each other, and the conclusions reached in the *Lysis* make the uncritical, acquisitive, reading of the *Symposium* impossible. We are bound to be left asking how Plato means us to take Diotima's story. But perhaps we should also be open to the possibility that some irony should be read into the *Lysis* itself in the light of the *Symposium*.

The *Lysis* is about loving. Most of the time it focuses on the term *philia*, but it also deals with both *eros* and *agape*. Three examples of love are particularly prominent in the dialogue:

1. Hippothales, a young man, is the lover (*erastes*) of Lysis, a boy; the whole dialogue is set up as an illustration of how a lover should address his boy.
2. The boy Lysis has a friend called Menexenus who is the same age; they are fond of each other.
3. Lysis claims, when asked (207d), that his parents love him.

In the course of the dialogue all three of these examples of love are shown to be impossible on the assumption that love is something self-seeking that expects to gain something of benefit to the lover. In the case of Lysis' parents, it appears that they could only love him if he were wise and good and able to bring some benefit to them. Yet Lysis is a mere boy and not apparently loved for any wisdom or virtue he already possesses or anything he does for his

[19] Considerations about possible dates can be found in M. M. Mackenzie, 'Impasse and Explanation: From the *Lysis* to the *Phaedo*', *Archiv für Geschichte der Philosophie*, 70 (1988), 15–45, and cf. David Bolotin, *Plato's Dialogue on Friendship* (Ithaca, NY and London, 1979), and G. Vlastos, 'Is the *Lysis* a Vehicle of Platonic Doctrine?', in Vlastos, *Platonic Studies*. In suggesting that there is some doubt about the date of the *Lysis*, I do not mean to say that the date matters to my analysis here, though it might seem more plausible that it radically undermines any possible self-interested reading of the *Symposium* if it is given a date after that dialogue, or is intended to be read after that dialogue.

parents. Hence, the argument concludes, Lysis' parents do not love him[20] (and nor apparently could anyone else, including his lover). Furthermore, the dialogue suggests,[21] Lysis and Menexenus cannot really be friends since they are too alike and neither has anything to offer that the other needs and has not got himself. Thirdly, Hippothales' love for Lysis turns out to be impossible if it is explained as a desire for something that is properly his but which he lacks and needs, an explanation which has obvious echoes of the analysis offered by Diotima; if that is so the love would have to be mutual, since Lysis will stand in the same relation to Hippothales as Hippothales does to Lysis.[22] But the relationship between a lover and his boy plainly is not mutual, and if non-mutual love turns out to be impossible this type of relationship will be inexplicable.

In theory there might be two ways of reading this sequence of arguments: we might take them at face value as Plato's attempt to show that certain relationships that we normally think of as love cannot actually be explained on the analysis of love to which we are committed, so that we have to conclude that parents, friends, and lovers do not love their respective objects. Or, on the more appropriate interpretation, the dialogue leads to a serious impasse, because we perceive that these are the most classic examples of love, and that if they are inexplicable something has gone seriously wrong with the analysis of love. It would be a reductio of any theory of love if it failed to account for these clear examples. On this view there will be Platonic irony (as well as Socratic irony)[23] in so far as Plato is inviting his readers to reject the analysis of love that has led to the absurd impasse in which Socrates and his companions find themselves. In each case the argument goes wrong as a result of an assumption that love seeks to gain from the beloved; in these classic cases it proves difficult to find anything, or anything sufficiently unique, to be gained, so as to account for the relationship in question.

Whatever response the reader of the *Lysis* is to make to the difficulties raised about acquisitive love, it remains true that the

---

[20] 210d.

[21] 215a–b.

[22] 222ab.

[23] Socratic irony appears in so far as Socrates is more wise than his interlocutors; Platonic irony appears when Plato is offering a different solution to his readers from that offered by Socrates to his interlocutors.

dialogue puts up for scrutiny another kind of love that is not susceptible (or not plainly susceptible) to the analysis associated with Diotima's theory in the *Symposium*. In the *Lysis* Socrates is himself presented as the model of the true lover who loves a boy not because he is wise or good or beautiful already but because the boy is ignorant, prepared to admit his ignorance and ready to learn.[24] Nor will the boy immediately love Socrates for the humiliation which Socrates applies to get him to recognize his ignorance. Socrates is presented as a lover of wisdom, but also an expert on the kind of love that cares for those who are not wise but have the capacity to become lovers of wisdom.

What the *Lysis* does is to offer three examples of a love that is not based on acquisitive motives. The conversation reveals that such a non-acquisitive love is a familiar part of the common-sense understanding of love brought to the dialogue by Hippothales and the boys that Socrates is talking to. They all suppose without difficulty that parents love their children, friends love each other, and lovers love their boys. It is only when Socrates asks what they love them *for* that they find themselves at a loss to give an explanation.

The point will by now be clear. It is apparent from the *Lysis* that Plato could convincingly represent the common assumptions of Athenians about love as being incompatible with an acquisitive analysis of love. It suggests that there is good reason to think that the ordinary way of thinking presupposed that love did not have to be explained in self-interested terms; Diotima's account in the *Symposium* would be at the very least a radical reassessment of the explanation of love, if it seriously presented such a desire-oriented rationale as an account of love. It would not be an expression of how the Greeks in general thought about love. Hence it would be wrong to suppose that Greek thought knew of no model of unselfish affection; indeed, there is no reason to think that Plato himself is leaving us with a self-interested explanation of love. If the *Lysis* is taken seriously, Plato is actually offering us precisely the material we need to establish that the conventional interpretation of Diotima's

[24] In the *Symposium* too Socrates is presented as the archetypal lover, but the ambiguity of his relationship with Alcibiades and other potential candidates for his affections in the *Symposium* leaves it an open question whether the love in which Socrates is expert is a love of what is already beautiful, good, and wise, as Diotima's analysis would require. On Socrates as the type of Love, see Ch. 4.

speech will not do as an analysis of love, and hence that either the account offered in the *Symposium* is not seriously to be adopted, or it must be read in another way.

This means that when we turn to the work of the Fathers of the Church we have no reason to suppose the only view of love that was available in their classical background was the acquisitive one. Even if the Fathers were unaware of other Platonic dialogues besides the *Symposium,* including the *Phaedrus* as well as the *Lysis,* we need not suppose that they were unaware that Diotima's account in the *Symposium* was unconventional in its analysis of love. It is plain that the conventions of Greek ideology were familiar with a less self-centred picture of the lover than is presented on the usual interpretation of the *Symposium.* We may reasonably suppose that the Fathers had a choice of models, even within their Greek heritage, that they might adopt in seeking to analyse the love of God and humankind.

### 3. ARROWS

Arrows rarely feature in contemporary theories of the explanation and motivation of love. I shall be introducing two types of arrows into my analysis in this context. One of these is the kind of arrows used in archery. I shall be returning to discuss the significance of these ancient missiles for the business of love later in this chapter. The other kind of arrow that we shall need now is a visual symbol, convenient simply to indicate direction, in this case the direction of care or affection bestowed on a beloved object and the direction of benefits given or received. If I love you, we are inclined to think that my love (or affection or goodwill or whatever) is directed *towards* you, whether or not you are aware of it or accept it. If you *return* my love the relationship is mutual and the same kind of benevolence is directed *from* you *to* me as *from* me *to* you.[25]

The direction of affection may or may not differ from the direction in which benefits are given or received in a relationship. If I love you, I may give you a rose, yet get nothing from you. Both the

---

[25] In certain circumstances the kind of response might not be exactly the same on the part of both parties, but precisely what kind of benevolence or goodwill is returned is unimportant for now.

love and the benefit are directed from me to you. None the less, my love for you might still include a desire or expectation that I might receive some return from you. Alternatively you might give me a rose for some other reason, even though you did not feel any return of affection. Hence benefits may be exchanged regardless of the direction any affection may take.

In Christianity there are a number of classic relationships that are characterized as open to analysis in terms of love. In the relationship between God and humanity it is said both that God loves humankind, and that we should love God. Thirdly we are told that we should love our neighbours, and fourthly it is said that we are to love our enemies. In the requirement that we are to love our enemies it seems plain that both the affection and the benefits are to pass in one direction only; we enter as lover into a relationship in which we expect no return of affection, and no benefits, either material or otherwise, to be bestowed by the beloved:[26]

> The Christian loves her enemy.
> The Christian gives her coat to her enemy who took her cloak.

In the case of love toward neighbours it is less clear whether returns might be expected. The distinction between neighbour and enemy is plainly that the former bears you no ill-will, while the latter is likely to return harm in place of benefit. But the classic example in the Gospels of the Good Samaritan suggests that, for the New Testament at any rate, love of neighbour cannot include expectation of return from the neighbour, either as a source of motivation for action or as a contingent result; the action is directed to an unknown stranger in no position to promise repayment, and the Samaritan leaves apparently with no expectation that he will see the victim (as opposed to the innkeeper) on his return. It seems that the most the lover can anticipate is that the beloved will return gratitude for the lover's care, but even this might be excluded if the lover acts anonymously or unbeknown to the neighbour. Again the relation-

---

[26] The possibility that we might hope for benefits from another source (e.g. that we go to heaven if we keep this commandment) need not alter the fact that the beloved individual is not loved as the source of such benefits. This example shows that the motivation may be complex: we might fulfil this commandment (*a*) because we actually cared for the beloved, (*b*) because we wished to please someone else (God) whom we care for, (*c*) because we wished for paradise for ourselves, or all three.

ship is not properly mutual, and the benefits are given only from the lover to the beloved.

Humanity's relation with God is complicated because each partner is said to love the other.

> We love God.                •
> God loves us.

But while the arrows of affection go both ways, we may yet ask whether the relationship could properly be mutual, and whether any benefits could be reciprocated. First we may ask whether the character of the love would be the same in both cases. But we might also be tempted to ask, as many have asked when considering this issue, whether the motivation of the love could be similar in each of the two cases. This second kind of question is, I shall be suggesting, fundamentally inappropriate. It asks about the motives for love, as though love were not itself a motive, but were motivated by non-loving considerations. The question arises because we can discern an exchange of benefits in relations of love, and we are tempted to see those benefits as a causal explanation of the relationship. That inference is, I am suggesting, entirely misplaced.

For the present I want to suggest that we adopt, for the sake of argument, the assumption that such questions about motivation make sense. Could the motives of the lovers be the same in both cases? We might start to answer this question, as many have started in the past, by considering whether a self-interested analysis, such as that in Diotima's speech about *eros,* could conceivably be applied to these relationships, and if so what the implications would be. This approach is liable to be doubly misleading, because one may be tempted to conclude that if a self-interested analysis of *eros* is logically possible for the relationship in question, then that must be what is intended. We should therefore start by reminding ourselves that the logical coherence of such an analysis does not imply that anyone held it to be correct. If we find it morally repugnant, it may well be that others would have ruled it out on the same grounds, or indeed on other grounds that suited their own preconceptions.

Is it possible to analyse the relationship between God and humankind as a case of desire for that which is good, beautiful, or pleasing? It seems plain that there is some difference in this respect between our love for God and his love for us. An analysis in terms of desire seems more readily available for the first case:

We love God.

In this case the beloved clearly is good and beautiful and the provider of benefits that are pleasing to humankind. That our love for God might be motivated by the desire to obtain those benefits, or to obtain union with the divine, is certainly possible. There is no denying that benefits are in fact given.

God gives good things to us.
We love God.

What remains unclear is whether there is any connection between these two transactions. It is worth noticing, of course, that the fact that God actually provides benefits is not required for desire to form the basis of our relationship. We might relate to an angry God in some way such as this:

God might (but never did yet) show mercy to us.
We desire mercy and offer grovelling devotion to God

Here our devotion to God is based on hope for something that we need. But would we call this desire love? It is certainly a longing for what the object of devotion is able to provide, and it manifests itself in actions which are perhaps virtually indistinguishable from the devoted service of the grateful recipient. But it seems that the mere desire is not sufficient to qualify for our term 'love', even though in certain cases we might identify love combined with an expectation of benefits not yet received:

God promises that he will grant mercy to us.
We hope for that mercy and offer loving service to God.

Here our desire is for the mercy God offers, but our love is, I take it, something different, and will relate to our response to a God who promises and shows himself willing to give. We might say it is a response to a promise already given (or if not an explicit promise, at least an indication of kindly disposition). But it does not follow that it is *caused* or motivated by gratitude for what has been given or by desire for what will be expected. It would thus be a confusion either to suggest that our *love* for God could *be* merely desire for the benefits he could give, or indeed to suggest that it was motivated by such desire. But none the less it seems that desire might enter into the picture of what follows from our love: because we love we both desire what God can offer, and seek to offer our own service and devotion to God; similarly we may feel gratitude for past benefits or promises received. But these are features that spring from our attitude to God. It is those desires that depend on and give evidence of our love, not our love that reveals our desire.

Thus it seems that an account of our love for God may include both the expectation of future benefits and gratitude for those already received. In this sense it might seem to be open to some kinds of analysis in self-interested terms. What about the inverse relationship, God's regard for humankind? Here the traditional response is to observe that, since God is self-sufficient, there cannot be anything that he stands to gain from humanity; hence his love cannot be described in self-interested terms. But this plainly will not do. There obviously are certain things that God obtains from no other source;[27] he cannot obtain the worship of human beings unless they perform it; similarly if he delights in burnt offerings, or contrite hearts, or fine music and art, or upright dealings and acts of mercy and charity, for all these he must turn to the free acts of humankind to satisfy his desire. Indeed, to suggest that God did not delight in such things, or did not take any interest in such matters at all, would already imply that God was aloof and careless of humanity. Hence if we are to attribute any love or concern for humanity to God it had better be an interest that appreciates what is good in human works, and is hurt by what is bad or undesirable. Thus it seems that we cannot attribute love to God without also attributing to him desires for what humanity, in its better moments, might be able to give.[28]

Thus it seems that *both* relationships, the love of God for humanity and the love humanity has for God, can be open to an analysis that focuses on self-interest. In both cases the beloved offers benefits to the other, which the other is bound to appreciate and treasure if he can be said to love the one who gives them at all. But is it *for the sake of* those benefits that he loves the other, or does he treasure those gifts *because* he loves the giver? Merely identifying

---

[27] That is as things stand now, given the limitations imposed by the independence of the created world and freedom on the part of the creatures. This is not to say that God would have been unable to secure provision of all his needs without recourse to outside help, had he never created the world as it now is; but creation of the world was a move that necessarily made him dependent on what is other.

[28] Again it should be noticed that we do not have to suppose that benefits are actually received, but only that God should have some hope that they might be offered.

the benefits that each receives will not establish that desire for those benefits motivates the recipient's love.

It appears, then, that there is less asymmetry between God's love for us and our love for God than we originally supposed. Yet Nygren would have us believe that it was only with regard to our love for God that the Fathers employed the notion of a love motivated by need or lack. Why should this be? One obvious answer is that in Diotima's analysis, in Plato's *Symposium*, the gods cannot have needs and cannot love. Love himself cannot be a god, since if he were he would have no need of anything. If it is Diotima's analysis to which the Fathers are assenting, then God cannot seek the things that delight him since he has it all already. There is then a problem, not just in the suggestion that humanity is motivated by need to seek the good things of God, but also in the implication that God can have neither love nor any other appreciation for good things outside himself.

If, on the other hand, we maintain, against Diotima, that God does value certain good things that may or may not accrue to him according to the whim of free agents in this world, it remains a logical possibility that his concern for humanity is motivated by the desire to procure those things, just as humanity's regard for God might be a recognition of benefits he provides. But while such an analysis might be possible for both relationships, it is not clear that it is right, nor that it is what the Fathers meant when they thought of the relationship as *eros*. We must also ask the same question about a non-appetitive analysis of such love. Does it make any sense to analyse the relation between humanity and God as a regard for the other rather than for the self?

Here again it seems that the two relations, God to mankind and mankind to God, are asymmetrical. In both cases we may note that benefits pass in the same direction as the affection:

> God loves us.
> God gives good things to us.
> We love God.
> We give service to God.

We might suggest that in both cases the giving of benefits serves as a token of the regard for the other that the lover professes. Because we care about God we try to do what pleases him; because God cares for us he gives us the good things we need. But can the two cases betoken the same *sort* of care for the other? We are hardly in a position to provide for the essential needs of God; what we offer is more a token of affection, as one might give someone a rose, not because she needs a rose but as a mark of one's own interest in her; doubtless it is important that she *likes* roses. In the same way we must believe that God will value our service and miss it if it is neglected. God, on the other hand, is in a position to care for our essential needs. Does he then have a different sort of regard for us?

Two issues arise in this connection. First, is the nature of our love determined by what we actually provide or by what we should like to provide in ideal circumstances? Secondly, is the nature of our love determined by the ability of the recipient to accept or value what is offered, or by our interests in offering it? In the first place it is clearly unsatisfactory to suggest that the measure of love is the value of the goods actually provided. If I have not the means to buy one red rose, it does not mean that I love you less than if I can afford ten roses every week; and the mother who has nothing for her starving child may be just as loving as the one with plenty for all her family. On the other hand, if the nature of the contribution differs it may reflect a different type of concern. If you are hungry and I bring you a rose, it may seem that I have less concern for your real benefit than I would have had I chosen to take you for a meal. The problem is that this comparison is only reasonable when the recipient is capable of accepting either kind of contribution. If you are well-satisfied it is pointless for me to offer you a meal as a token of my concern for your essential needs. And if God takes no delight in burnt offerings, then my willingness to provide one, if I could, will be the indicator of my love, not whether I actually succeed in getting him to accept one.

It seems, then, that the ability to give or receive benefits will not actually determine what the love or concern behind the giving might be. A failure to give when giving is possible and appropriate might seem to suggest a lack of love, and certain kinds of generosity might seem unlikely to occur in the absence of the appropriate kind of generous love. But the mere transfer of benefits will not in itself indicate that the giving was motivated by one or another sort of generous or self-interested concern.

Thus we must be cautious; for it is tempting to suppose that because God supplies us with some or all of the benefits that we need for a good life,[29] without formal conditions, his love must be supremely generous. But the fact *that* he supplies benefits does not in itself give us the reason *why* he supplies those benefits or whether he has a purpose in doing so. He might still look for some response, just as the loving parent will grieve if the child responds to her care with ill-will and bad temper. The desire to gain a loving response *might* be the purpose of providing for the beloved's needs in the first place; or the provision might be for the sake of the beloved alone, and the desire for a response merely part of the desire that the benefits should be of value to the beloved. Consider the following two explanations of the purpose behind Piglet's gift to Eeyore:[30]

A.  1. Piglet loves Eeyore for Eeyore's own sake.
    2. Piglet gives Eeyore the balloon for the sake of pleasing him.
    3. Piglet hopes that Eeyore will express pleasure and gratitude to confirm that the gift satisfies the goal expressed in 2.

B.  1. Piglet loves Eeyore for the sake of the gifts he could give in return.[31]
    2. Piglet gives Eeyore the balloon in order to elicit Eeyore's gifts in return.
    3. Piglet hopes Eeyore will respond with gratitude and give him the gifts.

In both cases it is plain that Piglet would be giving the same gift, and in both cases he would be interested in Eeyore's response and

---

[29] There is a tendency in discussions of this sort to suppose that God appears unfailingly generous. It is worth remembering that there are occasions when the basic necessities for a decent life appear to be denied to some individuals through no obvious human fault. While there may be ways to avoid laying blame for such suffering at God's door, it is important to recognize that the failure to give when giving is possible and would be appropriate ought to indicate a lack of generous love.

[30] A. A. Milne, *Winnie-the-Pooh* (London, 1926), Ch. 6. In the story Eeyore is not a natural giver; Piglet's urgent desire to make Eeyore's day is sabotaged by his accidentally bursting the balloon on the way and turning up with a piece of limp rag instead. Further destroyed by the discovery that the balloon *would* have been the perfect present had it *been* a balloon, Piglet's joy is miraculously restored when it turns out that Eeyore does after all take an unexpected delight in the limp rag.

[31] This formulation sounds odd, since we would not usually say that Piglet 'loved' Eeyore in such circumstances. That is what we should expect in accordance with my claim that we do not love for a motive. We are assuming in the present discussion that such loving for the sake of something might be thought to make sense, hence the curious formula.

pleased to find him expressing gratitude. But the reason why he sought Eeyore's gratitude would differ, because in the one case it would indicate the success of his effort to please Eeyore, regardless of any reward, whereas in the other case it would indicate the success of his effort to win a favour in return. In the first case Eeyore's delight is his immediate and only concern; in the other case Eeyore's pleasure is only his immediate concern, the ultimate concern being his own satisfaction. In both cases he would, of course, be pleased to have succeeded.

Thus we might suggest that it is not immediately obvious, simply from the fact that God supplies some benefits, that he does so from a purely generous motive. He might seek our welfare as an end in itself, or as a means to his own satisfaction. Either way he will be concerned to see that we appreciate his gifts and respond with gratitude.

It seems clear from this analysis that we are dealing not simply with an easy dichotomy between two types of love, the self-seeking *eros* of Diotima's speech and the generous love of Nygren's *agape*. The motives for giving to the other, or for treasuring the favours one receives from another, may be various. Within the Greek tradition of *eros* it is necessary to account for the other-regarding devotion to a beloved whose benefit is sought for her own sake; and within the Christian account of love and charity it is plain that the generosity shown to the beloved can, or should, also be a joy to the giver. In both cases the loving relationship can be more than a one-sided transaction. But even if one assumes a simple dichotomy between, on the one hand, love that is directed towards the other, and, on the other hand, a self-seeking love, both *eros* and *agape* can be found to incorporate both kinds of love in parallel ways. The term *agape* characteristically belongs in the context of family affection; but in this context we encounter not only the affection of the parent for the child who can offer nothing in return, such as was the focus of attention in Plato's *Lysis*, but also the affection of the child for the parent which is nurtured in response to love and care. The child's affection is clearly not caused or motivated by benefits or love received, but it is an affection directed at one who provides things that the dependent child needs. In this sense it is plainly parallel to the kind of *eros* depicted in Diotima's speech.

On the other hand, within the tradition recognizable as *eros* we find two kinds of attachment: first, the concern of the Socratic lover to realize, in the beloved boy, such capacities for wisdom and beauty as he may possess, regardless of the boy's present inferiority and without requiring any favour or reciprocal feeling; and, second, the self-seeking desire for the beloved whose beauty Diotima's lover yearns to possess for his own fulfilment. Thus both *eros* and *agape* can be used to designate love characterized by *either* generous *or* self-interested concerns; neither the direction of affection from superior to inferior or vice versa, nor the direction of benefits from lover to beloved or the reverse, can be sufficient to define the difference between *eros* and *agape*. Hence we are in no position as yet to decide that only one of these terms could be applicable to the relationship between man and God.

Aware, no doubt, of these parallel features of *agape* and *eros*, Gregory of Nyssa suggests that the distinction between the two kinds of love is merely in their intensity. 'For heightened *agape* is called *eros*', he says in his homilies on the Song of Songs.[32] Origen's discussion seems, at first, to imply that there is no significant difference between the two terms at all: 'Hence it is of no consequence whether God is said to be the object of *eros* or of *agape*, nor do I think one could be blamed if one were to call God *Eros* just as John called him *Agape*.'[33] But Origen does not actually claim that there is no difference in sense. His comment comes in the context of a passage that aims to show that both terms have their good and bad uses. *Both* can be used of types of love that are inappropriate as analogies for spiritual love; the terminology of *diligere* or *caritas*[34] can be used in examples such as the love of money or of sensual pleasures. There is thus nothing magic about these terms that means they always carry a virtuous sense free of corrupting interpretations. Hence there is no clear reason for excluding *eros* or *amor* on the grounds that it occurs in the context of carnal love. That term too can be used in non-spiritual contexts for a love that is corrupt or sensual, but that does not mean that it cannot be used in a morally pure way, any more than the worldly contexts of the other terms for love preclude them being used in a spiritual sense.

---

[32] ἐπιτεταμένη γὰρ ἀγάπη ἔρως λέγεται, Gregory of Nyssa, *HomCt* 13, p. 383 (M 1048C).

[33] 'Non ergo interest utrum amari dicatur Deus aut diligi, nec puto quod culpari possit, si quis Deum, sicut Iohannes "caritatem", ita ipse amorem nominet.' Origen, *ComCt*, prologue, 71.

[34] The commentary exists only in the Latin translation. These terms are the standard translation for *agape* and its related verb.

Hence Origen's claim may still be that the difference between the terms is not negligible; but is not a difference between a morally pure term and a morally objectionable one. In this view he would clearly be at odds with Nygren.

## 4. ARROWS AGAIN

I have suggested that it is a confusion to seek to explain love by seeking motives for love, or by identifying possible aims and rewards that are sought or desired. The failure of attempts to explain love in those terms invites us to return to the notion of arrows; this time the arrows we need are the missiles employed by Cupid (or Eros) to strike the lover in the heart. The image of Cupid with his arrows captures in picturesque form the idea that love is not susceptible to analysis in terms of desire for benefits or reciprocal love, or, if it appears susceptible to such an analysis, that the result of such an analysis seems inadequate. The motif of Cupid is traditional in Greek literature, though it might seem that its place is more in poetry and the visual arts than in philosophy (though it is, of course, the topic of conversation in Plato's *Symposium*).[35] In fact it is essential to incorporate it into any discussion of the implications of *eros* in Greek thought and in early Christian texts, for two reasons. One is that it radically changes the kind of analysis we are likely to offer for *eros,* particularly with regard to explanation of the origin and motivation for the lover's regard for the beloved; the other is that the motif is explicitly used by Origen in his comments on love, and lies behind other texts in the Fathers on the same subject. It is unreasonable, then, to criticize the Fathers' use of the term *eros* without scrutinizing the implications of the arrows Eros employs.

[35] The darts employed by Eros are actually missing from the *Symposium*'s tale of his birth and character. This fact is clearly important in that it invites an explanation of love in terms of the needs of the lover, not a cause unrelated to the previous condition of the lover. The motif of darts or arrows as a weapon of love appears in Euripides (*Hippolytus,* 525–34; *Medea,* 530 ff. *Iphigeneia in Aulis,* 548 ff.). Sometimes, as in the *Hippolytus,* the weapons belong to Aphrodite but are sent by Eros. Euripides appears to be the first explicit literary allusion, but cf. the missiles of Aphrodite in Pindar, *Pythian,* 4. 213. These references precede Plato's work, so that the absence of the motif in Plato is not merely historical accident.

Up to now we have been looking at who loves whom, and for what end. But when we add in a third factor, Eros with his darts, we are offering a causal explanation that eliminates the need to ask 'what for?' and avoids looking to features inherent in the lover or the beloved for the reason why that purpose should apply in the case of those individuals. Invoking Eros as an explanation is a way of answering the question 'why does A love B?' that does not involve saying that B is desirable or lovable or has something to offer, nor that A had any prior need of B. A loves B because Eros has caused A to love B, regardless of whether B looks attractive on any objective criteria.

Now, it might look as if this sort of explanation is unhelpful: it amounts to no more than saying that A loves B because A has conceived a love for B. It is not a real explanation. That would be true; but the significant point is that it shows that the inexplicability of loving someone is central to the traditional notion of *eros*. We cannot seek a further explanation for why A conceived a love for B; the search for an explanation has to stop at the stage when we claim that Eros did it, for Eros is a wilful child who selects his victims at random or for mischief. And the need to invoke Eros as such an unpredictable cause is precisely to avoid the suggestion that we might seek an explanation in the desirability of the beloved object. Eros accounts for the fact that one can fall in love with someone who is not beautiful and lovely except in the eyes of the afflicted lover.[36]

Origen, in his prologue to the commentary on the Song of Songs, suggests that God is Eros,[37] and invokes the motif of arrows. Having claimed that scripture uses *agape* and compounds of *agape* in place of *eros*,[38] Origen suggests that when, in the Song of Songs 5: 8, the bride says 'I am wounded with love'[39] she means that she has been struck with God's arrow (that is the special arrow that is referred

[36] Compare the idea that the lover is mad or crazy, prominent in Plato's *Phaedrus.*

[37] 'Nor do I think one could be blamed if one were to call God *Eros*', Origen, *ComCt,* 71. In Rufinus' translation the term is *Amor.* It is evident that *amor* systematically translates *eros.* Cf. *ComCt,* 194.

[38] *ComCt,* 68. That is, the intention is to convey the sense that would be conveyed by the terms related to *eros,* but the writers, for reasons that Origen discusses, felt constrained to exclude the term *eros* for fear of misleading some readers. Again the inference that Origen was discussing the term *agape* is based on the systematic translation by Rufinus; here *caritas* and *dilectio* translate *agape.*

[39] i.e. *agape.*

to in Isaiah 49: 2).[40] Recognizing that the motif of wounding with arrows carries connotations of violence and hostility, Origen sees that it is necessary to consider the propriety of God's responsibility for such trauma in the soul. He affirms that wounding the soul in this way is proper and fitting for God.[41]

In this passage Origen varies between using *caritas,* the biblical word for love that translates *agape,* on the one hand, and *amor,* which translates *eros,* on the other.[42] Furthermore, in an earlier passage where he considers the text in 1 John 4: 7–8 which claims that 'God is love' Origen suggests that we should take this 'love' (*agape*) as straightforwardly equivalent to *amor* (or *eros*).[43] The effect of this claim is that when John says 'God is love', he might as well have said 'God is Eros'. Origen, as we have observed, has no objection to that idea.

Nor do I think one could be blamed if one were to call God *Eros,* just as John called him *'Agape'.* And besides I remember that one of the saints named Ignatius said of Christ, 'But my *eros* has been crucified.'[44]

The arrows which belong to the motif of the god Eros are there in Origen's account of love too. They introduce a kind of explanation of why someone loves; one loves because one is wounded with the arrow sent by the god of love. The importance of this motif lies in the fact that explanation is not sought in the desire of the lover for the beloved, nor in the attraction that the beloved holds for the lover. The reason why the lover loves the beloved is not related to any lack on the part of the lover nor to any quality possessed by the

[40] The RSV reads, 'He made me a polished arrow, in his quiver he hid me away'; The Latin version of Origen, translating the Septuagint, reads, 'et posuit me sicut iaculum electum, et in pharetra sua abscondit me', *ComCt,* 194. The 'chosen arrow' represents Christ, of course, in Origen's interpretation, so that the wound of this arrow is the wound of the arrow of love, since God is love.

[41] *ComCt,* 194. 15.

[42] *ComCt,* 194. At line 6 one is said to burn with the *amor* of the Word of God. The description of the emotional state of one so afflicted with the wound of love (lines 7–12) is clearly intended to be reminiscent of one in love in the conventional erotic sense: he sighs day and night with desire for the beloved, can speak of nothing else, wishes to hear nothing else, is unable to think of anything else, and is incapable of entertaining any other desire or wish or hope.

[43] *ComCt,* 69–71.

[44] *ComCt,* 71–2. The reference to Ignatius is to the *Epistle to the Romans,* 7. 2. There has been some debate as to whether Origen has misinterpreted Ignatius' meaning, though the current consensus is probably that he has not seriously mistaken the sense. The issue is not immediately important to the present concern with Origen's own view on the use of terminology of love.

beloved; on the contrary it is clear that no such features need enter the explanation at all. The love that the soul has for God is adequately explained by appealing to the notion that God has inflicted the wound of his arrow. God is a sufficient cause for love, regardless of the earlier inclinations or condition of the soul that is now inspired to love.

## 5. EXPLANATION AND THE SOUL'S LOVE FOR GOD

In arguing that God could properly be said to be Eros, Origen wants to suggest that God demands or expects a like response in us. God is Eros not just in that he shows love towards us (though in fact the Saviour does himself follow the precepts he commends) but primarily in the fact that he prescribes and expects the loving response in us towards himself and towards our neighbour. Love requires in us a response like himself: we are to love because God is love.[45] This does not mean that we are to love him because he first loves us. We are to love because he is love and the inspiration for love. It is because he is causally responsible for love in this way that he becomes involved in following his own precepts such as the kind of behaviour illustrated in the story of the good Samaritan; thus the Saviour, like the good Samaritan, did not pass us by when we were in distress;[46] but it is not that he can be called 'love' because he displays such love, but that he displays such love because he is the god of love.

Origen focuses on two types of love: first, the love that the bride has for the bridegroom, which represents the love of the soul for the Word of God or the love of the Church for Christ;[47] second, the notion that God is Love, the cause of the love that the bride has for the bridegroom. Both of these centre attention on the demand for an explanation of the love that the human soul has for God. The first raises, and the second goes some way towards answering, the question of how it can be correct and seemly to suggest that the human soul is in love with God. In effect Origen's answer looks something like this: it is correct to say that the soul is in love with

[45] *ComCt*, 70.
[46] *ComCt*, 70. 27–9.
[47] See especially *ComCt*, prologue, 61. 5–9; bk. 1, 89. 10–13.

God for two reasons; for one because love is from God and God-given inasmuch as God is Love; secondly because the proper object for the love which is from God is God himself. It remains true that we may also love our neighbours, but that love will be derivative from our love for God because we recognize in the neighbour a kinship with the divine that is the first object of our love.[48]

This focus on our love for God might seem remarkable. Why, we might ask, does Origen have so little to say on the subject of God's love for mankind, and such ready enthusiasm for the notion that we can have erotic love for God? There are two issues that lie behind this question: first, is it appropriate to think of our relation to God on the model of *eros*? And secondly, is it that model that has diverted Origen's attention from God's love for us? It might, for example, seem impossible to use the model of *eros* as a proper illustration of the love of God for humankind. If that is so (a claim I aim to reject in the course of the studies in this book) it might be suggested that Origen ignores the love of God for mankind precisely because he is tied to the erotic model of love. We shall therefore need to ask whether he is attached to that model and for what reason, and whether it would be right to reject that model as an illustration of the love God has for us.

In the first place we should observe the context of Origen's remarks on love. He is not discussing *eros* in the abstract but in the context of a commentary on the Song of Songs. This gives him a justification for the use of erotic love as the model, and the only model, of love that he considers; that emphasis need not be because he could not conceive of any other type of love, but because no other type of love was relevant in this connection. It also justifies his preoccupation with the soul's love for God rather than God's love for us; the theme he identifies in the Song of Songs is the desire of the bride for her beloved. It is that attitude of desire that Origen must build into his account of the relation between soul and Word or between Church and Christ. That he finds that desire most plausibly illustrated in the love that the soul has for God, and the Church has for Christ, need not mean that he recognizes no inverse relation of love (albeit perhaps of a different sort) in God's love for us. Indeed, we have already looked at some passages that presuppose that God loves us, and the full extent of Origen's com-

---

[48] *ComCt*, prologue, 70. 29–32.

mitment to this idea will be explored in a later chapter.[49]

We should not suppose that Origen finds it unproblematic to transfer the notion of erotic love to the relation between humanity and God. On the contrary, this kind of love is explicitly treated as problematic, precisely because it carries with it certain connotations of appetitive and selfish desire. Origen faces a question as to whether that is a suitable kind of relationship towards God; he does not simply assume that it is. It is partly because the love that God shows to mankind is less problematic in this respect that Origen can afford to give less attention to it. He does allow that God is loving, but he does not dwell on it at length, since the problem of self-interest that might threaten in the case of our desire for God does not surface in the same way in respect of God. If God loves a human being, plainly we shall not be drawn to seek to explain it as due to a lack, or desire to gain advantage.

Nygren's dissatisfaction with the motif of erotic love arose because that love appeared selfish and he took it that it depended on a motivation inspired by need. But does Origen allow erotic love to look selfish? It is true that he reminds us, at the start of his prologue, of Plato's *Symposium* and the tradition of Greek philosophical discussion on love.[50] If we took that tradition to be confined to a self-interested analysis of love as motivated by desire, then we might infer that Origen was taking over the same analysis. But this would be a mistake for two reasons; first because, as we have seen, it is probably wrong to take the *Symposium* that way and Origen never implies that he does; and secondly because Origen is not putting forward the *Symposium* as his model for the account of love that he will give. He mentions the *Symposium* as an example of a work which, like the Song of Songs, treats of love as a means of drawing the soul up to the things of heaven, but which can also be an occasion of downfall for those who read the texts in a carnal way.

When he comes to his own account of love Origen leaves Plato's *Symposium* out of the picture. He does not presuppose, as Plato (or rather Plato's Diotima) seemed to do, that the soul's love for God is motivated by a need or lack, or that it is merely an appetite which God can satisfy. Indeed, he does not suggest that such love depends upon us recognizing benefits from God. On the contrary he invokes

---

[49] See below, Ch. 7.
[50] *ComCt*, prologue, 63. 6–16.

what we should call 'the inexplicability model': we love because we have received the wound of love, and the wound is given by God. Hence our love is directed to God not because God is desirable but because love toward God, and toward the perfect and incorruptible things that are God's, is God-given.

Origen is suggesting that what appears to be a selfish structure to the soul's desire for God need not be selfish in motive. The distinction between a desire that is motivated by the need to fulfil a lack, and love that happens to fulfil a lack though not motivated by need, is implicit in what Origen describes in his commentary about the origins of our desire for God. It is important to avoid supposing that love needs a further explanation. If love is the motive for our desires and actions, there can be no further explanation besides the fact that God gave, or struck us with, those motives.

## 6. MOTIVATION

We can fruitfully compare the idea of love as a motive in itself with what Gregory of Nyssa has to say in his analysis of the motivation for virtuous conduct. Here Gregory takes account of the fact that the same outward behaviour may spring from a variety of internal states:

For in the writings we have here the soul is, in a way, led out as a bride to the incorporeal and spiritual and undefiled marriage of God; for he who wishes that all should be saved and that all should come to knowledge of truth indicates here the most perfect and blessed manner of salvation—I mean salvation through love. For salvation also occurs through fear for some people, when we look at the threats of punishment in Hell, and separate ourselves from evil for that reason. And there are others who also act in accordance with virtue through the hope of rewards that is reserved for those who live well; they are won over not by the love of the good but by the expectation of the returns. But the one who achieves perfection casts aside fear (for when it is not out of love that one stays with the master, but through fear of the beating that one does not run away, that is the condition of a slave) and he disdains the actual rewards, that he might not seem to consider the reward as more important than the one who gives the benefit; rather he loves, with heart and soul and might, not one of the things that come from God, but God himself who is the source of the good things.[51]

We may act in accordance with virtue because we are afraid of the punishments in store for those who do otherwise; we may choose to act virtuously because we desire and hope for rewards promised to those who fulfil the requirements of virtue. But Gregory's third kind of motivation, where we act virtuously neither through fear nor hope, is motivation by love (*agape*). Love here is incompatible with fear, and also with the attitude that values the gifts above the giver. Hence Gregory is presupposing not that love can be motivated by desire for benefits, but that love is distinct from such desire, is a different kind of motivation, indeed one which values the beloved rather than the benefits that the beloved happens to provide. A relationship based on desire is not a relationship of love.

It will be noticed, of course, that Gregory uses the traditional terminology of *agape* in this passage. Plainly he thinks that motivation by fear or desire is incompatible with *agape*, but does it follow that he also thinks *eros* is not based on desire? Does he recognize a distinction between these two terms in this respect?

The answer is no, for two reasons. One is that Gregory himself is not recommending motivation by need and desire as the appropriate relation for the soul to God. On the contrary, in this passage from book one of his commentary on the Song of Songs he is precisely saying that the motivation God seeks to instil in us is that of love that has no place for fear or desire. Given this view it would be inconsistent for him to treat *eros* as an appropriate attitude for the soul to have to God, were he to suppose that such an attitude was motivated by desire. If Gregory does allow that *eros* is appropriate, as in fact he does, then we must suppose that he takes *eros* to be as unmotivated as this passage requires our relation to God to be. Otherwise he would be inconsistent.

The other reason is that Gregory himself, affirming the idea that the soul is wounded with a dart of *eros*, argues not only that *eros* is effectively the same kind of thing as *agape* (only more intense), but also that there is nothing shameful in *eros* provided that it is immaterial and not 'according to the flesh'.[52] Carnal love may be shameful, but it is not in virtue of being erotic that it is shameful,

---

[51] Gregory of Nyssa, *HomCt* 1, p. 15 (M 765). Compare the similar passages in Clement of Alexandria, *Stromateis*, 7. 66–88; 4. 29. 4.
[52] Gregory of Nyssa, *HomCt* 13, p. 383 (M 1048. 6–14).

but in virtue of being carnal. There is, for Gregory, nothing wrong with the erotic as such. Indeed, there is nothing that he regards as important to differentiate *eros* from *agape*. Thus our conclusion will need to be that Gregory is entirely consistent in his view that *eros* imports no shameful connotations in itself, and that it is a proper relation for the soul to have for God. He understands *eros* not as an attitude motivated by desire but as an unmotivated devotion to the beloved, like *agape*.

We can use this analysis in Gregory of Nyssa to confirm our interpretation of Origen. What is explicit in Gregory, and probably should be understood in Origen too, is that rather than distinguish a *type of love* motivated by need and another type that is unmotivated, we should distinguish love as one sort of motivation where need or desire or fear are other sorts of motivation. Love is not itself motivated by some other force; love is a force that motivates us to do certain kinds of action and to value certain kinds of thing. The same kinds of response can be found due to other motives; but where love is the motive it means that desire or fear is not the motive. It cannot then make sense to say that love arises from this or that motive. To invoke love as an explanation is to deny that other motives are relevant. Hence when we ask what is the explanation of love—why I love this individual and not that one—we are not seeking a motive such as need or lack; motives explain responses and those are already explained by love. For the explanation of love we seek a cause, and that has to be supplied, for Origen and Gregory, by love's arrows; the reason is precisely because there is no available explanation in terms of perceived rewards or threats, as there might be in the case of the other kinds of motivation.

### 7. GOD'S LOVE FOR MANKIND

It seemed, to begin with, that the love of the soul for God was problematic because it appeared self-interested. A clarification of the distinction between kinds of motives and kinds of love has suggested that Origen and Gregory of Nyssa were not introducing a self-interested desire into the soul's relation with God. No charge that their notion of erotic love is inappropriate on those grounds will stand up.

There might, however, seem now to be a new difficulty for supposing that God could love mankind. We are no longer admitting an explanation of love in terms of the capacity of the lover to give or receive benefits. But this means that we cannot account for the idea that God loves mankind simply on the basis that humanity is weak and stands in need of the gifts of God's grace. Just as the presence of desirable benefits is not sufficient to explain why the lover loves in the case where she stands to gain, so the opportunity to give will not account for why the lover loves in the case where she can bestow benefit. But if we want to say that God's love is 'generous love', that will not be to say that his love is caused or occasioned by the need of the beloved. Rather we should wish to say that he loves regardless of the condition of the beloved, but that the love manifests itself in a concern to provide for the needs of the beloved. Otherwise we shall find ourselves committed to the view that God is limited by what is available as the object of his love.

There is a sense in which we might want to say that God is limited in the circumstances that arise from his love. That is to say that, in loving another, God, like any lover, must become concerned about, and hence vulnerable to, the limitations and weaknesses of the beloved. But this is a limitation that arises within the relationship of love. We are not obliged to admit the idea that the scope of God's love should be limited to certain individuals, or that the nature of the love is defined by the nature of its object. If God could love only those capable of receiving his gifts it would mean that some individuals would, in theory at least, be unlovable. Furthermore it would presuppose that the cause of God's love lay in the beloved object, that God's attitude was inspired by some feature of what is outside himself.

Is this a problem? There seem to be two difficulties. One is parallel to the case of love inspired by what is fine and beautiful in the beloved, in that it appears to make the relationship of love dependent on some other motivation; in this case I love you because I want to be generous and you are one I can be generous to. In neither case does it seem satisfactory to speak of such a motive for love, since love itself provides a motive for being generous. The other difficulty arises from the fact that love dependent on a feature of the beloved seems to put God into a position of subjection: his capacity to love depends not on himself but on the nature of what is outside himself. But this seems unsatisfactory, perhaps partly because the nature of what is outside himself is not fully independent; it means that God's attitude towards his own creation is decided by the nature of his own creation, for which he is in any case responsible. Secondly, it will make God's ability to love dependent on the presence of sin or weakness in the world: if God can love only what could be an object of generosity, he can love only what remains in a state of imperfection with room for improvement. Thus God would be obliged to make an imperfect world in order to have the option of loving it in an other-regarding way. Though this might seem a possible account of the origin of evil, it makes an inadequate justification of it.

Plainly, then, we shall need to allow that God can love the objects of his creation without regard to whether they have or lack perfection. He must be free to show a concern for what is already lovely and fine, and not only to care for what is bad and needy. It cannot be, then, that the cause of his affection is his perception of the needy state of the world. His generous response had better not be a need to give, but rather a desire to give motivated by love. But if that is so what is the source of his love? For Origen the explanation of our love for God was given in the image of love's arrows, a love that was God-given and Godward. The love that God gives is essentially directed towards God, and only secondarily towards what is derivative from God.[53] Clearly we might suggest that God himself, the God of love, is also the source of his own love. But then it becomes problematic how he can love what is outside himself, given that the love given by God is always primarily directed Godwards. It seems that God will have a love primarily for himself, and secondarily perhaps for the finer and more godly aspects of his creation. But the love that is from God does not form an attachment to what is ungodly or corrupt, in Origen's analysis. Thus it seems impossible for God to love what is less perfect than himself. We find ourselves in the paradoxical position of attributing to God a love that is essentially self-centred and to humanity a love that is entirely other-regarding.

Origen does not find this position unsatisfactory. Part of the reason is that self-love was not self-evidently improper, given its place in the tradition of Greek Ethics.[54] But that is not the main

---

[53] Origen, *ComCt*, 70. 29–30; 71. 19–20.

[54] Self-love finds a place in Aristotle's Ethics, esp. *Nicomachean Ethics*, 9, ch. 8. See below, Ch. 6. Self-love is considered basic to our love in Augustine, *De doctrina Christiana*, 1. 22–35, and cf. Thomas Aquinas, *Summa Theol*, 2a 2ae, 23–7. But against self-love see also Augustine *Confessions*, 10. 39.

point. Origen's primary concern, in the text we are considering, is with spirituality, the relation of the individual soul to God. Within that context he seeks to show that love is properly directed God-wards. It might seem that he takes as his basis the idea that the propriety of love depends upon it being directed towards a worthy object. No love towards God could be unseemly on that analysis, since God is, of course, always the most worthy and excellent object of love. On this basis, then, it would be absurd to suggest that God's love for himself was improper, since it could hardly be said to be directed at an unworthy object.

But is it right to attribute to Origen the notion that the worth of the love is determined by the nature of the object, that we ought to love only what is finest and best?[55] When Origen raises this question explicitly he answers no. Should we, he asks, love the person of good and upright life more than the person who is engaged in wickedness?[56] Two illustrations are given to support the claim that different *kinds* of love are appropriate to different people: first Origen observes that a man is commanded to love his wife, but plainly love of other women is also commended. It would be correct to observe a difference between the two cases. But it does not follow that the love will be unequal, greater in quantity for one woman rather than another, and it certainly does not follow that love will depend upon how good the beloved is. The second example makes this even more plain. Origen here uses God's own love for his people as the exemplar that defines the perfect way to love. God, however, loved both the Egyptians and the Hebrews equally, but he did not love them similarly. The point made here is that God's love, which was equal in quantity for both peoples, nevertheless differed in kind in so far as the objects of the love differed.

It is clear from this passage that Origen does not claim that we should love only those of upright life. God quite properly loved the Egyptians just as much as the Hebrews, and we are to do likewise. Impropriety follows not from the fact that we love an unworthy object but from the way we love it. We are to avoid inordinate love, not because the quantity of love is too great but because it is a

---

[55] The idea that love is properly directed to what is good does, of course, appear in Aquinas in the view that one may love the sinner but not her sin. Similarly Aristotle is committed to the view that proper friendship will be with a virtuous man.

[56] *ComCt,* 186. See further on this section of the commentary in Ch. 7 below.

failure to distinguish the kind of relationship that is appropriate to the beloved object.

If this is Origen's view, plainly nothing prevents us from supposing that he would be happy to allow to God the other-regarding love for humankind that is in any case assumed in the illustration of God's universal love for Hebrews and Egyptians alike. But there is another response that we might want to make, and that is to consider why we are to avoid the inordinate love that arises in cases of inappropriate devotion to the unworthy object of love? When Origen raises the issue of inordinate love he suggests that the soul or bride is afraid of doing something inordinate and receiving a wound of love. What would be the harm if she were to find herself involved in inordinate love? One possibility is that she would find herself ashamed, guilty of improper affection. But that will not really explain the allusion to the wound of love's arrow. She seems to be afraid that she will be hurt. Origen does later allow that there are arrows of evil that can wound a soul not protected by faith,[57] but here the soul refers to a wound of love. It seems unclear at this point whether God himself can be responsible for causing wounds of inordinate love in those whose devotion is out of line and inappropriate.

In the context of the love of the human soul for God and for others it seems clear that Origen can work on the assumption that inordinate love is undesirable; it causes shame and hurt on the part of the lover because it involves an improper kind of love for an object that should be loved in a different way. What is less clear is whether Origen is right to assume that exactly the same rules apply in the case of God's love for mankind. Origen uses God's love for the Egyptians as a straightforward example: this is how love is properly ordered with regard to various kinds of object. Similarly, when Origen introduces the story of the Good Samaritan to demonstrate that neighbourly love extends to every human being no matter how fallen into wickedness, he moves directly from our obligation to love our neighbour as the Samaritan did, to the fact that Christ himself loved us like this in that he did not pass us by when we lay half dead from the wounds of robbers.[58] Our obligations to the other members of the human race exactly match God's love

[57] *ComCt,* 194.
[58] *ComCt,* prologue, 70. 17–29.

to us in the Incarnation. But it seems less clear in the case of God that the rules of propriety are respected. Is it not the case that in the Incarnation God goes beyond the kind of love that would be proper and appropriate; that he does more than could be expected for souls that are unworthy, and hence that he incurs the pain and the shame that is the wound of love that was feared by the bride in the Song of Songs?

It may be right to suggest that in the Incarnation God becomes involved in a love that commits him to pain and shame in some sense, but Origen is surely right to suggest that the obligation to love like that, to love every individual as neighbour regardless of worth, can be transferred to the duty of the Christian soul. The problem is that we then find that both God and the follower of Christ paradoxically have an obligation to do something that is beyond what duty requires; even the correctly ordered love will require that we love all individuals equally. Hence the soul's desire to escape the wound of love by avoiding the mistake of inordinate love will, in a sense, be hopeless, given that God is responsible for inflicting that wound in the demand that we love God and neighbour without respect to worth. That love is bound to involve a wound because it requires that we go beyond the measure of what would be reasonable, and commit ourselves in devotion to those who are not perfect. Love for God in itself will not involve that vulnerability since God is not imperfect, but in so far as commitment to God involves commitment to the love of others, it will commit us to a love of what is not fine and hence to a love that involves shame and pain.

## 8. CONCLUSION

The speculations of the last paragraph have gone beyond what is explicit in Origen's own text. Nevertheless, it is plain that Origen himself is committed to a position that is not unacceptable. He allows that the soul has a relation towards God that can be described in the terminology of *eros*, but that love is inspired not by a desire for the beauty of God or for the benefits he gives, but by the wound of the arrows of divine love. The explanation lies outside the lover and is independent of the needs of the lover and of the goodness of the beloved. In the same way Origen is committed to the view that

God also loves mankind, and again the love is conceived as taking no account of the worth of the object, except in so far as a different kind of love will be appropriate to a different individual. In both cases love involves not so much a desire to possess the beloved as a commitment to the concerns of the other. It seems not inappropriate to see in the notion of the wound of love's arrow the idea that that commitment to the other will involve some hurt and shame, rather than gratification, on the part of the lover. Origen never shows any inclination towards an appetitive analysis of love such as Nygren found in Plato's *Symposium.*

# 4

## Eros, the Socratic Spirit:
## Inside and Outside the *Symposium*

### I. THE UPWARD PATH

Several of Plato's dialogues begin with a journey. That is not strictly true of the *Symposium*, since here the dialogue starts[1] with a conversation between Apollodorus and a group of friends which forms the frame within which Apollodorus tells his story, although we never recall that frame at the end.[2] For most of the dialogue Apollodorus is the unobserved narrator. But where, we might ask, does the conversation take place? Where are Apollodorus and his friends when he tells the tale?

There is no indication at the start of the dialogue of where the conversation takes place. We come in in the middle; the others have clearly just asked Apollodorus about the famous drinking party that Socrates once attended, and the first thing we get is Apollodorus' reply, 'What you're asking me about is something I seem to be hardly unpractised at.'[3] In fact he had just had to go through the same story two days previously. However, we still do not know what the occasion of the present conversation is. Are Apollodorus and his companions walking together, as Apollodorus and Glaucon were on the last time he told the tale? Perhaps not, for Apollodorus dissociates himself from his listeners, who do not share his fanatical devotion to philosophy but are, he suggests, wealthy and materialistic men whose concerns he finds unproductive.[4] As the tale progresses it becomes apparent that the pursuit of philosophy is a kind of journey along a road; but it seems plain that Apollodorus' present listeners are not on that road as yet. Apollodorus had

---

[1] *Symposium*, 172a.
[2] The dialogue ends with the end of Apollodorus' account, when Socrates goes home from the symposium.
[3] 172a.
[4] 173cd.

himself only recently found the route, when he became a follower of Socrates:

Before that I went around wherever chance led me; I thought I was getting something done, but really I was more wretched than anyone—in fact no less wretched than you yourself are now, thinking that one ought to do anything rather than philosophy.   (173a)

To follow Socrates is to take a journey on the road of philosophy, and Apollodorus had found that road and begun his journey on it less than three years ago.

It makes a difference, then, whether the listeners to Apollodorus' tale are, like Apollodorus, travellers on a philosophical journey. Today's listeners apparently are not. But Glaucon, to whom the tale was told before, did not lag so very far behind. Glaucon had called out from behind Apollodorus on the road up to the city,[5] and Apollodorus had stopped and waited for him. Glaucon's position behind Apollodorus on the road to the city matches his backward state with regard to knowledge of the truth; previously he had heard an account of the famous party that was so garbled as to be unintelligible; he had heard it from someone else, who had heard it from Phoenix the son of Philip.[6] Apollodorus points out that Phoenix had originally heard it from Aristodemus, the same Aristodemus who had been the source of Apollodorus' own knowledge of the story. Hence the version Glaucon had heard before had been at third hand and far from clear.[7] Glaucon is trying to get closer to the truth. By listening to Apollodorus he can get one step nearer to the original, since Apollodorus' version is only at second hand, although Glaucon had been hoping that it would be a first-hand account. He had been under the impression that Apollodorus had himself been at the party and could narrate it from his own experience. Apollodorus can further Glaucon's pursuit of the truth by taking him through the conversation.

Two features emerge from the discussion in these opening pages of the dialogue. Apollodorus points out how long ago the party in question took place. Glaucon had supposed that Apollodorus had been present, but that would be impossible, since it had been years

[5]  172a.
[6]  172b3.
[7]  172b4.

ago when he and Glaucon were both still boys,[8] and Agathon had won the prize for his first tragedy. By remarking so clearly on the time elapsed between the original party and the present time, Apollodorus also establishes a sequence of priority for the followers of Socrates. He emphasizes the fact that Aristodemus, who was already a devoted follower of Socrates when the party took place, has clocked up many more years of service than he has himself. Since it was Aristodemus who told the tale to Apollodorus we may suppose that he is still around, or at least was until recently.[9] So Apollodorus is tagging along considerably behind Aristodemus as a follower of Socrates and a devotee of philosophy. He must have started his philosophical pilgrimage some ten or twenty years behind.

But there are others still further behind, among them Glaucon, who is the first to ask Apollodorus to narrate the tale. Apollodorus was leaving his home district of Phaleron to travel to the city of Athens when Glaucon hailed him from behind. The journey from his home to the city matches his departure from his old, non-philosophical lifestyle to the new Socratic life. We are made aware that Phaleron is his original home by the pompous greeting of his friend: 'Hail, thou man of Phaleron, Apollodorus, wilt thou not wait?'[10] and Apollodorus himself says that he was coming from his home. Why is he leaving his home to go to the city? The city of Athens is, of course, the characteristic haunt of Socrates, and as a convert to the Socratic way of life Apollodorus will make the journey from the port that was his home to the city that is Socrates' home. The narrative concerning Socrates which Apollodorus proceeds to relate takes place almost entirely within the confines of the city.[11]

Other Platonic dialogues also start with travellers on the road from A to B. Most notable is the *Republic*, where Socrates and Glaucon are making a very similar journey from Athens' other

---

[8] 173a5.

[9] The details describing Aristodemus at 173b give no indication of whether he is currently part of the scene. He is said to be small, always barefoot, and a member of the deme of Kudathenaion. At the time of the party he was one of the chief lovers of Socrates.

[10] 172a.

[11] Socrates walks with Aristodemus to Agathon's house, which appears to have been in the city and where the main discussion takes place. At the end of the dialogue he goes to the Lyceum, a gymnasium outside the walls.

port, the Peiraeus, up to the city when they are waylaid from behind by Polemarchus and a whole group of others. But there, unlike in the *Symposium*, they do not go on together to the city, but persuade Socrates to stay behind with them in the port. Many have seen in this the correlate of the philosopher kings, forcibly detained in the lower world to govern the routine day-to-day life of the city, rather than spending their time in contemplation of the truth of perfect reality. In the port, the centre of commerce and trade, Socrates concerns himself with the practicalities of politics and social theory; up in the city he pursues the vision of truth and reality that the philosophers achieve when they make their way up out of the cave. Hence it is significant that the *Symposium* starts with a journey up to the city, and that its account of the love of truth and beauty takes place in Agathon's house within the confines of the city of Athens.

Before Apollodorus became a follower of Socrates he had not known where he was heading, but now he is on his way up to the city where Socratic philosophy belongs. It is an uphill journey[12] and the motif of ascent in this journey coincides with the motif of ascent in Diotima's speech at the symposium itself. In that speech the philosophical lover makes progress towards a vision of true beauty, and that progress is spoken of as an upward journey. Diotima introduces the metaphor of travel at 210a:

If one is to progress correctly towards this thing, one must start as a young man by progressing to beautiful bodies, and first, if the leader takes him the right way, he must fall in love with one body, and engender beautiful discourses in it.

A little later, as she describes the ultimate achievement, Diotima goes on (210e):

The one who has been escorted thus far in the direction of matters of love, and who in the correct manner has gazed in turn upon things that are beautiful, at length progresses to the goal of the matters of love and suddenly catches sight of something amazing and beautiful in nature.

Thus far it is clear that Diotima describes education in erotics as a journey, a progress from A to B. But is it an upward journey? The motif of ascent begins at 211b when Diotima sums up the progress of the lover towards the goal of perfect beauty:

---

[12] 'I was going up from my home at Phaleron to the City', 172a.

When someone had made his way up from these things by means of the love of boys correctly practised, and had begun to perceive that other beauty, he would be virtually touching the finish. This is just what it is to progress correctly to matters of love, or to be guided by another, that is starting from these beautiful things always to go on up for the sake of that beauty, as if using steps, from one to two and from two to all the beautiful bodies, and from the beautiful bodies to the beautiful pursuits, and from the beautiful pursuits to the beautiful discoveries, and from discoveries to finish at that discovery that is none other than the discovery of that beautiful itself . . .

The word used for 'going up' in this passage is basically the same as the one Apollodorus used to refer to the fact that he was going up from Phaleron to the city, when he began his tale.[13] His ascent from ordinary life to Socratic philosophy, which matches his ascent from his coastal home-district to Athens, is also a step on the upward path of erotics in which he, as a follower of Socrates, is now serving as a guide.

### 2. GUIDES AND LEADERS

Apollodorus is ahead of Glaucon on the road to Athens, and in taking him on with him, and recounting the tale of the famous party, he acts as his guide for the journey to the city and as his guide in philosophy. But for both kinds of journey Apollodorus is not the only guide we meet in the dialogue.

Apollodorus' story is based on Aristodemus' memory of the occasion, and in that sense Aristodemus was Apollodorus' guide. Aristodemus' story starts with a journey; he tells how he met Socrates bathed and dressed for a party,[14] and how Socrates persuaded him to come along to the party too. Thus Socrates is taking Aristodemus to the party, and becomes Aristodemus' guide. At 174b2 Aristodemus submits to Socrates' guidance by agreeing to do whatever Socrates tells him to do. Thus it appears that while Aristodemus is the authority to whom Apollodorus looks for guidance, Socrates is the guide to whom Aristodemus owes allegiance.

Now, however, an odd reversal takes place. Whereas Socrates had

---

[13] ἀνιών, 172a; ἐπανιών, 211b; ἐπανιέναι, 211c.
[14] 174a.

set out to take Aristodemus to the party, Aristodemus shortly finds himself ahead. Guide and follower have changed places, as Socrates lags behind and eventually comes to a standstill in someone's porch. Aristodemus turns up at Agathon's house first and alone. The point of this absurd episode is not merely to illustrate Socrates' eccentric habits, although that aspect is also significant, as I hope to show. But it also marks out the fact that on this particular occasion Aristodemus is actually more Socratic than Socrates. Socrates, on this occasion, though never elsewhere, has bathed and dressed in his best clothes and party shoes. Aristodemus, by contrast, is not dressed or washed for a party since he had not expected to go to one, and, as always, he is barefoot.[15] Aristodemus was a lover of Socrates, so Apollodorus tells us, and doubtless that explains why he adopts Socrates' ascetic lifestyle; but Socrates on this occasion is professing to be a lover of Agathon,[16] and hence is following Agathon in dress and lifestyle. This explains why Socrates appears in the suave and elegant image that Agathon will shortly ascribe to the god Eros in his speech at the party. Just for now Socrates is posing as a follower of that Eros, the Eros that is Agathon's love. Once we come to Socrates' own speech we shall discover that that image of love does not lead to the truth. The one that is a true guide in philosophy is a much more rugged image, and that is why Aristodemus, who on this occasion retains the rugged Socratic mould, temporarily overtakes the uncharacteristically refined Socrates on the road. Socrates is not dressed aright for making good progress on the path to truth.

Apollodorus takes Glaucon up to Athens, and Socrates takes Aristodemus to Agathon's. Further guides turn up in other sections of the dialogue. Most memorable is perhaps the entrance of Alcibiades towards the end of the party, drunk and with his ivy wreaths so fallen over his eyes that he cannot really see, and certainly cannot see Socrates. The first words the assembled company hear from Alcibiades are the demand that he 'be taken to Agathon'.[17] He is led by the servants in his blind and wandering state to a place

---

[15] Cf. 173b2.

[16] 174a9, Socrates says he has made himself beautiful for going to a beauty. Cf. also the banter at 213c, where Alcibiades is supposedly jealous of the fact that Socrates is bestowing his attentions on Agathon.

[17] 212d5. As Nussbaum has remarked (*The Fragility of Goodness*, 185), the resemblance of Agathon's name ('Ἀγάθων) to the word for the good (ἀγαθόν) makes this demand peculiarly appropriate after Socrates' speech.

alongside Agathon. But we are left to wonder whether that was the right place for him to go. He had asked to be led there only because he was unaware of the presence of Socrates, who, it transpires, is the real object of his desire.

Alcibiades needed a guide to lead him to his beloved. The task of leading men to their proper objects of love is one of the roles assigned to the god Eros in virtually all the speeches reported by Aristodemus.[18] Thus Phaedrus begins by suggesting that Love is the principle that ought to guide men in all their affairs;[19] Pausanias suggests that the proper sort of Love turns men to the correct sort of objects;[20] Aristophanes, after describing the human quest for one's original 'other half', assigns to Eros the role of guide, leading us to what is akin to ourselves;[21] Agathon suggests that Eros guides his subjects to success in the arts[22] and serves as the best pilot in all affairs and the best leader in life's choral dance.[23]

Everyone, it seems, is looking to Eros as the guide towards achieving the objects of their desire and their highest aims in life. It is true that Socrates does not explicitly assign such a guiding role to Eros in his own speech. Nevertheless, Diotima criticizes Socrates for a mistake resembling that of Agathon, who had supposed that Eros was himself beautiful. Such a mistake, we are told,[24] arises from misidentifying Eros as the object of love, rather than the lover. Diotima herself holds that Eros is one who seeks the beautiful, not one who is beautiful, and Socrates concludes his speech with the claim that Eros is our helper in achieving our desire:

Well, Phaedrus and the rest of you, this is what Diotima said and I am convinced; and because I am convinced I try to convince others as well that one would not easily get a better assistant than Eros towards this treasure for human nature.[25]

Thus, although Socrates does not call Eros a 'guide' in so many words, plainly he does not dissent from the view of Agathon and

---

[18] This role is not explicitly mentioned in Socrates' own speech, and it is absent from Eryximachus' speech.

[19] 178c5.

[20] 181a6; 193d2.

[21] 193b2; 193d2.

[22] 197a7.

[23] 197e1–2.

[24] 204c.

[25] 212b1–4.

the others that Eros is the guide who helps us in our search for the beautiful object we long for. In these circumstances it seems reasonable to take the allusions in Diotima's speech to a guide in the ascent towards the true beauty to refer to Eros.

If Diotima means that Eros is our guide why does she not say so?

If one is to progress correctly towards this thing, one must start as a young man by progressing to beautiful bodies, and first, if the leader takes him the right way, he must fall in love with one body . . .[26]

One is led, educated, escorted, or guided along the path up to beauty,[27] but it is always left vague just who is doing the leading. The reason seems to be that the progress in love is progress in philosophy, and hence the guide will be not only an expert in love, but also a philosophy teacher. In this very dialogue we meet a number of such guides. For Socrates the guide is Diotima; for those at Agathon's party Socrates served as guide; and for Apollodorus the guide had been Aristodemus. But in each case the archetype that they embody is the philosopher-god Eros whose role is to direct us to the correct love of wisdom and of beauty.

### 3 . BARE FEET

The chief example of the guide in both love and philosophy is, of course, Socrates, and several features emphasized in the dialogue alert us to the implicit identification of Socrates and the god Eros. The first of these is Socrates' stance with regard to wisdom and knowledge. As often, Socrates adopts a stance of ignorance, disclaiming wisdom on the simplest matters when questioned by Diotima.[28] Indeed, the fact that he resigns authority to Diotima and cites her as the origin of all that he knows about love is itself an example of the Socratic denial of knowledge, though perhaps slightly moderated to the extent that he does now claim to have learnt from Diotima, and hence to have some knowledge concerning love that is derivative from her expertise in that area. Ignorance is a well-known Socratic characteristic, but it is peculiarly relevant here given that as the analysis proceeds we shall find love identified

---

[26] 210a4–7.
[27] 210e3, 211c1.
[28] Cf. 201e–202e.

with the philosopher's desire for wisdom; that desire, we are persuaded,[29] cannot occur in one who is already wise, but only in one who lacks wisdom. Only if one lacks can one love, and hence Eros, the archetype of the lover and the philosopher, must be one who lacks both wisdom and beauty. Socrates, like Eros, is notorious for being one who lacks wisdom and desires the knowledge that he lacks.

Socrates' appeal to his own need for a teacher is part and parcel of his identification with the real Eros.[30] That resemblance is fleshed out in Alcibiades' speech describing Socrates' characteristics and habits. Indeed, Alcibiades implicitly identifies Socrates with Eros when he volunteers, or is persuaded, to praise Socrates, in place of the encomium on Eros that was in order.[31] But Socrates' similarity to Eros had been hinted at long before, in Socrates' own speech. Socrates' speech makes some revisions to the images of love presented in the preceding set of speeches, and one effect of these revisions is to make Socrates' portrait of love resemble Plato's portrait of Socrates; thus, while Socrates' speech debunks Eros, Alcibiades' speech debunks Socrates, and both underscore the resemblance between Eros and Socrates. This resemblance was noticed by Ficino, and has often been remarked on since.[32] But the fact that the parallel is with the portrait of Socrates *in this dialogue* is generally overlooked by those who cite general allusions to Socrates in Xenophon or Cicero.

We may run briefly through some of the features that alert us to the assimilation of Eros and Socrates in Diotima's description. In addition to the passage where she argues that Eros must be neither ignorant nor wise,[33] to which we shall return, the main text is the account of the birth of Eros at 203b–d. Diotima corrects Agathon's classic picture of Eros as delicate and beautiful;[34] far from it, he is really hardened, unkempt, barefoot, homeless, always sleeping

---

[29] 204a.

[30] 207c.

[31] 214d2–10.

[32] See Ficino, *Symposium Commentary*, oratio 7. Others who notice the resemblance include L. Robin, *La Théorie platonicienne de l'amour* (2nd edn., Paris, 1964), 161–4; J. Gould, *Platonic Love* (London, 1963), 45 ff.; R. G. Bury, *The Symposium* (2nd edn., Cambridge, 1932), pp. lx–lxi. Stanley Rosen, *Plato's Symposium* (New Haven, Conn., 1968), 233 ff. attempts to minimize the resemblance, not wholly convincingly.

[33] 204a–b.

[34] ἁπαλός τε καὶ καλός, 203c6–7. Cf. 195c6–196b3.

rough and without a blanket, bedding down in doorways and on the streets under the stars, and impoverished.[35]

Some of these are, in any case, familiar characteristics of Socrates, but they are given a particular prominence in the *Symposium*. Eros is said to be homeless, sleeping rough without a blanket. What Diotima means by Eros' homelessness is not, of course, that he lacked a city that was his home town. Doubtless that would also be true, but Diotima does not say that he lacked a *polis* but that he lacked an *oikos*.[36] Thus the fact that Socrates is clearly at home in Athens is not a reason to deny that he resembles Eros in being 'homeless'.[37] Perhaps Socrates was not literally without a home, but Plato almost never portrays him at home; like Eros he is generally in someone else's home, at large in the city or outside the walls, or in the gymnasia and wrestling schools.[38] In the *Symposium* itself Socrates is away from home all night, and all the following day. Only in the evening does he finally make his way home, notably in the last two words of the dialogue.[39] Likewise Alcibiades describes Socrates away from home throughout: it is Alcibiades who invites Socrates to dinner or to the gymnasium,[40] and it is at Alcibiades' house that they spend the night together.[41] Similarly on military service Socrates is out on camp at Potidaea and in battle at Delium. In this dialogue we catch no glimpse of Socrates as a domestic man with a home life or economic interests.[42] In this sense he is *aoikos*, homeless.

Eros sleeps rough. Socrates seems to have a habit of staying out all night. At the symposium at Agathon's house Socrates actually never goes to sleep at all, and it is not clear that he did at Alcibiades' house either;[43] similarly at Potidaea Socrates spends a summer night awake, standing rapt in thought from one sunrise to the next, while the other soldiers bring out their beds and go to sleep round

---

[35] 203c6–d3.

[36] i.e. a home, house, or household. ἄοικος, 203d1.

[37] Rosen, *Plato's Symposium*, 234, seems to take the homelessness of Eros as political.

[38] The *Protagoras* is a counter-example since the dialogue starts at Socrates' home.

[39] καὶ οὕτω διατρίψαντα εἰς ἑσπέραν οἴκοι ἀναπαύεσθαι, 223d12.

[40] 217b7; 217c7; 217d3.

[41] 217d6–7.

[42] Except perhaps in his desire to leave after dining with Alcibiades, 217d2, 5, but it is not said that he would go *home*, only that he wished to go.

[43] 218c3–4; 219b–d.

him.[44] Thus although Socrates is not one to *sleep* out he does regularly spend the night out under the stars.

Sleeping without a blanket also fits the picture. Alcibiades enfolds Socrates in his own *himation* when he finds him huddled under no more than his usual thin cloak on a winter night,[45] and again at Potidaea, in the bitterest winter weather, Socrates ventures out with no more than his usual *himation*.[46] Coverings, or the lack of them, are part of the image of Socrates that Alcibiades depicts. As to bedding down in doorways, again Socrates is not one for bedding down; but doing philosophy in doorways is certainly his thing. The reader will not have forgotten that Aristodemus had left Socrates behind on the way to Agathon's house, and that he arrives hours late after sitting in the neighbours' porch.[47] As Aristodemus assures us, this is entirely in keeping with Socrates' habits.[48]

Socrates, like Eros, is a liminal figure, always at the door. Indeed, there is a great deal of arriving at doors in the *Symposium*. Just as Poverty, the mother of Eros, hangs about the door at the party to celebrate the birth of Aphrodite, so people keep turning up outside the door at Agathon's party to celebrate his successful play, hoping to get in. Not only Aristodemus, who arrives uninvited ahead of Socrates, and, of course, Alcibiades, but in addition a whole host of gatecrashers turn up at the door at 223b, and turn the party into a disorderly drinking session. There is clearly a sense in which Agathon's party represents the vision of beauty that everyone yearns to be included in, though only Socrates has the stamina to survive the rigours that ensue. Just as Aphrodite, at whose birthday party Eros was conceived, is a beauty to which Eros is devoted,[49] so Beauty itself, and the vision of it revealed at Agathon's party, is the object of Socrates' passionate devotion.

Perhaps most characteristically Socratic are Eros' unshod feet. We know from the *Phaedrus* that Socrates regularly went barefoot.[50] The *Phaedrus* is another dialogue about love, but in that case,

---

[44] 220c3–d5.
[45] 219b5–7.
[46] 220b.
[47] 175a8.
[48] 175b1–2.
[49] 203c1–4.
[50] *Phaedrus*, 229a3–4. According to Xenophon, *Memorabilia*, 1. 6. 2, this reflected both poverty and a preoccupation with philosophy. See also Aristophanes, *Clouds*, 103 and 362.

instead of going *up* towards the city as they do in the *Symposium*, Socrates and his interlocutor go outside the walls and *down* the valley of the river Ilissus. On that occasion Socrates was, as usual, barefoot, while Phaedrus, though not normally barefoot, was for once, on that particular occasion, without shoes. Clearly there is an inversion between the *Phaedrus* and the *Symposium*; whereas in one Socrates is typically barefoot, in the other he is untypically shod; whereas in the *Phaedrus* the interlocutor is untypically barefoot, in the *Symposium* Aristodemus is typically barefoot. And in both dialogues there is some question as to who is leading whom on the journey; Phaedrus volunteers to guide Socrates down the Ilissus valley, but in practice it is Socrates who knows the history and cultural significance of the features they pass, and who can correctly identify the geography of the place, although he had professed to be unfamiliar with it.[51]

Bare feet seem to make a difference to the search for the truth about beauty and love, and to one's ability to take the lead in that search. In each case it is the one who typically goes barefoot who makes accurate progress. If we are right that Eros, in Diotima's speech, is to be the guide on the ascent to the vision, it is not irrelevant that he too is barefoot.[52] And indeed the matter of wearing shoes becomes a recurrent theme in the *Symposium*.

To start with, one of the first things, indeed almost the only thing, that we learn about Aristodemus (who first told the story to Apollodorus) is that he was always barefoot.[53] The point is partly to indicate that Aristodemus was already a committed follower of Socrates; indeed, Apollodorus says that he thinks he was a lover of Socrates. But the significance is greater than that. Two other things we are told about him are that he was small, and that he belonged to the deme of Kudathenaion.[54] The significance of his diminutive stature is not obvious, though traditionally Eros himself appears to be small. But it may well also be important that Aristodemus is

---

[51] The area outside the walls is not one we associate with Socrates' vision of the ascent of love. Phaedrus proves to be a bad guide in matters of love, and Socrates has to recant after his initial speech that has denigrated the nature of love. The image in the myth, of love as a struggle against the parts of the soul that pull us down, suggests that we are to see the descent outside the city walls with Phaedrus as guide as a distraction from the ascent of love that leads to the vision of truth.

[52] 203d1.

[53] 173b2.

[54] 173b2.

from Kudathenaion, which is a deme within the city walls of Athens, unlike Socrates' own deme, Alopeke, which was just outside the walls, across the Ilissus valley.[55] The motif of ascent implied that the city was identified with the summit of the journey to the vision of beauty, and hence it is unsurprising to find that Aristodemus belongs in the city and has, in this respect, a head start over Socrates on the philosophical track. Socrates still needs to tag along behind Aristodemus to Agathon's house, and behind Diotima on the ascent to knowledge. Aristodemus, on the other hand, is already a lover, already barefoot, already a city-dweller. In some sense he no longer needs a guide, but he serves as the guide for those who subsequently seek to find out. He seems to stand for one who, by following Socrates, has already arrived. It is no wonder, then, that in one sense he never speaks—many have wondered that Aristodemus does not list himself among those who took their turn at speaking— and in another sense he speaks throughout, since it is in his words that the whole episode is narrated. He is, after all, our first authority on love; but he is not, as the other speakers are, still engaged in the search for a guide to truth. He is the real lover who has already mastered the technique.

The tale that Aristodemus tells begins by commenting on the fact that Socrates was, on the occasion of the symposium, wearing shoes.[56] We have already noted the way in which Socrates had dressed to play the part of Agathon's lover at Agathon's party. His style corresponds to the image of the elegant Eros that Agathon will describe in his speech. Aristodemus remarks on how unusual it was for Socrates to appear bathed or shod. It is true that at the very end of the dialogue when all the rest have fallen asleep, Socrates goes off to the Lyceum and has a wash before beginning the day's business.[57] But that routine wash[58] is not going to affect the overall presentation of the person, as the bath[59] had done before the party.

---

[55] The location of Socrates' deme is important, since it means that Socrates must be familiar with the Ilissus valley when he walks there with Phaedrus in the *Phaedrus*. Phaedrus' assumption that it is unfamiliar is symbolic, because Socrates' love is philosophical, not wordly. Love is seen as a kind of attention: Socrates' attention belongs in the city, not in the country.

[56] 174a3–4.

[57] 223d10–11.

[58] ἀπονιψάμενον, 223d11.

[59] λελουμένον, 174a3.

Bathing clearly merits remark as something quite out of the ordinary for Socrates.[60]

Now we can understand why it is that Socrates, in this dialogue, has resigned the position of leader in love to Aristodemus and Diotima. His uncharacteristic appearance and footwear show that he has adopted the model of love put forward by Agathon. That is what Socrates says at the start of his speech, when he observes that he had made claims about love essentially identical to those put forward by Agathon,[61] and that it was Diotima who was in a position to correct and teach him. His appearance supports his contention that he is ignorant on the subject,[62] whereas Aristodemus' appearance supports the idea that he is a lover modelled on the Eros of Diotima's speech: unshod and lacking.

We know that Aristodemus was not just usually barefoot but also barefoot on this particular occasion. When he arrives at Agathon's party, before he can recline on the couch, a slave has to come and wash his feet.[63] If he had had shoes on, the job of the slave would have been to take off his shoes, as is the case when Alcibiades comes in. *He* is taken to a place between Agathon and Socrates, where he first of all sits down.[64] Then Agathon has the slaves remove Alcibiades' shoes, whereupon he is ready to recline on the couch.[65]

Alcibiades, unlike Aristodemus, is not so devoted to Socrates as to imitate his barefoot habits. Describing Socrates' remarkable hardihood in the wintry campaign at Potidaea, Alcibiades stresses Socrates' lack of footwear:

Once when the ice was most dreadful, and everyone was either indoors and not going out, or if they went out they put on an amazing amount of clothes and footwear, bundling up their feet in woolly socks and sheepskin boots, this man Socrates went out in a woollen wrap such as he used to

---

[60] See K. J. Dover, Plato: *Symposium* (Cambridge, 1980), 81, and for other references to unwashed philosophers in Aristophanes see Bury's note *ad* 174a.

[61] 201e.

[62] Of course Socrates should not profess ignorance at the point at which he goes to Agathon's party, nor when he gives his speech, since he claims to have learnt the truth from Diotima some time beforehand. Both the suave and unphilosophical appearance, and the opening disclaimers of ignorance must in this sense be disingenuous: he is not really ignorant of the true nature of love but acts tonight as if he were.

[63] 175a6.

[64] 213a7.

[65] 213b5.

wear before, and got over the ice better in his bare feet than the others did in their boots.[66]

Clearly Alcibiades did not imitate Socrates at Potidaea, nor is he following his barefoot example now on the occasion of Agathon's party. Thus, although Alcibiades is fascinated by Socrates, he is in striking contrast to Aristodemus, the Socratic lover. Whereas Aristodemus never speaks the whole evening, Alcibiades is an unbridled chatterbox. But the whole of Alcibiades' speech, with its candid confession of his failed attempt to seduce Socrates, betrays just how far he is from understanding what makes Socrates tick. Among the features that indicate Alcibiades' confusion is his failure to appreciate the significance of the barefoot philosopher.

We have dealt so far with the features of Eros that derive from his mother, Poverty. But Diotima also notes that there is a resourceful side to his nature, supposedly inherited from his father Poros. These features also bear a resemblance to Socrates' character, less detailed perhaps than the poverty side, but recognizable. Eros is said to be one who lays traps for the beautiful and the good; he is daring, headstrong, and intense, a clever marksman, always contriving some schemes. He has a passion for wisdom, is resourceful, and spends his whole life philosophizing.[67] Alcibiades' account of his relationship with Socrates plainly reveals Socrates as one who ensnares the beautiful and good. Alcibiades had thought himself the master of love's arrows,[68] but Socrates, it emerges, was really the wizard at that.[69] Similarly the description of Eros as the lifelong philosopher with a passion for wisdom cannot fail to remind us of Socrates.

The resemblance between Diotima's picture of Eros and Plato's picture of Socrates is remarkable. It is also worth noticing because it shows us that the theory about the status of Eros and his role in philosophy is not just a piece of mythological demonology, but is also about Socrates and about Socratic philosophy. The text is first and foremost about the status of the philosopher and his relationship with truth, beauty, and the good.

Eros is an intermediary. So also is Socrates, whose task it is to

---

[66] 220b.
[67] 203d4–7.
[68] 219b3–4.
[69] 215c–216e; 217e6–218b5.

convey the wisdom of the priestess Diotima to the company at the party. Eros is neither ignorant nor wise; likewise Socrates knows at least that he needs to learn. Eros is neither mortal nor immortal; neither is the philosopher, whose love earns him the immortality he desires. Nevertheless, we should not *dismiss* the passage about Eros just because it portrays an image of Socrates. The image of Socrates presented by Plato in the *Symposium* is just as much an illustration of a theory of love as his account of love is a picture of Socrates. In other words, Plato chooses to stress certain features of Socrates in this dialogue as part of his definition of love.

## 4. EROS IN NEED

Diotima's account of love starts by making some basic philosophical distinctions which help to determine the status of Eros. These distinctions come into three categories.

### (i) *Opposites*

At 201e8–10 Diotima makes laborious work of explaining to Socrates (whose wits seem slow at this point) a rather elementary point about the neutral middle ground between contraries such as 'good' and 'bad', or 'beautiful' and 'ugly'. The point is then made again at 202a2–10 for 'wise' and 'ignorant',[70] and also at 202d8–13 for 'mortal' and 'immortal'. The aim is partly to stress Socrates' own lack of wisdom, the condition necessary for being a philosopher; but in this case his lack of wisdom is specifically in the field of what is 'in between', including the epistemological state between knowledge and ignorance, though not only that. By this means it becomes clear that the state of being neither one thing nor the other, but in between, is fundamental to the theory of love that is being offered.

### (ii) *The notion of* lover

Diotima turns the analysis of love away from the beloved (which had been the focus of attention in all the earlier speeches) and seeks

---

[70] Cf. 204b1–2.

an explanation in terms of the lover. Socrates had already, at 199d, drawn attention to the relational character of love. This paves the way for Diotima's claim, at 204c1–6, that to explain love we need to look at that which loves, not that which is loved.[71] She rejects any attempt to explain love on the basis of the beauty of the beloved, and locates the explanatory force in the lover, specifically in the need or lack on the part of the lover. Hence we start with an analysis of love as desire, or more specifically the desire to possess some class of good things, which happen to be the property of certain individuals. Hence it is the desirable properties, not the individual who possesses them, that take on the role of object in a desire-analysis of love. And the motivation becomes self-interest. It is Socrates who suggests that the lover wants the fine things to 'accrue to him',[72] but at this point no other option is available since love has been analysed in terms of fulfilling a need. The direction of the analysis was determined from the point at which Socrates secured agreement from Agathon to the principle that one could not love what one already possessed.

### (iii) *Begetting*

Although the analysis initially starts from desire to possess (204d–206a) this is modified in the famous passage concerning 'begetting in the beautiful' (206b–212a), where the emphasis changes from *possessing* the beautiful to *gazing* on beauty and goodness itself, while the need to possess is a need to possess immortality in order to gaze for ever on the beautiful itself. Thus at this stage, although Diotima does not remark on the fact, a wedge has been inserted between the desire to possess and what constitutes true love. The motivation is still self-interest, and the focus of attention is still the lover, but the ultimate aim of his love is not possession of good things but a vision of unfailing beauty.[73] His relation to individual beautiful things is likewise not to possess or consume, but the creative relationship of 'begetting'.[74] Only immortality is desired

---

[71] τὸ ἐρῶν not τὸ ἐρώμενον, 204c1–6. Diotima does not consider the possibility of a middle term here.

[72] γενέσθαι αὐτῷ, 204d7.

[73] 210e3–211b7; 211d1–3. Notice the change of terminology from κτήσει ἀγαθῶν ('acquisition of goods', 205a1) to τὸ ἀγαθὸν αὐτῷ εἶναι ἀεί ('that the good should be there for him for ever', 206a11).

[74] 209a8–c7; cf. 210a4–8.

for possession,[75] and then as a means to the permanent enjoyment of other things, not as an end in itself.[76] At 206e2 Diotima remarks on the revision of the original analysis.

Given this outline of the progress of Diotima's analysis of love, we can arrive at a kind of explanation of the status of Eros in Diotima's account. 1. In Diotima's view Eros is the lover, not the beloved. 2. The lover is one who desires beauty, not one who possesses beauty, so Eros must be lacking in beauty and those other fine things he loves. 3. In order to desire something one must be intermediate, not so lacking as to have no sense of what one lacks. Hence Eros must be intermediate in the relevant respects. 4. Since love also desires immortality, Eros must be intermediate between mortal and immortal.

The mythical description of love and his parentage occurs in the framework of the initial, possessive, account of love. The subsequent revision, in terms of creative begetting, is never plugged into the portrait of Eros, but the desire for immortality, introduced in the transitional passage[77] but a subsidiary pursuit in the second analysis, continues to be conceived on the same model of acquisitive desire that was central to the first analysis of love.[78]

## 5. THEOLOGY

We have already two kinds of explanation of Eros' liminal status: first that Eros serves as an image of Socrates and of the true philosopher; secondly that he illustrates Diotima's first, acquisitive, analysis of love in which desire is explained by the intermediate status of the lover and by his need. However, neither of these excludes the possibility of a third kind of analysis, in terms of what it is to be, or not to be, a god. If Eros marks the gap between gods

---

[75] 208b5–6; 210a1–2.

[76] Cf. 206e8–207a2.

[77] 206a–207a.

[78] In the first analysis the possession of the good things is also a subsidiary goal, where the final goal is to be happy ($\epsilon\vec{v}\delta\alpha\acute{\iota}\mu\omega\nu$ 205a1–3), though it is probable that being happy consists in possessing various kinds of good thing, and hence to acquire those things is to acquire happiness. In the second analysis *possession* of things that are *kalon* is not a goal at all; rather the subsidiary goals are *begetting* beautiful *logoi* and so on *in what is kalon*, and *possessing* immortality.

and men, can we see what makes a god a god and a non-god not a god?

The main part of my analysis will be concerned with the grounds on which Diotima denies to Eros the status of god. Secondly I shall ask why intermediates could or should exist, and thirdly whether there are theological advantages in positing them.

### (i) *Why not a god?*

When and why does Diotima claim that Eros cannot be a god? The first mention of his divinity in Socrates' speech is at 201e5 and is dramatically prominent because it marks the beginning of Socrates' disagreement with the previous speakers, all of whom had either assumed or stated explicitly that Eros was a god.[79] But in fact Diotima's first challenge is not to the divinity of Eros, but to the claim that he is beautiful or good.[80] This first refutation supposedly delivered by Diotima is not narrated by Socrates, who says it took the same form as his conversation with Agathon.[81] Thus, when Diotima's discussion begins at 201e8 Socrates has already been convinced that Eros cannot be beautiful and good. It remains to show that he need not be ugly and bad either, since it is possible to be neither good nor bad but intermediate.

Thus Diotima's first objection is actually to the claim that Eros is beautiful and good, and makes no reference to theology. It is completed at 202b2–5 with the observation that if Eros is not beautiful and good it need not follow that he is ugly and bad. It is Socrates who introduces theology at this point: 'Yet on the other hand, I said, it is universally agreed that he is a great god.'[82] Socrates introduces this as a new point;[83] the precise connection between beauty and divine status has yet to be examined.

Diotima proceeds to ask[84] whether the view that Eros is a god is held by people who do not know, or by those who know as well.

---

[79] Phaedrus' speech, 178a7; 180b6–9. Pausanias' speech, 180d6–e4. Eryximachus' speech, 186b1. Aristophanes' speech, 189c4–d3. Agathon's speech, 195a5–8; cf. 197e.

[80] *kalos* or *agathos*, 201e7.

[81] 201e6–7, referring to 199c3–201c9.

[82] 202b6.

[83] καὶ μήν, 202b6.

[84] 202b8.

Her division into knowers and non-knowers[85] carefully complies with the principle she has just enunciated concerning the middle ground between knowledge and ignorance.[86] Socrates' suggestion that the view is held by knowers and non-knowers alike meets with derision from Diotima, who claims that there are at least two people who hold that Eros is not a god at all, Socrates for one and Diotima for another.[87]

Socrates is surprised to find himself credited with such a radical view. It seems to be the opposite of what he has just proposed.[88] Diotima has to persuade him that he is already committed to it in virtue of his agreement to the proposition that Eros is not beautiful and good. This she does in a meticulous exposition of the theological implications of his position:

What do you mean by that? I said.

Easy, she said. Tell me, don't you think all the gods are happy and beautiful? Or would you be prepared to say that one of the gods was not beautiful and happy?

Not I, by Zeus, I said.

But don't you say the happy are the ones who have got good and beautiful things?

Yes for sure.

But you just agreed that it was due to his lack of good and beautiful things that Eros had a desire for those things that he lacked.

Yes I did.

How then could one who had no share of beautiful and good things be a god?

No way, so it seems.

So you see, she said, that you too think Eros is not a god.[89]

This passage is interesting. Diotima does not move directly from Socrates' agreement that Eros is not himself beautiful and good to the conclusion that he cannot be a god. To do that she would have had to claim that any god must necessarily be good and beautiful.

[85] τῶν μὴ εἰδότων, ἔφη, πάντων λέγεις, ἢ καὶ τῶν εἰδότων; 202b8.

[86] 202a2–10.

[87] Whether Diotima would put herself and Socrates in the class of knowers or non-knowers is never made clear. It seems that Socrates is portraying himself as qualifying for true judgement (ὀρθὰ δοξάζειν, 202a5) at the very most.

[88] Socrates does not literally propose that Eros is a god at this point, 206b6, since he merely observes that it is universally agreed. He had apparently proposed such a view earlier (201e5).

[89] 202c5–d7.

It is not clear that that principle could be demonstrated at this point,[90] but Diotima takes a point specifically related to Eros, namely his lack of good things. Happiness (or blessedness, *eudaimonia*) is a feature of the gods, and if happiness consists in having what you want, then Eros plainly cannot have it, for he is by definition one who is always in want of something.

Diotima inserts the notion of *eudaimonia* to add plausibility to the idea that lack of fine possessions is incompatible with godhead. She also seems to hold that lacking good things means that one is not oneself good,[91] and lacking fine things means that one is not fine, but these are not the immediate basis on which she argues, and would perhaps not stand up to scrutiny. She takes it for granted that being beautiful and being blessed go together. Eros is neither beautiful nor blessed, and hence cannot be a god.

The next step in Diotima's account is an outline of what it is to be a *daimon* or spirit;[92] it is taken for granted (202d8–9) that Eros is not mortal, and the only remaining possibility is that he comes into the intermediate state of *daimon*. Before considering this discussion of what a daimon is we should look first at one other passage concerning the criteria for divinity. At 203e5, at the end of the account of the birth of Eros, Diotima says that he is in between wisdom and ignorance. She then expands the point:

It's like this. None of the gods is a philosopher or desires to become wise— for god is wise—nor will anyone else who is wise be a philosopher. Nor again do the ignorant practise philosophy or desire to become wise; for ignorance is a problem precisely for the fact that one thinks one is O K when one is in fact neither fine nor good nor sensible. So the one who does not suppose he is in need does not desire what he does not suppose he needs.[93]

Diotima cannot argue that because Eros is not a god, therefore he must be a philosopher, since she does not hold that all who are not gods are philosophers. On the contrary, she allows that some who are not gods might be wise,[94] and certainly some are supposed to

---

[90] There is also a problem about the meaning of 'good' since Eros' difficulty is not that he is not good to others, but rather that he lacks what is good for himself. Hence Diotima cannot proceed by showing that any lack of goodness is incompatible with godhead; in this case it must be failure to obtain what is good.

[91] Cf. 201b6–c5; 201e6.

[92] 202d13 ff.

[93] 204a1–7.

[94] 204a2.

be ignorant and hence not to know what it is to be a philosopher or why one should be one. Nor does it follow that because Eros is intermediate between gods and mortals he must be a philosopher; again it is allowed that some of those between gods and mortals might not be philosophers. Diotima does not argue from Eros' divine status (or lack of it) to his being a philosopher.

On the contrary, Diotima's argument is designed to establish that Eros has an intermediate status, starting from the premiss that he is a lover of the beautiful. The argument is explained at 204a8–b5; Socrates, singularly dim-witted on this occasion, has already forgotten what he was told at 202a about the intermediate state between knowledge and ignorance. He is puzzled as to who could qualify as a philosopher:

Who are the philosophers then, Diotima, if they are neither the wise nor the ignorant? I said.

This much is plain even to a child, she said, that it's the ones between the two, among whom would be Eros as well. For wisdom is one of the most beautiful things, and Eros is love for the beautiful, so that Eros must necessarily be a philosopher, and if a philosopher then in between wise and ignorant.[95]

Thus Eros' desire for wisdom is just one aspect of his desire for all fine things. Since desire presupposes lack he must lack wisdom, but he cannot lack it to the extent of ignorance since then he would not desire it.[96] Thus we have here, as we did not in the case of the god/mortal dichotomy at 202a, a reason why Eros must be in-between. And once we have established that Eros is between wisdom and ignorance, we can infer that he is excluded from the ranks of the gods since they all possess wisdom.[97]

Eros' lack of immortality, mentioned at 203d8 ff. but never explored in detail, must prevent him from being a god, just as his lack of wisdom does, since we are told at 208ab that gods have immortality in a way peculiar to themselves:

For it is in this way that every mortal being is preserved, not by being entirely the same for ever as the divine is, but through what is departing

---

[95] 204a8–b5. Notice that his status between wise and ignorant is the conclusion. That Eros is a philosopher is a preliminary conclusion, drawn from the premisses that he desires what is *kalon* and that wisdom is *kalon*.

[96] For this part of the argument see 204a3–7.

[97] 204a1.

and ageing leaving behind it a new one such as it was itself. This is the scheme, Socrates, by which what is mortal partakes of immortality (both bodies and all other things), she said. But what is immortal does so in a different way.[98]

Diotima leaves no room here for intermediates between mortal and immortal. She is no longer talking specifically about Eros the daimon, but has moved on to her later analysis of the progress of the true philosopher towards the vision of true beauty. Unlike this philosopher, who achieves both the vision and some form of immortality, Eros as he was described before could achieve neither possession of the goods he desired nor immortality.[99] Eros is in fact responsible for mortals' yearning, but not for the achievement of their ambition. Though mortals do achieve some half-baked version of immortality, by leaving offspring or by begetting true virtue, Eros permanently lacks even that.

## (ii) *Why a daimon?*

Diotima has suggested three criteria for gods: (1) all gods are happy and beautiful, 202c; (2) all gods are wise, 204a; (3) gods (and gods alone) have pukka immortality, 208a. Eros fails on all three, so he cannot be a god. But given that he is not a god, are we in a position to infer that he is a daimon? Socrates himself professes to be unfamiliar with the notion (202d8–e2) so we should take the cue from him and ask what is the point of daimones?[100]

As we observed, Diotima does not, initially, offer any reason why Eros could not be a mortal,[101] but in response to Socrates' ignorance she offers an account of the nature and function of daimones at 202e–203a. It is here that we should look for a reason, if there is one, for there being intermediates between gods and mortals. The function she describes is entirely concerned with communication:

Interpreting and conveying to the gods the things from men and to men

---

[98]  208a7–b4.

[99]  212a7. Note that here the immortality achieved by the philosopher seems to be distinct from that of merely leaving a replica as mentioned in 208ab. Cf. I. M. Crombie, *An Examination of Plato's Doctrines*, vol. i (London, 1962), 361–3.

[100]  For general accounts of 'demonology' in Plato see Robin, *La Théorie platonicienne*, 110–15, and A. Levi, 'Sulla demonologia Platonica', *Athenaeum*, 24 (1946), 119–28.

[101]  202d8–9.

the things from the gods, from men their prayers and offerings, from gods their commands and returns; being in the middle the daimon completes both, so that the whole is bound itself to itself.[102]

She goes on to explain that prophecy, priestly art, divination, and so on are all facilitated by the daimon: 'For god does not mix with humanity, but all the intercourse and communication that gods have with human beings, whether awake or asleep, is through the daimon.'[103] Diotima seems to suppose that two problems would ensue if no intermediate existed: (*a*) communication between gods and humanity would break down; and (*b*) the universe would fall apart because the divine part would not be joined to the mortal part. But she does not explain why we should think either consequence likely. Is it not merely a result of positing an intermediate that the extremes are too far apart to meet? It seems that if we dispensed with daimones then gods and men would be adjacent and not divided by any gulf. Whereas if we do suppose there is a difficulty about bridging the gap between gods and mortals, will there not also be a similar difficulty between daimones and mortals, or daimones and gods?

I want to offer two kinds of defence against the charge that Diotima is merely multiplying the celestial hierarchies to no effect. (*a*) First we should observe that gods and men are treated not as adjacent links on a more extensive chain of being, as might be the case for example if animals and plants were under consideration, but rather as polar opposites. God is at one extreme of a scale of which humanity is the opposite end; the pair god and mortal is treated as logically similar to the pairs beautiful and ugly, good and bad, and wise and ignorant that we had met earlier in Diotima's speech as examples of opposites which allow for an intermediate state that is neither one nor the other.[104]

Thus, whereas the insertion of extra links in a continuous chain would elongate the chain and increase the distance between what had been adjacent links, Diotima's intermediates are used to fill a gap that was a maximum divide between extremes. This is one reason why it is important for Plato, or Diotima, to explain the nature of contraries that allow such logical space for intermediates.

[102] 202e3–7.
[103] 203a1–4.
[104] See 202d7–11; 201e10–11; 202b2; 202a2–3.

It seems that Diotima's universe would be in danger of falling into two parts if intermediates were denied, due to a kind of dualism that treats what are properly contraries as if they were contradictories.

(*b*) Daimones are posited because such intermediates are held to be a logical possibility. But why should Eros in particular be a daimon? It seems that the communication for which Eros finds himself peculiarly responsible is that of desiring to possess what one lacks, and indeed perceiving that one lacks it in the first place. Eros serves as a daimon in that he enables mortals to perceive their lack of divine qualities and hence to desire to possess them, providing a link between the divine and the mortal.

On the other hand, there seem to be difficulties. Certainly the gods are happy, beautiful, wise, and immortal, and these are the features that mortals lack and that are the object of the desire aroused by Eros. Without Eros the mortals would not only lack those features but be so far from appreciating them that they would not even perceive their lack or the desirability of the features they lacked. Eros is responsible for their ability to perceive a lack and their desire to make good the lack. That desire can only occur when they come near enough to being wise or beautiful to perceive what it would be. That much is clear.

Two problems seem to arise. (1) As Socrates agrees at 205a5–b2, all humans seem to have the relevant desires, to some extent, and indeed even animals reveal a desire for immortality, according to Diotima (207a7–d2), so that it seems impossible to locate any example of mortal nature in its wholly unregenerate state. (2) It seems possible for mortals not merely to desire to become like the gods, but also to some extent to achieve their desire. Yet if gods and mortals are defined as contraries it seems impossible that what is mortal should acquire the features of the divine and yet remain what it is.

The first difficulty is not a real problem; indeed it clarifies why mortals and gods are introduced as opposites in the first place. The fact that we cannot locate an example of mortal nature untouched by the effects of Eros does not mean that we cannot infer what mortal nature would be in the absence of Eros. Diotima's point would be that no mortal without Eros would desire wisdom or beauty and the rest. In that unaspiring state they would indeed be the antithesis of the divine. Then the second difficulty can be explained on the same lines. The fact that mortals can acquire the divine characteristics to some degree does not mean that we should not define mortality itself as the total absence of those characteristics. With the assistance of Eros mortals cease to be the unerotic creatures they would have been in their purely mortal state. What is anomalous is the fact that we continue to call them mortals even after they have lost the defining features of mortality and acquired some vestiges of divine characteristics.

(iii) *Are there theological advantages in positing daimones?*

Diotima implies that we need daimones to avoid a kind of dualism and bipartition of the universe. That need arises first from positing a profound opposition between god and mortal nature. Given that opposition we then need some means of accounting for the fact that mortals do, in practice, recognize and desire communion with divine beauty and goodness.

The same sort of issue arises in the Judaeo-Christian tradition when humanity is considered in its fallen state. Even if originally created beautiful and good, postlapsarian humanity is often conceived as fundamentally divided from God, in a state somewhat comparable to what Diotima assigns to mortals without Eros. If humankind is so utterly without virtue, how can it possibly achieve relations with the divine? Much theological controversy has turned on whether the source of the grace that enables us to achieve communion with the divine lies in our own nature, or is provided by some mediator between ourselves and God, or derives from God's direct intervention in the mortal realm.

Diotima, for sure, does not envisage the divine stepping out of its cosy heaven to intervene in the mortal sphere; in her scheme the divine is beautiful and happy in virtue of its possession of good things, and it has no need to share. Nor does mortal nature have the ability to pull itself up by its own bootstraps. Thus we are likely to admit that if, with Diotima, we hold (*a*) a low estimate of human nature as such, (*b*) a high estimate of the degree to which it can rise to the level of divinity, and (*c*) the total non-involvement of the divine in providing for that progress in mortals, then to posit a non-divine intermediary as what we might call a 'soteriological device' is probably the best option.

## 6. PLOTINUS

Plotinus comments in a rather random fashion on the myth of the birth of Eros in Plato's *Symposium*, at *Ennead* 3. 5.[105] He returns several times to the issue of why Eros should be a daimon and not a god,[106] but it appears that for him the function of Eros is rather different from the function we have just outlined from a reading of Plato himself. I shall consider two of the relevant passages in Plotinus.

### (i) *Ennead* 3. 5. 6

In chapter 6 Plotinus starts on his exegesis of the birth of Eros. The first question is why Poros and Penia are appropriate parents for Eros. In fact Plotinus does not deal with Poros and Penia as individuals until chapter 7. In the meantime he considers the fact that they, like Eros, must be daimones.[107] What are daimones?

Let us then consider how we distinguish gods from daimones; not as we frequently say that daimones also are gods—but rather when we are speaking of them as being different classes, gods one sort and daimones another. The fact is that we think of and speak of the class of gods as impassible (ἀπαθές), but we ascribe feelings (πάθη) to daimones, saying they are eternal, but next in line after the gods already some degree in our direction, that is between the gods and our kind.[108]

Plotinus goes on to explore how the daimones fell into this condition; the details need not concern us. What we notice here is that whereas in Plato the daimones lacked what the gods possessed (namely happiness and fine things) here the daimones possess what the gods lack (namely feelings, πάθη).[109] Impassibility (*apatheia*) is the mark of the gods, and *apatheia* is a freedom and independence

---

[105] This passage is discussed by Robin, *La Théorie platonicienne*, 104–6, and by J. Dillon, '*Ennead* III. 5: Plotinus' Exegesis of the *Symposium* Myth', *ΑΓΩΝ* 3 (1969), 24–44.

[106] These passages are left aside by Dillon, '*Ennead* III. 5' since he is not concerned with demonology.

[107] Plotinus assumes that these two have the status of daimones, though this is not explicit in Plato's text. In fact Plato seems to include Poros among the gods, 203b2–3.

[108] *Ennead* 3. 5. 6. 7–13.

[109] πάθη include emotions other than desire. Not every daimon is an eros, *Ennead* 3. 5. 6. 27–33. πάθος is the subject of *Ennead* 3. 6 (chronologically earlier).

preserved by those who have not become involved with matter.[110]
So in Plotinus the daimones are the ones who have, and the gods
are the ones who lack.

The difference from Plato's picture is, in a sense, a theological one
because it reflects the fact that for Plotinus everything, including the
daimones and mortals, theoretically derives from the divine state
of *apatheia* and independence. There is no need to explain why
things that were originally opposed should be drawn together, since
Plotinus does not suppose that they are originally opposed. Because
the divine is their place of origin, mortals naturally have some
desires or aspirations upwards toward divinity. The further they
are from perfection the greater and more pathetic their desires, and,
of course, the harder of fulfilment. Hence for Plotinus Eros is not
required to explain mortals' aspirations, unless he explains the *fall*
from unity, not the return to it. For Plotinus Eros is one example
of the desiring nature of what is not divine, as anything that is one
step down from divinity will be caught up in desire for what is
above.

Given this view we can see that Plotinus does not need Eros as a
'soteriological device', because the desire of the lower for the higher
is innate and natural. Plotinus has an apophatic theology, defining
the divine by its *lack* of the constraints that characterize the
material, mortal, pathetic, and worldly. Diotima, by contrast, gave
us an apophatic anthropology, defining mortals by their *lack* of all
that the gods possessed, attributes which she ascribes cataphatically
to the divine.

## (ii) Ennead *3. 5. 7*

In this passage Plotinus considers the features of Eros in particular,
not of daimones in general. Now he carries out his task of interpreting the parentage of Eros. He says little about Poros, who, we
infer in lines 9–12, provides Eros with his status as a *logos*, but
Penia is said to be responsible for the incompleteness of Eros and
his lack of self-sufficiency:

Hence because logos entered into what is not logos, but an indeterminate
impulse, an obscure entity, it made the offspring not perfect nor sufficient,
but lacking, in that it was the product of an indeterminate impulse and a

---

[110] *Ennead* 3. 5. 6. 35–45.

sufficient logos. And this logos is not pure, in that it includes an indeterminate, irrational, indefinite impulse; for it will never be replenished as
long as it has the nature of the indeterminate in it.[111]

This is the nearest that Plotinus comes to elucidating Plato's
concern with lack in Eros; but whereas for Diotima what Eros
lacked were good and fine things, in Plotinus he lacks determinacy
and rationality. This explains not his desire as such, but the insta-
bility of his desire:

And Eros is like a gadfly,[112] needy by nature; so that even when he strikes
lucky he is immediately in need again. For he is not capable of being
replenished, because mixture is not; the only thing that is really replenished
is what is already replete in its own nature; but what craves because of an
inherent lack, even if it is momentarily replenished, leaks again at once.[113]

Thus it is the indeterminacy, inherited from his mother and modified only slightly by his fatherly heritage of rationality, that explains
Eros' neediness and craving. Eros is born an insatiably leaky vessel.
Thus Plotinus explores, as Plato did not, why Eros cannot get and
keep the things he lacks. He is leaky because he has not got proper
edges, his walls are porous; he is a mixture of the finite and the
indefinite.

Plotinus is not concerned, as Plato was, to make Eros a boundary-
crosser. His concern with boundaries is only to place Eros outside
the sphere of intellectual, definite things, and inside the realm of
mixture where definition is lost, and where pathos and craving
belong.

## 7. CONCLUSION

If my analysis is right it seems that Plotinus is more concerned
about pathos and emotion than Diotima was. It would be nice to
be able to offer an explanation for this change. Initially it seemed
plausible that an explanation might be sought in the fact that
Plotinus was aware of a threat from Christianity, a factor plainly
not significant for Plato. Perhaps it was because Christianity's God

---

[111] *Ennead* 3. 5. 7. 9–15.
[112] For the gadfly see Plato, *Apology*, 30e (where it is μύωψ) and *Phaedrus*, 240d1
(οἶστρος as here).
[113] *Ennead* 3. 5. 7. 19–24.

appeared to be subject to pathos and emotion that Plotinus was particularly concerned to attribute *apatheia* to the gods as an essential part of the divine nature. In Plotinus' theology no god could suffer, nor love.

But this concern will not explain why the notion of lack, so prominent in Plato, should have disappeared from view in Plotinus. That notion too might well have figured in an attack on Christianity, given that Christianity affirms the self-emptying of the divine logos as a central tenet. This suggests that seeking an explanation in terms of the presence of Christianity is not helpful. The difference between Plato and Plotinus is probably better analysed in terms of the distinct anthropological theories advanced in the two passages. It is not, perhaps, that they think differently about god so much as that they present different accounts of humanity. Diotima's polarity between god and mortal nature in its unredeemed state means that mortal nature in its unredeemed unerotic state is wholly apathetic: it neither knows nor desires the things it lacks. Hence it is without longing, without passion, without aspirations. That state of *apatheia* is impossible in Plotinus, except in one who has achieved union with the divine. Hence for Plotinus pathos invariably characterizes the lower forms of life.

Thus what is absent in Plotinus is Plato's (or rather Diotima's) antithesis between gods and mortals that makes human beings so far from the divine that they have no inclination to seek what is good. Plotinus places mortals closer to the divine as part of its fallout, not as an opposite kind of being. If Plotinus' view were a response to Christianity, which in any case I doubt, it would have to be a rejection of the anthropological views, rather than the theological views, of the theory it rejected. In fact it would need to be a response that said that soteriology is simply unnecessary. There is not, and never has been, any need for a redeemer since humanity was never so far lost as to lack the aspirations, and the means, to draw itself back to communion with the divine, from its own innate resources. For Plotinus humanity is, in itself, fundamentally erotic.

The contrast between Plotinus and Plato shows us something about what is important in the account of love in the *Symposium*. Diotima had diverted our attention from an explanation of love in terms of the beauty of the object to an explanation in terms of the lover. That move is important because we are to look at the aspirations we have to improve our lot. But what Eros accounts for is the very fact that we perceive the objects as desirable and worth having. It is not that the beauty provides the motivation, but that we have to be inspired even to see the beautiful as something to love. And that perception of the beloved as desirable is something inspired by the work of Eros, that transforms us from mere mortals without erotic aspirations to philosophers who yearn for what they perceive as good. So it is wrong to suppose that love is motivated by desire, or inspired by a beauty that is perceived independently of love. Rather we should see Plato as attempting to capture the notion that our very perception of the beloved as good is dependent on our first seeing with the vision of love. It is an attitude that takes us outside ourselves, to see ourselves as lacking and inadequate, and which enables us to proceed on the road of philosophy, a road that we should never set out on if we did not first remove our shoes and follow the spirit of Socrates, or Eros, who can inspire us with the love of wisdom.

# 5

# The Power of the Beloved:
# Aristotle on the Unmoved Mover

This chapter sets out to ask whether the sun, moon, stars, and planets are alive, and whether we need to attribute consciousness to them. That may seem a rather odd and antiquated question to ask; but I am inclined to think that it is not really any more odd as a question now than it was in the days of Aristotle and of Aquinas, when it was a real issue and much ink was spilt on the subject.[1] Their texts are going to serve as my starting point.

## I. WAS IT AN ODD QUESTION TO ASK WHETHER THE SUN, MOON, AND STARS WERE ALIVE WHEN ARISTOTLE ASKED THE QUESTION?

Aristotle was, of course, keenly interested in biology and an expert on the behaviour of animals and on the structure and functions of their parts. It seems unlikely that the observations available in the field of astronomy would offer much to suggest an analogy between the behaviour or the bodily structure of the heavenly bodies and that of familiar living organisms on Earth.[2]

The best way to get at an answer to whether the issue was an odd question or not is to ask whether anything has substantially changed in our understanding of the universe or its behaviour to make the issue of life or consciousness more absurd now than it was then. Obviously some things have changed, but do those changes have any bearing on the issue of life? It seems that our views about the nature and behaviour of the universe and the bodies in it have changed in four, or possibly five, ways.

---

[1] It was also a controversial issue when Origen wrote. Its importance has recently been explored by Alan Scott, *Origen and the Life of the Stars* (Oxford, 1991).

[2] Aristotle denies that the stars have bodies constructed like animal bodies (*De Caelo*, 290a29–b11). This is a reason for supposing that they are not intended to be self-moving creatures, 290a32–5.

1. One obvious difference is that we take a different view from Aristotle on the question of which bodies move relative to which other ones. He supposed that the sun went round the Earth; we tend to suppose it is the reverse—and that affects what the rest of the stars and planets do. But this will not change very much. Neither theory determines what the absolute motion going on is, if any; and it makes little difference precisely which bodies are moving, as regards how we are going to explain the motion or other behaviour. If the Earth is moving, along with the other planets, we shall need to reclassify the Earth as one of the bodies whose motion requires explanation. But this will hardly make a fundamental difference: it still remains true that the planets in general can be considered as candidates for the description 'alive'—we should just have to agree that Earth was too.

On the other hand the stars no longer rotate about the Earth but 'stand still'. If the stars are stationary perhaps we shall not have any reason to attribute life to them after all, given that motion or capacity for motion appears to be the only feature that ever suggested they were animate in the first place. But two cautions must be entered here. First, the relative stillness of the fixed stars as regards the Earth tells us nothing about whether they move absolutely, so that we are not entitled to infer that the stars are actually incapable of motion; it remains an open question whether they might move.

Secondly, it may well be wrong to suppose that ultimately it is the motion of the heavenly bodies that leads Aristotle or any other thinker to think they are alive. Aristotle is perfectly well aware that motion occurs in things that are inanimate, and indeed the archetypal natural motions occur in the inanimate elements. The reasons for attributing life to the rotating heavens are more complicated, and I shall be looking in more detail at what they might be shortly.

2. The second change in our understanding of the workings of the universe is simply a consequence of the first. Because we now have a different view of which bodies move relative to which other ones, we also describe their paths differently. What difference does that make? The main change is in the planets, as regards the details of their paths. They were called 'wanderers' because their path round a stationary Earth was less simple than that of the stars.

They seemed to go back and forth and turn epicycles all over the place. Now that they go round the sun we can describe their paths by means of relatively simple ellipses. The change in the paths described by the planets might seem significant in so far as a simple motion is more likely to be explained mechanically than a complex one. If the ancients really thought that the planets wandered, then they would need to attribute soul to them to account for the spontaneous variation in their movements. On the other hand, all ancient astronomy worked on the basis that the motions of all the heavenly bodies was, in principle, entirely predictable, and the planets were no exception. Predicting the paths of the planets might be more complicated, but it was axiomatic that it must be possible; and there was no suggestion that their motion should be attributed to soul while that of more regular bodies should be explained mechanically.[3] Thus it does not appear that anyone seriously took the errant paths of the planets as an indication that they were alive, or that they were free agents in a way that the rest were not. All the heavenly bodies were treated the same, regardless of whether their motion was wandering or simple. There was never much doubt, after the Presocratic period, that the paths of all of them were regular and predictable.

(3) The third change in our perception of the heavenly bodies concerns the matter and composition of the stars and planets. Aristotle, notoriously, thought that the stars, and the spheres on which they were carried, were all made of a stuff totally distinct from the elements we encounter here on earth: the fifth element has characteristics that make it behave in a different way.

We differ from Aristotle in this respect. We generally work on the assumption that the material composition of Earth and things on Earth is basically similar to that of the other planets, and that the processes that go to make the sun and stars appear as they do are roughly similar to processes that can be replicated with the elements familiar on Earth. There is not a fundamental difference for us between the material and behaviour of sublunary bodies and that of other bodies in our universe.

This might seem to give us a rather different outlook on things. It seems that we have a more earthy estimation of the nature of the

---

[3] On the contrary Aristotle regards the greater complexity of their motion as due to their being less alive than the more regular sphere (*De Caelo*, 2. 12).

heavenly bodies. Their composition is, quite literally, not so ethereal as it was for Aristotle. But I doubt that this should make any real difference on the matter of life. There is, in fact, no necessary connection between Aristotle's fifth element and soul or life. On the contrary it seems that the fifth element was introduced partly to avoid having to appeal to self-moving souls as the explanation of the motion of the heavenly bodies. The reason why Aristotle introduces the fifth element in *De Caelo* 1. 2 is that the natural motions of ordinary sublunary elements are, in his view, rectilinear motions: fire moves up and earth moves down.[4] In order that the motions of the heavenly bodies should be simple and natural in the same way as the movement of heavy and light bodies on earth is, he proposes that there should be an unfamiliar element, the aether, whose natural motion is circular. This is an attempt to make the heavenly bodies rotate in a way that is as natural to them as it is natural for a light body to rise upwards. Just as fire moves up because it is light, so heavenly bodies go round because they are (neither heavy nor light but) made of aether. In terms of life and consciousness there is no significant difference between being made of one element or another.

Part of Aristotle's problem was created by his assumption that circular motion was a simple motion and not a complex one. Given that he wished to maintain (perhaps misguidedly) that each form of simple motion was natural to some natural body,[5] then it seemed to follow that there must be some body whose natural simple motion was circular. All these assumptions seem to be pathetically ill-supported, but they do not substantially affect our present case. Had Aristotle allowed that circular motion was not simple but complex he would have had no need to appeal to a further simple body. The motion of the heavenly bodies could have been explained as a combination of more than one rectilinear motion, and the composition of the bodies could have been identified as elements of the same nature as the ordinary four.[6]

Thus Aristotle's introduction of the fifth element does not contribute to any project for attributing soul or consciousness to the

---

[4] Aristotle, *De Caelo*, 1. 268b11–269b17.

[5] *De Caelo*, 269b2–3.

[6] The pressure to explain the motion and composition of the bodies as simple stems from the traditional view that simple is more perfect and more lasting. Aristotle also holds that circular motion is superior to rectilinear, 269a19–28.

heavenly bodies. On the contrary it enables Aristotle to argue that the motion of the heavenly bodies is natural to their elemental composition, and hence is to be explained like the motion of inanimate heavy and light elements, and not as requiring any further source of movement.

Does it make any difference to us that we think of the stars and planets as made of the same sort of stuffs as we meet on Earth? An unreflective response might say that we cannot think of those bodies as alive if they are only made of the same stuff as our Earth. But that response clearly will not do, for two reasons. First, our decision as to whether something (or someone) is alive, in the ordinary course of events, is not decided by what elements he, she, or it is made of. We are all, animate and inanimate alike, made of the familiar earthly elements. That does not preclude us from classifying some things as alive or animate or conscious, and others as dead or inanimate or devoid of consciousness. When we make that distinction we do not seem to be introducing some extra stuff in the material composition of the ones that are alive.

Secondly, we might diagnose our difficulty as resulting from the fact that we do not, generally, regard planet Earth as alive. If planet Earth is not alive and planet Earth is one of the same kind as the other heavenly bodies, then we have some reason to hesitate about attributing life to the other bodies. On the other hand, this difficulty also is nothing to do with the material composition of the Earth, or only incidentally so. It might indeed appear that the bodily composition of most living creatures was not identical to the material structure and composition of the Earth; but we would need to establish that it was impossible for such a body to be alive before we could conclude that the planets could not be alive because their bodies are inappropriate. To establish that conclusion it would not be sufficient merely to observe that we normally draw the line between living and non-living round a more restricted class of bodies. The question was: should we be extending that class to include this sort of body after all?

While it is true that the man in the street probably does not usually speak of planet Earth as alive, there is an area of scientific thought in which this sort of language is not, after all, wholly inappropriate. This view depends on the recognition that the Earth (known in this case as 'Gaia' because it is viewed not merely as an inert collection of matter, but as a functioning system in which form is as essential as matter) behaves in many (or all) respects as a living organism.[7] Now, it might seem that the meaning of 'as' in 'behaves as a living organism' is important here: are we merely likening the way in which the ecological balance of the Earth is maintained to the way in which a living healthy organism maintains its chemical balance, so that the Earth functions as if it were a living organism; or are we saying that the Earth is, in practice, a living organism and functions as such? Does the 'as' mark an analogy or an identity?

It seems to me that we could take the claim either way. Lovelock and his adherents are pointing out that the chemical composition of the Earth and its atmosphere can only be explained if we take seriously the idea that the whole planet, including its dependent organisms, functions in just the way that a single living organism functions. If that claim is pressed it would be nonsense to make a distinction or even to ask the question, 'is it actually a living organism, or does it merely function in every respect as if it were one?' We should be hard-pressed to find a criterion for deciding whether something was alive other than its characteristic processes and behaviour. If those processes are exactly replicated in another object could we coherently deny that that too was a living organism?

On the other hand, that may be taking the Gaia hypothesis as stronger than it was meant to be. It would be possible to maintain that all the processes and behaviour of the Earth taken as a unit could be paralleled in organisms we classify as living things, but that certain types of behaviour are lacking in the case of the Earth. In other words the Earth has some, but not all, the typical features of a living organism, though all the features it does have are typical features of living organisms. For example, we might argue that it had functions analogous to respiration, nutrition, and excretion—the functions that maintain a healthy chemical balance—but no function like reproduction. In this case it would be right to say that the Earth functions somewhat as if it were a living organism, and yet maintain that we are not committed to saying that it is a living organism.

In any case two implications seem to be apparent. One is that it is not self-evidently nonsense to ask whether Earth is a living

---

[7] The classic and influential work on this theory is J. E. Lovelock, *Gaia: A New Look at Life on Earth* (Oxford, 1979).

organism, given that some aspects of its nature invite such a description; the other is that the biological functions in question do not include consciousness. It might be tolerably clear what is meant by suggesting that processes analogous to nutrition are evident in the ecology of Earth, but the mind boggles once we ask even about reproduction, let alone consciousness, as a feature observable in the world we know. But if these seem like meaningless questions for us, there is no good reason to think they had more meaning for Aristotle. He was happy to suggest a hierarchy of functions for living organisms, such that the lower creature possessed only the simplest functions while higher creatures possessed those and the higher functions in addition.[8] But in the case of the stars it seems unlikely that such a theory can apply. We require a different criterion for life: asking whether a body can reproduce will not be relevant, as it would for a plant or micro-organism. Aristotle cannot treat the issue as a straightforward matter of biology, any more than we can.

4. The fourth respect in which our assumptions differ from Aristotle's is in the field of dynamics. Aristotle divided motion into two categories, natural motion and forced motion. In general natural motion is caused by a body seeking its natural place in the world, forced motion by some body pushing the projectile throughout its period of motion.[9] Aristotle had no concept of inertia.

Now, this makes it slightly problematic to explain the eternal motion of the heavens. If the motion is to be forced motion that will require an infinite force to account for motion during an infinite time.[10] Aristotle wavers between explaining the eternal motion by means of natural place[11] or an unmoved mover[12] or perhaps a combination of the two; but in no case does his need for an explanation that fits in with his theory of dynamics lead him to suppose that the source of motion in the heavenly spheres is a self-moving soul. In fact he explicitly rejects the idea (which is basically Platonic) that a self-moving soul explains the rotation of the

[8] Aristotle, *De anima*, 2, chs. 2–3.
[9] Cf. Aristotle, *Physics*, 8. 10, 266b30–267a12.
[10] Aristotle, *Physics*, 8. 266a12–24; 267b22–4.
[11] *De Caelo*, 1. 3. Cf. *Physics*, 4. 1.
[12] *Physics*, 8. 6.

heavens.[13] He is not inclined to invoke the animate nature of the heavenly bodies as a means of avoiding problems in dynamics. On the contrary he seems to hold that the movement of the bodies in question cannot be satisfactorily explained by appeal to a soul, but must be explained in the manner of the natural motion of inanimate elements.

5. That makes the basic four ways in which our views might differ from Aristotle's; but none of them, I would suggest, makes any significant difference to his or our expectations about life or consciousness in astronomical explanations. Aristotle is just as reluctant to invoke the soul in these respects as we would be.

There remains a fifth area in which we might or might not wish to dissent from Aristotle's initial assumption, and that is over the possibility of an infinite chain of causes. Arguably Aristotle shared with the later Wittgenstein the view that to speak of an actual infinity as existing was incoherent;[14] certainly he was prepared to acknowledge the potentially infinite in the case of what could always go on further, but he is consistently reluctant to envisage the completion of an actual infinity of real things. One idea that he rejects as totally incoherent is the idea that there might be an infinite chain of causes: such an infinity would have actually to exist, since a cause cannot cause the next event unless it is itself actual. Given a universe without beginning, there seems to be a threat that we may already have traversed an infinite chain of actually existent causes, each caused by something else.[15]

Aristotle's objections to an infinite chain of causes apply, in fact, not so much to an infinite sequence occurring one after the other

---

[13] *De Caelo*, 2. 1, 284a27–35. Aristotle also argues in *De Caelo* 2. 8 that the stars are not like animals in being self-moving; their lack of organs for movement shows that they are not, like animals, designed to move of their own accord.

[14] See e.g. L. Wittgenstein, *Philosophical Grammar*, ed. Rush Rhees, trans. A. Kenny (Oxford, 1974), II. 10; *Lectures on the Foundations of Mathematics* (Hassocks, 1976; 2nd edn. Chicago, 1989), 31–2. There is some doubt as to whether Aristotle is an ally for Wittgenstein or an opponent in this case. The more subtle reading of Aristotle makes him an ally and gives a better sense to his thought. See A. W. Moore, *The Infinite* (London, 1990), 137–41, and 207. Cf. also R. Sorabji, *Time, Creation and the Continuum* (London, 1983), 210–28.

[15] It might seem that allowing that the universe is without beginning already contravenes Aristotle's ban on actual traversed infinities. Surely the universe has already completed an infinite time? But in fact this may be less problematic than Philoponus, for one, seems to have thought (cf. Sorabji, *Time, Creation and the Continuum*, 228–9), since the motions and events of time are only potentially countable, and have not been actually enumerated.

in time—it remains unclear whether Aristotle would be happy to allow that an infinite set of changes could occur in an infinite time. The problem is rather that an infinite chain of causes requires an actual infinity to occur in a finite time, since cause and effect must be simultaneous; thus, if the effect takes place in a finite time, all the infinite changes that bring about that effect must take place in that same finite time.[16] Hence an infinite chain of causes is incoherent in itself, regardless of whether we should be prepared to allow that change and motion could continue indefinitely given an infinite time. Aristotle is thus committed to the view that any particular change or motion is ultimately derived, directly or indirectly, from a first cause. The number of intermediate instrumental causes will always be finite. And the first cause must not itself be undergoing change in order to cause the process of change, since if it were it would not after all be the first cause: its own change would be caused by a further source of change.

Thus the incoherence of supposing the infinite simultaneously and actually in existence leads Aristotle to posit a first-mover to explain any change or motion. If we share his objections to real infinities we may be disposed to agree. In any case it might seem that infinite chains of explanation are incoherent, though that would not necessarily preclude the need for an infinite chain of causes.

Regardless of whether we share Aristotle's distaste for endless chains, it does not make an immediate difference to whether we shall have to invoke life in explaining the behaviour of the universe. It should be noted that Aristotle's solution is not to make the basic motion of the spheres an example of self-motion, the motion of animate beings. On the contrary, self-motion fails to provide a solution, since so called self-movers can be further analysed into mover and moved.[17] What is required is an unmoved mover, and Aristotle's apparently preferred solution is not to propose that the stars have souls, but that there is an independent Prime Mover.

[16] Aristotle, *Physics*, 7. 242a49–b53/242a15–b19 (there are two versions of *Physics* 7, Ch. 1). See R. Wardy, *The Chain of Change* (Cambridge, 1990), 99–120.
[17] Aristotle, *Physics*, 7. 1.

## 2. FIVE REASONS IN FAVOUR OF ATTRIBUTING LIFE TO THE STARS

So much for the possible differences between Aristotle and ourselves that might make us feel that it was less odd in Aristotle's day to propose that the stars were alive; in practice it remains just as odd on Aristotle's assumptions, I would argue, as it does on ours. And furthermore in none of these cases does Aristotle actually respond by suggesting that the stars are alive. On the contrary he specifically observes that soul will not provide an adequate account in these respects.

If these reasons are not sufficient to induce Aristotle to attribute life to the heavenly bodies, or the spheres that carry them, what reasons are sufficient? If it was for him an odd idea, what makes him consider it despite the weight of evidence against it? This question is not easily answered from Aristotle's own texts, since it is not clear that he maintained any consistent position on the matter; in his major works he concentrates on stressing the explanatory role of the matter out of which the stars are made and of the external unmoved mover, and minimizes the place of the soul or consciousness. Indeed, this looks like a deliberate rejection of the position associated with Plato, a position to which Aristotle himself probably subscribed in his early work, the *De Philosophia*. In his later works Aristotle rejects the idea that the presence of soul will be a sufficient explanation of the motion of the heavens; but he does not abandon the idea of souls altogether. What reasons could have persuaded him to retain them?

To explore an answer to this question I propose to look not directly to Aristotle, but to the clear summary of reasons given by Aquinas. Aquinas' own position is that strictly speaking the stars are not alive,[18] or, at least, that to say they are animate does not mean the same as to say that an animal or plant is. But before reaching this conclusion he sets out a number of reasons why one might (or in particular Aristotle might) be committed to the view that the stars have soul. He offers five arguments in favour;[19] I shall begin with the first.

[18] *Summa Theol*, 1a. 70. 3.
[19] He replies with objections to these arguments in the second part of the article. His replies are not precisely the same as I offer here.

1. The first argument depends upon a notion of hierarchy. The more noble a thing is the more noble its attributes and adornments ought to be. Thus, given that an inferior body (the Earth or its constituent bodies) is adorned with animate creatures, it should follow that the heaven would be adorned with animate bodies too.

Two interesting features of this argument should be noticed. First, it assumes without question that things with soul are a noble adornment and superior to things without soul. If the reverse were the case it would be fitting that the best things should lack animate creatures. Aquinas simply assumes that living things are worth having.

Secondly, the argument seems to depend upon the assumption that the outer heavens are superior to, more noble than, the Earth. Given that the heaven is more noble, presumably, it is unfitting that it should be less well-endowed than the lower regions. This assumption is interesting only in respect of the fact that we are dealing with a geocentric theory. It is worth noticing that the geocentric theory does not assume that the central body is a noble body; on the contrary, it is less noble than the outer regions.

None of the premises of this argument seems to me to command any acceptance. The idea that what is noble ought to have noble attributes clearly goes the wrong way round. We might infer from the fact that something had noble attributes that it should be described as noble, but there seems no reason first to decide, arbitrarily, that something is noble, and then infer that it will have corresponding attributes. The idea that soul is itself noble again begs the question: we need first to establish whether we characteristically regard living things as noble. This seems doubtful when we consider candidates such as slugs, fleas, and stinging nettles. Thirdly, we shall obviously have more difficulty than Aquinas did with the idea that certain parts of the universe are inherently more noble than other parts. We do not subscribe to a geocentric theory, so we do not automatically infer that the Earth is inferior to the moon, sun, or other planets as Aristotle did. But nor are we inclined to suppose that it is superior either. Hence it will not be possible to deduce anything about the appropriate attributes of particular bodies in the sky on the basis of relative nobility.

2. Aquinas's second point is rather similar. The more noble a body the more noble its form is. The lights of the sky are more

noble bodies than plants and animals. Hence they must have a nobler form. And the soul is the noblest sort of form.

Again the argument assumes that the lights of the sky are noble— this time more noble than plants and animals. We might raise similar objections as we did over whether the heavens were more noble than earth. The other idea introduced here is that soul is a form, and in particular the noblest form. It seems impossible to establish that soul is the most noble kind of form. Again we need a criterion for what makes a thing noble.

3. The third argument Aquinas produces concerns causation. It depends upon the traditional principle that a cause is greater than its effect. It goes like this:

A cause is nobler than its effect.

The sun and moon etc. are causes of life.

Therefore they must themselves be alive.

Why Aquinas says 'nobler' here seems unclear: the point in fact depends not on how noble the cause is but on the idea that it must possess the quality that it imparts to other things in a greater degree or at least as great a degree as that which the result then displays.

This principle that the cause is greater than the effect has come in for considerable criticism in recent philosophical discussion.[20] The objections centre on two aspects of the theory: first, the idea that causation is a matter of transmission of some quality from the cause to the effect; there seem at first sight to be plenty of examples of causes that do not themselves possess the feature that they cause in others. Secondly, objections have been raised against the strong version of the theory, namely the claim that the cause must be not merely equal in the relevant respect but greater. It seems that even if a transmission theory of causation were acceptable it could only justify the weaker version, that the cause must be at least equal.

Take, for example, the classic illustration. A warm body gets into a cold bath of water. As a result heat will be transferred from the warm body to the cold water and will raise the temperature of the water to resemble the temperature of the body. It is the fact that the body is warm that causes the water to become warm, and there

---

[20] Most recently Stephen Makin, 'An Ancient Principle about Causation', *Proceedings of the Aristotelian Society*, 91 (1990–1), 135–52. See also Bernard Williams, *Descartes: The Project of Pure Enquiry* (London, 1978), 135–8. A more positive assessment of its stengths and weaknesses is provided by A. C. Lloyd, 'The Principle that the Cause is Greater than its Effect', *Phronesis*, 21 (1976), 146–56.

is a limit to how warm it could cause the water to become. It cannot make it warmer than it is itself. But there does not seem to be reason to infer that the water must end up less hot than the body.

Or does there? This example shows that it is not so clear that the cause will produce an equal result. In fact a hot body will heat the water not to the temperature it had originally, but until the two are the same temperature. In imparting heat to the water the hot body will cool down. The eventual temperature of both will be cooler than the body was before it got into the bath. Thus there is, even on a transmission theory of causation, a prima facie case for the view that the effect will always be less than the original cause.

It has been argued that Aristotle need not be committed to the stronger version, but could consistently hold merely the weaker view that the cause is at least as great as the effect. Aquinas, on the other hand, is committed to the stronger version. However, he does not require the stronger version for this argument; all he needs to show is that a cause of life must have life; he need not show that it has more life than that which it causes.

The objection that all causes cannot be accounted for by transmission seems more damaging, but I think the difficulties are overestimated. Of course the murderer is not more dead than the man he killed. But it seems clear that Aristotle would regard that description of the cause as inaccurate—it is not in as much as he is a man that he causes the death of the dead man, nor in respect of being alive. There are plenty of other men, and alive ones at that, who do not cause the death of another. So the cause is inaccurately described in such a case—we have not yet identified what the immediate cause of death was. Nor does the description of the case give us the means to do so.

Furthermore, the causal theory is clearly meant to account for more types of cause than the examples so far considered. Aristotle developed a scheme of 'four causes' precisely to alert us to the idea that not all types of explanation bear the same relation to the feature they are supposed to explain. The examples we have taken so far— the murderer causes the victim's death, the hot body causes the water to warm up—are clearly examples of cause in the sense of a source of change. But even within that class of causes there are a variety of ways of explaining the result. Was it the murderer that caused the death, or was it the dagger he used, or what he did with the dagger, or some response in the victim (e.g. a heart failure, or bleeding) that was the real cause of the death? Clearly the principle that the cause is actually like the result, only more so, can be made to look more or less plausible depending what restrictions you place on what counts as the real or immediate source of the change in question. What is certain is that you cannot hold that it applies to all the possible candidates in any case of change.

Two possible responses are available to defend the plausibility of the principle.

(*a*) One is that it applies more appropriately to formal and final causes than to the cause that actually initiates change. Thus the form of a thing constitutes an explanation of what it is (an octave is explained as a ratio $2:1$),[21] though it does not explain any change in it. It does, however, seem self-evident that the formal cause resembles what it explains in the relevant sense, though it is doubtful whether it can be 'greater' than its effect. The final cause fits even better. The final cause explains what a product is aiming to be. Clearly there is an important sense in which the final cause must resemble its effect and be greater than it. A healthy diet is healthy because it aims at and contributes to health. But it will only manage to be healthy to the extent that it succeeds in approximating to the ideal of healthiness at which it aims. Thus it makes some sense to say that the end in view is something greater.

(*b*) If not all the things that we, or Aristotle, would call causes do conform to the so-called 'causal resemblance' aspect of the principle—not all causes do themselves possess the feature that they bring about or explain in something else—it might seem reasonable to suggest a weaker version of the principle. In those cases where it is true to say that the cause explains the presence of an attribute in something else in virtue of possessing that attribute itself—in those cases we may infer that the cause possesses the attribute to at least as great a degree, or to a greater degree, than the thing whose attribute it is to explain. If it is *qua* wet that the rain causes the ground to become wet, then it must be that the rain is wetter than the ground becomes (or at least that the wetness of the rain is as great as the eventual wetness of the ground). But if the rain causes a seed to germinate, it is again in virtue of being wet that it does so. But the effect on the seed is not wetness (or not only wetness) but germination. The rain does not seem to possess that

---

[21] Aristotle, *Physics*, 2. 3.

attribute itself and hence cause and effect seem to be incommensurable. It does not make sense (or not very clear sense) to ask 'is the rain more wet than the seed is germinated?'

Thus we might allow that a weaker version of Aquinas's principle is acceptable; where the cause is responsible for producing a similar attribute, the effect will never be greater than the cause in that respect. But clearly this principle in its weaker version will not supply what Aquinas needs in this case. He wants to infer that since the sun and stars are a cause of life, therefore they must be alive themselves (only more so). For his purpose the question of the relative degree of cause and effect is actually unimportant;[22] what matters is that the cause should have the attribute it produces. But this is what our weaker version of the principle will not give him: if we know that the cause resembles the effect we may infer the relative degree, but even if we know that the cause is more noble (as Aquinas says) we cannot infer that it possesses the attribute it causes. Hence it seems that Aquinas's argument remains implausible to anyone who is unwilling to accept the strongest version of the principle that cause is greater than its effect.

4. The fifth argument that Aquinas offers concerns motion. It starts from the claim that the first thing that is in motion is the heavens itself—and then infers that since the first thing that is moved ought to be moved *per se* rather than by something else, hence the heavenly bodies must be alive. There seem to be several slippery patches in this argument.

First, what is said to be first moved is 'the heavens' (*caelum*). This ought to mean either the outermost sphere (which carries the fixed stars with it) or the entire structure of the universe as a whole. Either way it does not entitle us to infer that the bodies that are carried round in the course of the motion of the spheres are themselves animated by souls. On the contrary, it seems that the heavenly bodies themselves are not the first-moved nor self-moved in the requisite sense, because they are moved by the spheres that carry them.

Secondly, there is a problem about what constitutes being moved *per se*. Aquinas claims that what is moved *per se* is prior to what is moved by another. What is first moved cannot be dependent on

---

[22] It is important only in so far as it will establish that the stars do not (*a*) have life but (*b*) to a lesser degree than the creatures they affect.

something else being moved first. But it is not clear that the distinction between motion *per se* and motion by another will give him his required distinction between animate and inanimate motion. Rather it corresponds with the distinction between natural and forced motion. It would be possible to maintain (and Aristotle did maintain explicitly in the *De Caelo*[23]) that the motion of the heavens was the natural motion of an inanimate element. It is moved *per se*, by its own nature. But that does not mean it has a soul.

Thirdly, there is a difficulty as to whether animate motion should properly be said to be *per se*. In *Physics* 8. 4 Aristotle suggests on the one hand that the movement of living things is not strictly speaking self-motion, but rather the movement of one thing by another.[24] But the distinction between self-moving and movement by another is not the same as the distinction between *per se* and *per accidens*,[25] nor the distinction between natural and forced motion. Hence it is not correct to infer that if a thing is moved *per se* it is self-moved and hence alive.

5. There is one remaining argument in Aquinas's list, the fourth one. This seems to me to be the only one that retains some plausibility. Arguably it has some force not only for the Aristotelian view of the world, but also perhaps for our own; I propose to consider just how far we need to take it seriously.

The point is this. Aristotle wants to stop the infinite regress of causes of motion by positing at the start of any sequence of causes a mover that is itself unmoved. In the *Metaphysics* he argues that ultimately there is just one such unmoved mover[26] and that it causes movement (or change) in virtue of being an object of thought or desire. Aquinas's point is that in order for the first mover to act in this way, the object that it moves must be capable of apprehending it; we need to attribute consciousness to the first thing that is moved by the first unmoved mover, since an object of thought or desire cannot move something incapable of thinking or of desiring. Something, then, either the stars or what causes the stars to move, must be a conscious being that is moved as the one who desires is moved

---

[23] *De Caelo*, 1. 3 etc. In *De Caelo*, 2. 8 (290a7–290b12) Aristotle argues that the stars do not move *per se*.

[24] *Physics*, 8. 4, 254b27.

[25] Animals do move *per se*, but so do some things that are moved unnaturally. 254b7–14.

[26] 1074a31–8.

by the desired object.[27] This fits with Aristotle's own acknowledgement, in connection with the unmoved first mover, that there
is a hint of truth in the old tradition that the stars are gods. It
appears that he recognizes that he is committed to the view that the
spheres are moved on account of consciousness.

Aristotle's unmoved mover serves the role of God. It stems the
regress of caused causes by being the first cause of all change. It is
responsible for the initial motion of the heavenly bodies[28] and hence
for all subsequent caused motions and changes. And it is supreme
in that it moves by being actual and never potential. But what
Aquinas's point seems to suggest is that Aristotle is committed, in
virtue of this account, to two consequences: (*a*) that the stars, or
the spheres, somewhat contrary to our intuitions, must be conscious
beings; and (*b*) that the influence of God can extend directly only
to conscious beings. God cannot directly influence the changes or
motions of inanimate parts of the cosmos.

These two points are related. If Aristotle denies that the influence
of God is restricted to animate or conscious beings, then he can
deny the need for the stars to be conscious. We need to consider
whether Aristotle did, or should, have agreed with Aquinas's claim
that the unmoved mover bears upon conscious beings only. Aristotle has notoriously little to say about how the unmoved mover
actually has its effect, but it is worth paying close attention to what
he does say. In *Metaphysics Λ* chapter 7 he introduces the idea that
there must be something that causes movement but is not itself
moved. He then observes[29] that objects of thought and objects of
desire cause movement in this way; this need not mean that the
first mover is an object of thought or desire, but rather that those
objects serve as an illustration of how an unmoved object can cause
motion in another. How far are we supposed to infer that God
moves in precisely that way, or should we take it that causation is
somehow analogous in the case of God?

Aristotle proceeds with a brief analysis of appetite distinguishing
between (*a*) the object of desire (which is something that appears
to be fine) and (*b*) what we want, which is something that actually

[27] Aquinas goes on to suggest that the sentient substance is intrinsic to the stars
rather than external. It is unimportant precisely where consciousness is to be located.

[28] 'Initial' in the sense of primary. The universe does not have a first movement
in time.

[29] 1072a26.

is fine.[30] The distinction actually makes no difference to Aristotle's point. It would be wrong to suppose that he classifies the first mover in the category of what actually is fine at this point. Rather he introduces the distinction in order to show that it makes no difference to the manner in which the object of appetite moves the subject. In both cases, both desiring and wanting, what inspires the appetite for something is that that thing seems to us to be fine. The 'seeming fine' part of the process comes first: it seems to me that the apple is nice, so I desire the apple (whether it really is or only appears nice); it is not the case that I desire the apple and hence it appears to me that it is nice.[31] Thus Aristotle takes the 'seeming fine to me' to be a species of thought, and hence claims that desire is dependent on thought. The origin of desire is thought.

This move reduces Aristotle's two examples of unmoved movers (objects of desire and objects of thought) to one example. Objects of desire after all turn out to be a species of object of thought. Aristotle, then, establishes first that desire depends on thought, and secondly that it is correct to say that the object of thought can be said to cause movement. It seems more obvious that the object of appetite might be a source of movement; Aristotle suggests that in the case of thought too, the mind is moved by the object of thought. 'Moved' here is a word that Aristotle employs to cover all sorts of change. The mind is affected by the object of thought.

It still seems uncertain whether this excursus on objects of thought and desire is intended to illustrate a way in which some unmoved mover may bring about an effect in something else, or to describe the way in which the first mover itself does so. Aristotle's next move is to establish that the range of *per se* objects of thought, which are candidates for moving in this way, include not only substance itself but also what is fine and choice-worthy in itself. We can thus establish that what both is in actuality and is the finest and best thing will be one of the things capable of causing change as an object of thought or as an object of desire. God, it seems, in virtue

---

[30] 1072a27–8. W. D. Ross (*Aristotle's Metaphysics* (Oxford, 1924), ii. 376) introduces a distinction between rational and non-rational appetite, but this is not explicit in this text.

[31] Aristotle is thinking, apparently, of things for which we have a natural appetite. It seems less clear to me than it does to him that the 'seeming fine' comes first, and the appetite follows. We might equally argue that it seems fine to me because I have an appetite for it. And all this will be independent of the question under what aspect I see it, and whether that is affected by my state or the state of the object.

of being in actuality and being the best in itself, can be a cause in this way.

On the other hand, showing that God is the sort of object that could function as a cause in this way does not seem sufficient to establish that it does. In particular it seems clear that an object of thought can function in that way only if there are thinking subjects capable of apprehending it. Thus it appears that Aristotle must hold that God causes motion in precisely this way, as the object of desire, and if he is a cause at all that the causation can take effect only in a subject capable of thinking and desiring.

We might suggest two ways of excusing Aristotle from this consequence. One would be to say that the object of desire should serve only as an analogy for how an unmoved cause can produce an effect, but that the first mover should be thought of as operating in a way that does not require a conscious subject; the other would be to suggest that Aristotle is wrong about the link between desire and thought, and hence is wrong to infer that the good can only be an object of appetite to a conscious being.

The first alternative requires that we find some kind of cause that does operate in the requisite way without the subject being aware. It seems clear that for the most part Aristotle's final causes are supposed to operate in this way; things in nature are motivated by the relevant goal that serves as their final cause, only in the sense that that is what their functions are directed towards, not in the sense that they consciously perceive that as an end in view.

If the purpose of a pig is to feed a man, it need not follow that it perceives that purpose as its goal. Why, then, should not the best thing, in the form of God the Unmoved Mover, be the involuntary goal of the inanimate spheres of the heavens? Aristotle's theory will not admit that analysis partly because it is nature that directs the functions of pigs towards the goal in question, so that though the individual pig may not be aware of the relevant goal there is some sense in which the nature that governs its processes is aware of a goal. There is thus a kind of awareness that ultimately goes back to the appreciation of what is best, and the chain of causes will not stop until we reach something that is capable of that appreciation. Aristotle does not want to describe this as a choice, but it does seem to involve processes directed to a recognized goal.

Our second option in defence of Aristotle requires a very similar answer. Was it right, we asked, to make a close link between appetite and thought and to make appetite dependent on thought? Aristotle did this by suggesting that appetite depends upon something 'seeming to me' to be fine—and that 'seeming' originates in the *nous*—it is a form of thinking. It might seem that this is too strong a claim; it suggests that all appetite involves reflection, and perhaps conscious choice, whereas we might cite examples of plants that grow towards the light, or put their roots down for water, where the appetite to move towards what is good does not seem to depend upon thinking or reflecting that it is good or that it is better than some alternative. On the other hand, in the case of plants it would still be plausible to claim that appetite derived from some sort of awareness, and that the subject should be said to be alive. It is more difficult for us to suggest that appetite could be located in a subject that is not alive. For Aristotle the difficulty might seem less great, since his analysis of natural motion in inanimate objects depends upon the assumption that they have an intrinsic tendency to seek their natural place: fire goes up because it is inclined to travel to its proper place. Why is this not an example of appetite? Aristotle never does describe it as appetite.[32]

There is thus a form of natural tendency that is not appetite and does not require any sort of soul. But Aristotle does not use that explanation for the first mover and the motion of the heavens. The reason for introducing thought as essential to appetite seems to be not so much that no other explanation was possible, as that Aristotle must make God an object of thought in order that he could be the best thing and subject to the best sort of activity.[33] Thus the incoherence of supposing that the first mover moves inanimate objects involuntarily is not in the impossibility of such motion, but in the impossibility that that should be the activity of the best and most perfect cause. To be best, the first cause must be causing the best type of activity in the most perfect way.

Aristotle is thus committed to the view that the direct influence of God must be on intelligent beings. His causal role in the universe is thus restricted to initiating the first movement of the heavens, where a sentient soul is capable of apprehending the desirability of the good; the inanimate parts of nature are beyond the reach of

---

[32] At *Physics* 8. 4. 255b13–17 he says the reason for motion to its proper place is ὅτι πέφυκέν ποι. It just is the nature of the heavy or light to tend that way.

[33] *Metaphysics* Λ, Ch. 9.

such a god. He can have no direct control over anything that lacks soul.

### 3. GOD AS OBJECT OF LOVE

It remains to ask whether we need be impressed by Aristotle's requirement that the response to God come from a conscious being. Will this be an implication that we need to take on board if we are to allow that there is a God whose influence extends to the natural world? If we share the assumption that an infinite chain of causes is impossible we might find ourselves, with Aristotle, committed to the view that there must be a first cause responsible for a primary form of change in the universe. Will that cause be able to act on inanimate matter or could it only act on conscious beings? Aristotle's God, it should be noted, is not a creator and it is not clear what sense could be made of creation as a species of final causation; but we might still want to hold that even if creation is envisaged as a different type of causation, yet final causation of the type that Aristotle envisages should be one of the possible roles of God.

This issue becomes particularly relevant in connection with the issue of love. Aristotle says in *Metaphysics Λ* that God causes motion as the beloved causes motion.[34] This is clearly a re-expression of the notion of an object of desire, but here the word refers not to mere appetite but to 'love'. It seems more difficult to suppose in this case that love could be the response of a being that lacked consciousness. What Aristotle's theory raises is the issue of the power exercised by the beloved object over the loving subject; Aristotle uses this model because in his view it is the only purely independent power available: the beloved object is totally unmoved itself but causes motion in another; it is not dependent on any other cause either in itself or anything else for its effect on another perceiving subject.

The question of whether God can properly be said to be an object of love occasionally surfaces in philosophical discussions. In some cases this question arises on the assumption that the object of love must be something weak and powerless (an object of sympathy, concern, or benevolence). For Aristotle, by contrast, the object of

---

[34] κινεῖ δὲ ὡς ἐρώμενον, *Metaphysics*, 1072b3.

love is something powerful and perfect that exercises influence by attraction and contemplation. We shall need to be careful if we want to assert on the one hand that there can be an omnipotent and perfect God and on the other hand that his range of powers does not include the power of acting as object of love. In Aristotle's view that was the only appropriate causal power for God. On the other hand, if we do acknowledge that acting as object of love is the appropriate role (or is one of the appropriate roles) for a supreme God, will it then seem problematic if that role cannot be exercised over those parts of creation that are inanimate or lack consciousness and the ability to love? Would that amount to a limitation on the extent of the influence of such a God? It seems that the threat that some parts of the world are inaccessible to the power and influence of God might lead us to agree with Aristotle that there must be some sense in which the world is moved by an awareness of its cause. Hence it would be inconsistent to maintain both that there was a supreme God and that the stars and moon lacked consciousness.

# 6

## Friends, Friendship, and Loving Others: Aristotle and Aquinas

After Piglet and Christopher Robin had discovered what it was in the Heffalump trap, Piglet (who was embarrassed to find that he had been a very foolish Piglet) ran off to his own home and went to bed with a headache. But,

> Christopher Robin and Pooh went home to breakfast together.
> 'Oh Bear!' said Christopher Robin. 'How I do love you!'
> 'So do I,' said Pooh.[1]

You do not have to be very old to see the joke in these last words of chapter five of *Winnie-the-Pooh*. Clearly we all know, from a fairly early age, that Pooh and Christopher Robin are friends, and friends don't love themselves, they love each other.

In view of this it has sometimes seemed surprising to modern readers that Aristotle, when he discusses friendship in the *Ethics*, does not notice loving each other as a particular mark of friendship. Not only does he spend a large proportion of his time discussing business relationships and the like, in which loving hardly seems relevant at all, but when he does raise a question that looks like loving others, he explains it as an extension of how you regard yourself. Thus to Aristotle, apparently, it is not so very obvious that friends love each other; what is most obvious is that a friend, if he is a good man, will certainly love himself. If this impression of Aristotle's discussion is right, Aristotle would not have seen the joke in Winnie-the-Pooh's reply to Christopher Robin. It would have been perfectly proper for Pooh, as a worthy friend for Christopher Robin, to love himself.

The broad range of Aristotle's discussion of friendship has often

---

[1] A. A. Milne, *Winnie-the-Pooh* (London, 1926), 64.

been remarked upon. *Philia*, we are regularly reminded, means more than just our idea of friendship; it extends to include, in Anthony Price's terminology, 'positive interaction between human beings'[2] of all sorts and in all spheres. We find *philia* located in domestic family relationships, political alliances, civic partnerships, and in general where any two human beings perceive their common humanity as a reason for assistance or hospitality. This clearly suggests that our term 'friendship' does not comfortably fit all that falls under the Greek term *philia*.[3] But, we must still ask, does any part of what Aristotle regards as *philia* correspond to what we know as friendship? Price, for one, is convinced that Aristotle's favourite type of *philia*, the perfect *philia* of those who are good, corresponds to what we know as 'friendship'.[4] By assuming that such 'virtue friendship' is the main focus of Aristotle's attention, and that the broader use of the term *philia* is merely a concession to popular usage and secondary,[5] it is easy to conclude that what Aristotle is really interested in is what we call friendship after all. Thus we find ourselves no longer concerned, as we should be, about the breadth of his discussion as a whole.

In this chapter I shall question whether our notion of friendship fits even with 'virtue friendship' as it is often called; secondly I shall consider the meaning of the verb *philein*; thirdly, with the help of Aquinas, I shall analyse why it is that Aristotle's account has little to do with loving or liking; fourthly, rehabilitating the unfortunate Aquinas, I shall attempt to draw some analogies between *philia* and Christian charity, since the comparison is instructive.

## 1. WHERE, IF ANYWHERE, DOES FRIENDSHIP OCCUR IN THE *NICOMACHEAN ETHICS*?[6]

In the course of his discussion of *philia*, Aristotle occasionally refers

---

[2] A. W. Price, *Love and Friendship in Plato and Aristotle* (Oxford, 1989), 159–60.

[3] See also, for example, John M. Cooper, 'Aristotle on Friendship', in A. E. Rorty (ed.), *Essays on Aristotle's Ethics* (Berkeley, Calif., 1980), 301–40.

[4] Price, *Love and Friendship*, 131.

[5] But against this assumption see Cooper, 'Aristotle on Friendship', 316.

[6] For reasons of space and relevance I shall be focusing on the *Nicomachean Ethics* *(NE)* which is the text used by Aquinas. The discussion in the *Eudemian Ethics* corresponds in general outline with that found in the *Nicomachean Ethics*.

to 'comrades'.[7] These are people who enjoy each other's company, are similar in age and upbringing, and derive pleasure from being together and doing things together. Aristotle affirms that such friends have affection for each other,[8] and that their affection derives from their similarity and common upbringing, particularly among siblings.[9]

The characteristic feature of comrades is their equality; it is in this respect that comradeship is linked to timocracy in Aristotle's analogy between political systems and personal relationships.[10] Just as timocracy is only one of the acceptable forms of government (along with kingship and aristocracy), so the companionship of equals is only one of the proper forms of *philia*.

It seems plausible that Aristotle's notion of 'comrades' comes close to what we would, in normal conversation, call 'friends' in English: those who, like Winnie-the-Pooh and his friends in the forest, enjoy each other's company and share interests and pleasures in a relationship of equality. If we wanted to extend our notion wider, we might expect to include all those who took pleasure in each other's company, so as to include lovers for example, whether or not they were alike in age, or equal in every respect. Aristotle, however, is consistently unwilling to regard such relationships as perfect *philia*.[11]

If I am right, our unsophisticated use of 'friends' fits best with Aristotle's idea of 'comrades', and perhaps also with his idea of '*philia* due to pleasure' (in which lovers are a prime example). Now, so far as we can tell, Aristotle is willing to allow that the relationship of most, if not all, comrades is *philia* in the true and perfect sense of the word, but he does not hold that perfect *philia* always and only occurs among comrades of this sort; proper relationships of *philia*, based on proportion rather than strict equality, also occur between some individuals of superior and inferior status, such as husband and wife, or father and son.[12] Further, and more importantly, we cannot assume that it is in virtue of being comrades that

---

[7] ἑταῖροι. 'Comrades' are mentioned with brothers as two instances of *philia* at *NE* 1159b32; they are also mentioned at 1160a2 and a5. Cf. also 1161b12–13.

[8] στέργοντες ἀλλήλους, 1162a12.

[9] It is not clear whether young friends or siblings could be comrades. See 1158a18–20; 1156a32–56b1.

[10] 1160a31–1161a9.

[11] 1157a6–7; 1156b1–6; 1159b15–19.

[12] 1158b30–1159a4; 1159b1–2.

their relationship counts as *philia*. It may be that all comrades are, in fact, involved in *philia*, but in virtue of what are they included?

## 2. LIKING, LOVING, AND BEFRIENDING: THE MEANING OF *PHILEIN*

John Cooper, in his article on friendship in Aristotle, emphasizes how much active well-doing is involved in the notion of *philia*. It is, after all, not mere well-wishing or benevolence that makes one a true *philos*, but the appropriate behaviour that goes with it.[13] At 1166b30–67a10 Aristotle draws the distinction between benevolence (*eunoia*) and *philia* carefully. There are three distinctions: first, you can be benevolent towards one who is unaware of your good wishes; secondly, *philia* involves a certain amount of affection, whereas you can wish well to any old soccer-player or athlete; and, thirdly, *philia* clearly involves active commitment: a *philos* will get on to the pitch and join in, not simply stand by and watch.

So it is not possible to be *philoi* if you are not benevolent, but it does not follow that benevolent people are *philoi*; for they only wish for good things for those for whom they are benevolent, but would not take an active part with them, nor would they be put to any trouble over them.[14]

In this passage I have translated the verb *philein* as 'be *philoi*', which is no translation at all. It is worth noting that we cannot translate it as 'like' here,[15] since the discussion has nothing to do with whether the benevolent person likes the one he is well-disposed towards.[16] The problem is that the well-wisher may like her, but he does nothing for her. Arguably he might love her, but if he does not take on the practical part of a *philos* it is an empty goodwill, an

---

[13] Cooper, 'Aristotle on Friendship', 302. Cooper cites the *Rhetoric*'s definition of τὸ φιλεῖν (*Rhetoric*, 2. 4), according to which the inclination to *do* good to another is as important as the *wishing* good to the other. However Cooper renders the verb φιλεῖν as 'like' which implies that the important issue is feelings about a person, rather than behaviour towards her.

[14] 1167a7–10.

[15] Cooper argues for translating φιλεῖν as 'like' ('Aristotle on friendship', 302 n. 4).

[16] Though benevolence is said to involve a rather superficial level of affection, 1167a3.

unproductive relationship.[17] Thus, although there are occasions on which Aristotle uses the verb *philein* in the sense of 'like' or 'love', as in the case of 'love of wine',[18] in most of the circumstances in which he uses it we should do better to find a more practical translation, such as to 'befriend'. Befriending someone is not merely liking her, nor merely wishing her well, but doing something about it too.

Thus it is clear that there are practical implications to the verb *philein*. Similarly there are practical implications to being a *philos*. Again it is not merely a matter of well-wishing, nor is it a matter of taste: one is *philos* to a person not merely when one likes her, but when one acts as a *philos* acts. Of course it is also true that the word 'friend' in English can prescribe action as well as emotion or taste: this is particularly true in the phrase 'a real friend'. Again I quote from Winnie-the-Pooh:

'Eeyore,' he said solemnly, 'I, Winnie-the-Pooh, will find your tail for you.'
'Thank you, Pooh,' answered Eeyore. 'You're a real friend,' said he.
'Not Like Some,' he said.
So Winnie-the-Pooh went off to find Eeyore's tail.[19]

On the other hand, the connection of action with friendship in English differs in certain respects from what we find in Aristotle, I would suggest. It appears that the friendly action of finding Eeyore's tail merely confirms and demonstrates the love and care that Pooh feels for his friend. Arguably it is the affection that is the real friendship, while the action is the evidence that proves to the friend and others that that affection is real, lasting, and deep. This could be what Aristotle means by relating action to *philia*, but my impression is that the connection there is closer: action is part of what it is to be a *philos*, not merely the evidence that one has the affection that constitutes being *philos*; what constitutes *philia* is not the care that leads to action, but the co-operative or friendly action itself. This explains why Aristotle easily includes examples where affection is not obviously or necessarily involved.

Aristotle's notion of *philos* fits much better with the range of meanings of 'ally' in English, because an ally is anyone who co-

---

[17] ἀργὴν φιλίαν in 1167a12; absent friends are 'non-practising', 1157b5–11.
[18] 1155b27.
[19] Milne, *Winnie-the-Pooh*, 42.

operates with you for your own benefit, regardless of whether she does so out of mere liking for your character, or because she enjoys working with you, or because mutual co-operation is beneficial to both parties. Once we see Aristotle's discussion as a concern with alliances, whether political, civic, economic, or merely social and domestic, it is easy to see why it forms a major part of his ethical and political theory.

Aristotle is commending a view of society that stresses the place of co-operation, and not just competition, as an important and valuable feature of a good system of exchange and social intercourse. Hence he makes a distinction between justice and *philia*.[20] Both justice and *philia* belong in the same sphere of interpersonal relations, but justice is compatible with a competitive strategy, where you give back only what you strictly have to, while seeking to gain for yourself without regard to the well-being of your fellow-citizens. Co-operation, by contrast, takes as its aim the mutual well-being of both partners in any alliance or exchange; that is what *philia* is about, and that is why there is, in Aristotle's words, a 'different' justice in co-operative alliances.[21]

Aristotle's subject is, I am suggesting, all forms of co-operation that occur within society, whether between individuals or between larger groups such as alliances of cities or states. Alliances are, for the most part, based on an agreed exchange; hence Aristotle's lengthy concern with settling disputes between the parties to such an agreement.[22] His persistent preoccupation with what you get out of a relationship, and whether you or the other person are getting as much as you give, seems to fit ill with our notion of how friends regard each other. But once we see that we are talking about allies the rationale becomes clear. An ally is someone who contributes in a practical sphere, and if she ceases to do her bit the alliance is clearly in danger of falling apart and being broken off. This is why alliances that arise out of mutual usefulness are the simplest and most straightforward examples, in which the role of each ally is most easily analysed; it is not surprising that Aristotle keeps returning to such alliances to clarify his points.

On the other hand, it is to Aristotle's credit that he recognizes that economic motives are not the only ones that operate in the

[20] *NE* 1155a26–8; 1158b29–33.
[21] 1159b35–1160a8.
[22] In bk. 8, 1162b21–63b29, and in bk. 9, 1163b30–64b21.

sphere of human relations. There are a number of other factors that may cause people to co-operate as allies in exactly the same way as if it were for tangible economic advantages; some of these Aristotle lumps together under 'the useful'—such as co-operating as soldiers to win a victory, or political parties:

All societies are like parts of the political community; for they are working together for some benefit and providing one of the things that contributes to life. And the political community seems to arise originally and to endure for the sake of what is beneficial; and this is what lawgivers aim at, and they say that what is beneficial to society is 'just'. The other associations seek what is beneficial according to their individual lot, e.g. sailors seek what is beneficial in shipping with regard to manufacturing goods or the like, fellow-soldiers work for what is beneficial in military affairs, whether they desire goods or victory or a city, and similarly the members of a political unit such as a tribe or deme. All these seem to be subsets of the political community.'[23]

Others, however, are motivated not by specific advantages of this sort, but more generally by the pleasure that they derive from each other. This is a separate category in Aristotle's threefold analysis, but in most cases he treats alliances due to usefulness and alliances due to pleasure in the same breath, given that both provide some benefit to the allies. The third class of alliance is treated separately because it is not susceptible to analysis in strategic terms. This is what Aristotle calls 'the alliance of good people who are alike in virtue'.[24] We can see why he has to treat this as a separate phenomenon, because although as an alliance it works in exactly the same way as any other alliance motivated by mutual interests or benefit, and the two parties co-operate and work together for each other's good just as they would in any other partnership, the explanation for why they do so is not so clear. The alliance or relationship is not founded on a desire for gain. These people are allies not because they get something out of it, although they do in fact get both good and pleasure from the alliance.[25]

Thus Aristotle has to allow for some people who, purely because they are good and decent people, like to co-operate with other good and decent people, for no ulterior motive. In some cases these might

---

[23] 1160a8.
[24] 1156b7.
[25] 1156b12.

be family members or husband and wife,[26] in other cases they might be what we call 'friends'. But what Aristotle is interested in is not who they are but the ethical and social implications of the fact that they work together and co-operate as allies, because these family and comrade alliances are social forces of cohesion, just as the business and pleasure ones are too.

Coming at it in this way it might seem surprising that Aristotle should pay so much attention to these alliances of decent individuals, and why he should regard this as the most complete or 'perfect'[27] form of alliance. It seems at first surprising that Aristotle should think that any great significance can be attached to the idea that people might co-operate out of the goodness of their hearts, rather than out of self-interest. However, if we look at the text we can see very well why Aristotle thinks these alliances are actually a more complete sort of alliance, and indeed socially significant: the point is that they last.

> Those who want good things for their allies for the sake of those allies, are most of all allies; for they are like that not *per accidens* but in themselves. So the alliance of these people lasts as long as they are good, and virtue is lasting.[28]

Thus Aristotle would be maintaining not that virtuous alliances are more perfect because more virtuous, but rather that they are more co-operative, more committed, more lasting, and hence more of a total alliance between two individuals. One which breaks off quickly and easily because of a minor change in circumstances will not be the same profound alliance as one which lasts through time and change. Such an alliance is also with an individual, not with some benefit she may accidentally provide: 'But those who are allies due to usefulness dissolve the alliance along with the benefit; for they were not allies of each other but of the profit.'[29] Thus the perfect sort of alliance is an important feature in Aristotle's Ethics because it is the focus of real co-operation between individuals in society, and represents a lasting and effective cohesive force. Hence, although such alliances are relatively rare, as Aristotle admits at 1156b24–6, they are the stuff of a stable and cohesive society.

---

[26] e.g. 1162a24–7.
[27] τελεία, 1156b7.
[28] 1156b9. Cf. also 1157a20; 1156b17.
[29] 1157a14.

The point of this slightly tendentious outline of Aristotle's analysis may now be becoming clear. What I want to suggest is that Aristotle does, or would, classify what we know as friendship, the companionship of like-minded individuals, as a form of *philia*, provided that the relationship included practical co-operation. But he would do so not because the friends liked each other or were fond of each other, but because they behaved as allies, because they would work together and co-operate as a unit in society with joint interests, and not as separate and competing individuals. Hence friends are *philoi* not *qua* friends but *qua* allies; a *philos* is an ally, someone who takes the interests of another as a goal in her own deliberations and behaviour, no matter what the causes, motivations, or accompanying emotions.

### 3. AFFECTIONS AND SELF-LOVE

Two minor points may now briefly be cleared up.

### (i) *Affections and emotions*

First, if we are right that co-operative behaviour is the subject of Aristotle's analysis, we might well wonder why the subject of feelings or affections should ever need to surface in his account. Some have been surprised that he should not give more prominence to love,[30] but on this account the question of whether I love someone or merely co-operate with her, out of respect for her fine character and goodness, makes very little difference; as regards the practical

---

[30] Cooper, 'Aristotle on Friendship', 308 n. 9, argues, rather weakly, that the emotional bond is central to Aristotle's analysis, suggesting that he does not remark on it because he takes it as obvious. The best evidence falls outside Aristotle's systematic discussion of *philia* in bks 8 and 9, viz. in bk. 4, 1126b16–18 where the subject is the virtue of correct behaviour (which is like *philia*, only without the affection). We can see that Aristotle is pointing to the difference between a real ally, committed to the well-being of the other, and one who merely acts in that way out of habit or training. Whether he would analyse the difference as affection when he gets to the detailed account of precisely what constitutes *philia* is the question I am still asking. Julia Annas, 'Plato and Aristotle on Friendship and Altruism', *Mind*, 86 (1977), 532–54, simply assumes throughout that love is involved, as does Oswald Hanfling, 'Loving My Neighbour, Loving Myself', *Philosophy*, 68 (1993), 145–57, when he discusses Aristotle as someone who regarded 'self-love' as paradigmatic.

side of the alliance it is all one whether there is a deep emotional bond or not. I might co-operate with my fishmonger, or my bank manager, or my college tutor, in mutually beneficial exchange, just as I do with a friend.

Thus we should not be particularly surprised if the place of affection is not very prominent in Aristotle's account of alliance. On the other hand, we need not suggest that it should be absent altogether. There are two points on which it might be relevant to mention affections: first in explaining an alliance that is not due to mere usefulness or pleasure—why befriend one person rather than another?—and secondly in connection with breaking off an alliance, which may be harder if emotional attachment ties the parties together.

The occasions on which Aristotle actually discusses whether the parties are fond of each other (*stergousi*) are not many, though he occasionally takes it for granted that they would be, particularly in relationships due to pleasure such as love-affairs.[31] Affection is given some attention in connection with breaking off a love-affair,[32] once the lover and beloved are no longer getting what they wanted out of the affair. In that passage we are told that they often continue their alliance regardless, if they have grown accustomed to each other and fond of each other's characters. So affection is one factor in explaining why an alliance that ought to lapse, given an analysis merely in terms of advantage, may last.

Secondly, affection surfaces in the section on 'benevolence' (*eunoia*) at 1166b30. Mere benevolence, we are told, does not involve action; people who are benevolent, and not real allies, love only superficially.[33] Here affection is identified in a case that does not qualify as *philia*; but we are immediately told that benevolence, with its superficial affection, appears to be a source of *philia*. Affection is given a place in explaining the origin of a true practical alliance.[34]

Thirdly, there is a passage in which Aristotle himself clarifies the difference between 'love' (*philesis*) and co-operation (*philia*), arguing that the choice to act in accordance with another person's

---

[31] e.g. 1156a15; 1157a28; 1164a10. Also family affections, 1161b18 and 25; 1162a12. στέργειν can, of course, be a very weak affection or mere toleration.

[32] 1157a.

[33] ἐπιπολαίως στέργουσι, 1167a3.

[34] There is one further section in which love or affection (στέργειν and ἀγαπᾶν) comes in, and that concerns loving the object of benefaction, 1167b31.

goals proceeds from one's co-operative disposition towards that person (*philia*), not from one's emotional feeling for them (*philesis*), which can equally be directed towards some inanimate object.[35] Here it seems that love explains one's desire for something good for oneself, but the functioning of an alliance, in which someone else's good is chosen as an end in itself, is due not to the love one feels for that person but to the alliance established between the two. Love is relevant, then, but it is not the proper explanation of the co-operative behaviour of the partners in the resulting alliance.

## (ii) *Self-love*

Our second point concerns self-love. Given that Aristotle is interested more in the practicalities of co-operation than the psychological analysis of why we do so, it would be surprising if he were greatly interested in whether we love ourselves, or even whether we like ourselves. Surely this is no more relevant than the question of whether we love our greengrocers or philosophy teachers, indeed perhaps even less relevant. In fact we shall need to look afresh at the passages supposedly about loving oneself. Here too the emphasis is not on feelings, but practical behaviour and choices. Aristotle points out that you have to get your own act together if you are to work effectively with another.

There are two passages that talk about whether one can have a co-operative alliance with oneself, *Nicomachean Ethics* 9, chapters 4 and 8. It is important to distinguish the two since the first, chapter 4, only makes some preliminary observations reaching an aporetic conclusion at 1166a33–b25. Chapter 8 takes up the issue again, and indeed at 1168b3–6 it refers back to chapter 4.[36] But this time Aristotle uses the verb *philein*.[37]

Now, it is possible to translate *philein* as 'like' or 'love' as we have observed before. If we say 'like' the question asked in chapter 8 is this: 'There is a puzzle as to whether one ought to like oneself most of all, or another person.'[38] In that case it appears that we are talking

---

[35] 1157b25–34.

[36] Note that the terms are slightly different: 1166a1: τὰ φιλικὰ δὲ τὰ πρὸς τοὺς πέλας ... ἔοικεν ἐκ τῶν πρὸς ἑαυτὸν ἐληλυθέναι; 1168b5: εἴρηται γὰρ ὅτι ἀπ' αὐτοῦ πάντα τὰ φιλικὰ καὶ πρὸς τοὺς ἄλλους διήκει. Is it significant that he no longer says 'from co-operation with oneself', but rather 'from oneself'?

[37] ἀπορεῖται δὲ καὶ πότερον δεῖ φιλεῖν ἑαυτὸν μάλιστα ἢ ἄλλον τινά, 1168a28.

[38] 1168a28.

about educating our taste, so as to like the things we ought to like; otherwise it makes little sense to speak of whether we 'ought to like' someone. It may seem better to translate as 'love', so that the question concerns not so much taste as emotional bonding. Nevertheless, it still might not seem relevant to the subject of co-operative alliances whether one either liked or loved one person more than another. What matters is the practicality of whether we behave co-operatively towards them, as one might with oneself whether one liked or loved oneself or not.

I would argue, therefore, that in this chapter *philein* has practical implications: it alludes to the friendly behaviour discussed in Aristotle's earlier chapter (chapter 4), a meaning we might best translate 'befriend' or 'co-operate with'. Taken thus, chapter 8 is not concerned with emotional attachment to oneself, but rather with acting in one's own interests, as one's own best ally, and how far one should put one's own interests first and act 'in league with oneself':

But there is a puzzle as to whether one ought to befriend oneself most of all, or someone else. For people despise those who have a great affection (*agaposi*) for themselves, and they call them self-interested (a term of disgrace); and it is the bad man who seems to do everything for his own sake, and the more wicked he is the more he does so. And indeed they revile him, with accusations such as that he does not do anything altruistic. The decent person, on the other hand, acts on the basis of what is fine, and the better he is the more he acts on the basis of what is fine, and also for the sake of an ally, but ignores his own interests. But the facts disagree with these arguments, and not without reason. For they say that one ought most of all to befriend the one who is one's greatest ally, and the greatest ally is the one who wants goods, for the one he wants good things for, for that person's sake, even if no one will ever know. But these conditions apply particularly to one's relation with oneself, and the same with all the other conditions by which an ally is defined;[39] for as we said, it is from oneself that all co-operative actions come, including those towards others.

And all the proverbs agree—e.g. 'one soul' and 'allies share' and 'amity is equality' and 'the knee is closer than the thigh'. For all these things would apply most with regard to oneself; for one is one's own greatest ally; so one is to befriend oneself most of all.

[39] A reference to the definitions proposed in *NE* 9, ch. 4.

Hence there is a puzzle as to which arguments we ought to follow, given that both sets are convincing.[40]

Aristotle's solution to this puzzle is to distinguish clearly which part of yourself you ought to minister to, and what interests you are serving in each of the two senses of befriending oneself, or being self-interested. By suggesting that self-interest is best served by ministering to the higher elements of the self, and that this is done by doing good, which in itself benefits others as well as the self, he can argue that serving others not only follows from looking after number one but also contributes to that task.[41]

This may still seem to undermine altruistic behaviour done purely for the sake of others, but we might argue that it has nothing to do with whether I love someone else more or less than I love myself. Rather it concerns only whether one or other interest takes precedence in determining my course of action: whether I allow my interests to compete and win over those of another, or whether I submit my interests to those of somebody else in order to co-operate in promoting her good.

## 4. PRELIMINARY CONCLUSION

I have argued that Aristotle's analysis of *philia* is not concerned with loving others. Rather it is concerned with co-operating with, or befriending, others in such a way as to operate in society as if their goals were your own goals, or as if the pair of you, or group of you, had joint goals. Such alliances may be formed for various purposes, but how the parties feel about each other is not directly relevant to the practical and social implications of such partnerships. It is in this context that the question of priorities between one's own interests and those of others arises; and again the concern is not with how one feels about oneself, that is whether one loves oneself, but rather whether one ministers to one's own needs in

---

[40] 1168a28.
[41] My conclusions here about befriending oneself roughly coincide with the line on the absence of egoism in Aristotle taken by Richard Kraut, *Aristotle on the Human Good* (Princeton, NJ, 1989), especially 115–19, except that he takes it that Aristotle does not distinguish between loving and befriending, and he stresses a notion of competitive virtue which I think is at odds with Aristotle's notion of co-operation between friends and with oneself.

practice, and whether anyone, whoever she may be, will actually be co-operating with herself more than she is with any other ally.

### 5. AQUINAS ON ARISTOTLE

Given this pragmatic emphasis in Aristotle's analysis of co-operative alliances in the civic life of the ancient Greek city, it comes initially as a surprise to find that Thomas Aquinas takes these texts of Aristotle as his main authority on questions about Christian love for God and neighbour. In *Summa Theologiae secunda secundae*, Aquinas's subject of enquiry is charity.[42] It is possible that Aquinas's use of Aristotle has had an influence on the way subsequent readers have approached Aristotle's text; the very fact that it has been read for centuries as a text about friendship and love may be due to the fact that Aquinas and others, from the time that Aristotle regained a place in the libraries of the West, have been reading it as a text about love. That is why it is necessary to look again and see that it is a text about action and the practicalities of competing interests in society.

We ought rightly to be surprised at the way Aquinas uses Aristotle's treatise on *philia* as a text on Christian love. On the other hand, once we have noted the ways in which Aquinas's reading of Aristotle seems to do some violence to the spirit of Aristotle's discussion, and perhaps also to the Christian understanding of *caritas*, we may recognize that Aquinas is not so wide of the mark. On closer analysis we shall see that Aristotle's subject and St Thomas's subject have enough features in common for the comparison to be enlightening.

To illustrate Aquinas's use of Aristotle in his discussion of love, we may start by looking at Quaestio 25, article 4. This concerns the question whether one ought to love oneself.[43] Aquinas turns immediately to illuminate the question of love by reference to observations about 'friendship' (*amicitia*), and to base his obser-

---

[42] *caritas*, the Latin word that translates *agape* which is the New Testament word for 'love'.

[43] 'Utrum homo debeat seipsum ex caritate diligere.' There are parallel discussions elsewhere in Aquinas: see particularly *Sent.*, Bk. 3. 28. 6; *De caritate*, art. 7.

vations about friendship on Aristotle's discussion of *philia* in the *Ethics*:

With respect to the fourth article it goes thus.

It seems that one would not love oneself out of charity.[44]

1. For Gregory says, in a homily, that it is not possible to have charity among less than two. So no one has charity towards himself.

2. Furthermore, friendship in virtue of its very definition imports a return of love and equality, as is plain in the eighth book of the *Ethics*;[45] but return of love and equality cannot apply in the case of a person towards himself. But charity is an instance of friendship, as was said before.[46] Therefore, one cannot have charity towards oneself.

3. Furthermore what pertains to charity cannot be blameworthy: because 'charity does not do amiss' as it says in 1 Corinthians 13. But to love oneself is blameworthy; for it says in 2 Timothy 3 'In the last days perilous times shall come, and men shall be lovers of their own selves.' Therefore, one cannot love oneself out of charity.

But on the other hand there is the saying in Leviticus 19 'Thou shalt love thy friend as thyself'. But we love a friend out of charity. Therefore we must love ourselves out of charity as well.

In reply it must be said that, since charity is a form of friendship as was said before,[47] we can speak of charity in two ways. In one way according to the common definition of friendship. According to this it must be said that properly speaking it is not friendship that one has towards oneself, but something greater than friendship because friendship implies a certain union (for Dionysius says that love is a 'unifying force'[48]). But each individual has unity with himself, which is stronger than union. Hence just as unity is the origin of union, so the love with which someone loves himself is the form and root of friendship. For it is in this respect that we have friendship towards others, in that we relate to them as we do to ourselves. For it says in the ninth book of the *Ethics* that the friendly things that occur in relation to another derive from those that occur in relation to oneself.[49] Just as it is not science that we have about first principles, but something greater (namely intellectus).

---

[44] *Caritas*; Aquinas lacks a verb to correspond with the noun *caritas* (i.e. to translate the Greek verb ἀγαπᾶν) just as English lacks a verb for charity. Aquinas uses 'diligere ex caritate' to serve as his verb, and I am translating it literally 'love out of charity'.

[45] 1155b28 and 1158b28.

[46] This was argued in Q23 art. 1, on which see further below.

[47] Cf. Q23 art. 1.

[48] Dionysius the Areopagite, *DN* 4. See below, Ch. 8.

[49] 1166a1. Cf. 1168b5.

Although in this section Aquinas argues that the love that we have for ourselves is not, strictly speaking, friendship but something greater (unity rather than union), nevertheless he is still working on the assumption that the concept up for discussion (charity, Christian love for neighbours and self) is readily clarified with reference to friendship, and that the two are the same at least in the case of relationships directed not towards self but to others. Not only is he committed to the identity of charity and friendship, but also to the identity of charity and what Aristotle was analysing, namely *philia*, which Aquinas perhaps rightly translates *amicitia*, but which I have suggested fits less well with our current notion of 'friendship'. The identity of charity and friendship is assumed as Aquinas proceeds with the rest of this article:

In the other way we can speak about charity according to its proper definition, according to which friendship exists primarily from humanity towards God, and by consequence towards those things which belong to God. Among those are the human being himself who has the love. And thus among the rest of the things that he loves out of charity as pertaining to God, he loves himself out of charity as well.

In response to the first point then, it must be said that Gregory is speaking of charity according to the common definition of friendship. And the second point is also based on that too. In response to the third point it must be said that those who love themselves are blamed inasmuch as they love themselves according to sensible nature, to which they conform. That is not truly to love oneself according to rational nature, so as to wish for oneself those good things that pertain to the perfection of reason. And it is in this way that loving oneself most particularly pertains to charity.

Aquinas's commitment to the propriety of loving oneself is supported by arguments that owe a great deal to Aristotle's *Ethics*. He cites the *Nicomachean Ethics* explicitly twice in this article, once for an objection against self-love, and once in his response. But that is clearly not all. The whole argument depends upon the identification of *caritas* and the Aristotelian analysis of *amicitia*, though to bring in union and unity he also cites Dionysius.

The claim that charity is friendship had been made by Aquinas in an earlier article in the same part, Quaestio 23, article 1. In that article Aquinas sweeps aside three objections that suggest that Aristotle's concept of *amicitia* does not fit with the Christian concept of *caritas*: here I am translating *caritas* as 'love'.

23. 1: Whether love is friendship.

With respect to the first article it goes thus: it seems that love is not friendship.

   1. For as the philosopher says in the eighth book of the *Ethics*[50] nothing is so characteristic of friendship as a common life with one's friend;[51] but there is love of humanity towards God and towards angels, for whom there is no intercourse with humans, as it says in Daniel 2: 11. Hence love is not friendship.

   2. Furthermore, there is not friendship without return of affection, as it says in *Ethics* book 8.[52] But one can have love even towards enemies, according to Matthew 5: 44, 'Love your enemies'. Hence love is not friendship.

   3. Furthermore there are three sorts of friendship according to the philosopher in *Ethics* 8,[53] namely pleasurable, useful, and the friendship of the good. But love is not useful or pleasurable friendship; for Jerome says in his letter to Paulinus placed at the beginning of the Bible, 'that is the true intimacy, cemented with the glue of Christ, that is conjoined not by the usefulness of the friend's estate, nor by the presence of particular bodies, not by subtle and flattering adulation, but by the fear of God and the study of the Holy Scriptures.' Similarly it is not the friendship of the good, because we love even sinners; but the friendship of the good only extends to the virtuous, as it says in *Ethics* 8.[54] Hence love is not friendship.'

These three objections depend upon locating an apparent misfit between prominent features of the Aristotelian analysis of friendship in *Ethics* book 8 and the commonly accepted views on Christian charity supported by biblical quotations and Church Fathers. The three problem areas are:

   1. Aristotle's claim that friendship occurs between equals, and those who share a common life, which excludes humans from having such a relationship with God or angels;

   2. Aristotle's assumption that the relationship is mutual, whereas

---

[50] 1157b19.
[51] I am tempted to translate this symbiosis; but the Greek is actually συζῆν and refers to shared activities rather than complementary contributions to livelihood.
[52] 1155b28.
[53] 1156a7; 1155b21.
[54] 1157a18.

love for those who do not return affection is essential to the Christian love for enemies;

3. Aristotle's view that the only unmotivated form of friendship is friendship towards virtuous and like-minded individuals, whereas charity includes unmotivated love of sinners.

In reply Aquinas offers first a piece of counter evidence (the reference to 'friends' at John 15: 15), secondly a weak argument to the effect that there is in fact a communication route between humanity and God (namely one by which God communicates blessedness to mankind), and that a friendship ought to be founded on this (the 'ought' I take to be a moral obligation rather than a modal or logical inference), and that such a friendship founded on that communication would be charity. He nowhere shows that the Aristotelian demand for equality can be met, nor that the obligation for charity towards God is in fact equivalent to an obligation for 'friendship' with God.

Thirdly Aquinas offers detailed replies to the three objections. He argues that the difficulty over communication with God is a false one, since we do have communication with God in our spiritual selves; it is only in our corporeal and sensible lower selves that we lack a common life with God, though in the present life our relation with God is imperfect. Secondly he argues that the difficulty over mutuality can be solved by suggesting that we may not only love a mutual friend, but also love others (who do not love in return) for the sake of the friend who does. Hence we may love our enemies for the sake of our friend. Thirdly he argues that even love of sinners can be accounted for, if we take it as an extension of our primary love of a virtuous person. So we can love sinners if we love them for the sake of God. By this reasoning a kind of friendship extends to enemies and bad men, so that Aristotle and St Paul were, after all, both talking about the same thing.

Aquinas emerges with an account of charity that allows for love of sinners and enemies in the reduced sense that we always love them not for their own sake but for the sake of one who is really good and lovable, namely God who is in the end our only true friend. Thus we may feel that Aquinas has assimilated Christian charity to Aristotelian friendship at the expense not only of a distortion of Aristotle's account, but also of a reduction in the force of Christian charity. Whereas Aristotle's account never envisaged a relation of *philia* towards the unlovely, Aquinas would have us extend it to include sinners and enemies, as well as God; while in the case of Christian charity we might doubt whether the weak sense in which we may love our weaker brethren, but not for their own sake, does justice to the extremism of the Christian claim to love sinners and enemies. The Christian ethic of love of enemies and love of the unlovely sinner was supposed to be challenging or even shocking; indeed the same is probably true of the claim to love God. Aquinas finds it to be quite compatible with a classical ethic of mutually beneficial relationships between fine and virtuous aristocrats. Something seems to have gone awry.

## 6. CHARITY AND *PHILIA*: ARE THEY SO DIFFERENT?

Clearly something has gone wrong if the ethics of Christian charity emerge at Aquinas's hands indistinguishable from Aristotle's ethics of co-operation; it will be clear by now that I want to suggest that Aquinas's understanding of Aristotle in the light of Christian teaching does less justice to Aristotle's particular interests than we would wish, and also that his identification of Christian charity with Aristotle's theory undervalues what is novel and unconventional about the Christian ethic. But, that said, we have now, in the final section of this chapter, to recognize that the juxtaposition of the two subjects is instructive and indeed helpful in a positive way. Aquinas's reading of Aristotle brings out a number of features that are common to the Christian understanding of charity and the Aristotelian understanding of co-operative alliance; and recognizing these features can contribute to our understanding of the Christian view of love.

The point is this. We have seen that the tradition concerning *caritas* fails to coincide with Aristotle's theory of *philia* in the area of mutuality, equal social status, co-operation, equal benefits accruing to both parties. This is the area in which Aquinas has to do most violence to both sides, minimizing the demand for mutual benefit in Aristotle, and maximizing the requirement of virtue in the beloved object in the *caritas*-tradition. In the tradition that Aquinas inherits *caritas* is clearly not a co-operative virtue, but one that is directed *towards* another object, whereas *philia* implies give and take, a relationship *between* two not *towards* another. But on the other hand there are several features characteristic of *caritas* that do correspond to features of *philia* in Aristotle. These corresponding features are in four areas: (1) the practical character of the virtue; (2) obligation; (3) the place of taste or feelings; (4) self-interest and altruism. By exploring these aspects we shall see that *caritas* is not so different from *philia*: the comparison between the two will not lead us to identify them but will heighten our awareness of exactly what is distinctive in each case.

## (i) *Practicalities*

We have observed very clearly the practical and active side to Aristotle's notion of alliance; the ally is not merely a well-wisher but one who mucks in and fights for the good of the other. Mere benevolence is not sufficient,[55] though it is important and necessary.

It is clear that the practicalities of charity do not concern Aquinas so much. Unlike Aristotle he does not spend a great deal of time on the give and take of practical benefits in a loving relationship, and he never gets down to the nitty-gritty of what we have to *do* to love our neighbour. When he quotes Aristotle he does not stress the practical aspects of *philia*. Nevertheless, it becomes apparent from a number of the problems that Aquinas has to deal with that the practical aspect of *caritas* is strongly present in the tradition, and that he must at least take account of it if he is not prepared to make it central. The practical implications surface in Quaestio 23, article 3, where friendship is classified as a practical virtue:

Aristotle is not denying that friendship is a virtue, but rather says that it is 'a virtue or with virtue'.[56] For one could say that it is a moral virtue concerning actions that are directed towards another, but in accordance with a different rationale from justice; justice is about actions directed towards another according to the rationale of legal obligation, but friendship is according to the rationale of some friendly and moral obligation, or rather the rationale of a gratuitous benefit, as is clear from Aristotle.[57]

Furthermore, in Quaestio 25, article 9 the question arises whether we actually have to show our love for our enemies in practical ways.

---

[55] *NE* 1167a1–2 and 8–10.
[56] 1155a3.
[57] Q23 art. 3, reply to the first point.

It is clear from the way Aquinas responds that the initial evidence
all points to the conclusion that practical action is essential to the
*caritas*-tradition. Aquinas first acknowledges this tradition. His
reply cannot in the end eliminate all practical obligation from
charity, though he tries his best. He argues that it is only necessary
to be prepared to put our love into action in the event of urgent
need. To do so in other circumstances would be a mark of 'perfect
charity' and as such cannot be a necessity for those who are less
than perfect. Thus we shall be content with the minimum of practical action only if we are content with less than perfection; it is clear
that the practical nature of charity, at least when fully observed, is
undeniable.

## (ii) *Obligation*

Much of Aristotle's discussion of *philia* is taken up with whether
one *ought* to relate to various people in one way or another. If we
think he is talking about love that can seem a trifle odd. Can we
love to order? Exactly the same point arises in Aquinas, however.
In the section on love and the objects of love[58] we repeatedly find
questions concerning who, or what, we ought to love and to what
degree, while in Quaestio 44 Aquinas specifically asks whether love
is an appropriate subject for commands and obligations. He voices
some of our own hesitations, suggesting that the subject of commandments is the actions themselves and not the manner in which
they are performed, whereas love concerns the manner.[59] But his
response rejects that hesitation as ill-founded. On the contrary, he
argues in the response to Quaestio 44, article 1, the command to
love is the chief and greatest command in that it is commanded for
its own sake; while the reason why particular actions are the subject
of individual precepts, such as the ten commandments, is because
those actions promote, and contribute to, the fulfilment of the
command to love.

Thus, although it is correct, according to Aquinas, to say that
you cannot love under compulsion but only out of free choice,[60]
that does not mean that the free choice is not a choice to obey a

---

[58] 2a 2ae, QQ23–7.
[59] 2a 2ae, Q44 art. 1.
[60] Q44 art. 1, ad. 2. In fact if the subject were feelings it might be doubted whether
one could love 'by free choice'.

commandment or obligation. In Aquinas's view, therefore, love is the subject of obligations and duties, just as *philia* and its associated attitudes and behaviour are in Aristotle.


### (iii)  *Taste and feelings*

We have already seen that Aristotle allows for fondness between the parties to a co-operative relationship. But we also noted that co-operation is not restricted to cases where the partners are bound by affection, and that indeed was the main reason for arguing that Aristotle's subject is not friendship as such but the co-operative alliance that occurs in friendship and other joint enterprises.

Something of the same combination occurs in Aquinas's analysis of charity. The very fact that charity is a subject of obligations and commands suggests that it is not solely a matter of involuntary feelings and affections towards objects that are attractive. On the contrary we are obliged to have charity not only towards God and other lovable and virtuous people, but to enemies and sinners as well,[61] clearly those for whom we do not automatically have affectionate feelings; and although Aquinas explicates love of sinners as loving their good qualities and not loving the sin in them,[62] there is no doubt that we still will not necessarily find them obviously likeable or to our taste. Thus, in some cases of charity, the relationship is with one for whom we already feel affection, but in other cases charity is demanded towards those for whom we do not first have friendly feelings, regardless of whether we like them or not. On the other hand, Aquinas, like Aristotle, distinguishes charity from well-wishing (*benevolentia*) on precisely the same grounds as Aristotle had distinguished *philia* from well-wishing (*eunoia*), namely that charity implies a union of affections and more commitment to the individual concerned than mere well-wishing does.[63] Love cannot be a detached or general kindliness; it must be real concern for real individuals, not superficial but affectionate.

Clearly in both cases the place of affection is problematic. Neither writer is concerned simply with the affection that we readily feel for those who are likeable or good to us; rather they are trying to

[61]  Q23, *passim*.
[62]  Q25 art. 6.
[63]  2a 2ae, Q27 art. 2.

explain how the commitment found in that sort of relationship may in certain circumstances also occur in other relationships where there is not an obvious explanation in those terms. Aristotle is not, of course, interested in devotion to sinners or enemies, but rather with business relationships and joint enterprises in which both partners make a positive contribution, and to that extent he is not concerned with wholly disinterested affection as Aquinas is. But in both cases what needs explaining is not primarily affectionate feelings, but the commitment to furthering the goals of another individual. The place of affection is not irrelevant in either case, but it is not the whole story.

## (iv) *Self-interest and altruism*

Given that Aquinas's topic (charity) resembles Aristotle's topic (*philia*) both in the place it gives to affection and in the practical implications, it is hardly surprising that the matter of self-interest and altruism also arises in both cases in analogous ways. For both writers it is important to determine the priorities between concern for self and concern for another.

There is, however, some difference here, in that Aquinas pre-supposes that the goals of both the self and the other are subordinate to the goals of God, and hence the best interests of oneself are served by conformity with the will of God, not with the (possibly mistaken) desires of one's own will. Since the will and com-mandments of God prescribe that we should act in the interest of others, there is in theory no potential conflict between self-interest and the interest of another. Self-interest is best served by altruism.

This might seem an important difference from Aristotle, whose vision belongs squarely in the human context of the Greek polis. The will of God does not ever enter his picture. However, it is still worth noting the parallel between Aristotle and Aquinas in this respect. Aristotle does not need to invoke the divine will in order to justify the idea that co-operation and concern for others might be the best way of serving the interests of both. Not only does he admit a class of alliances in which mutual benefit is the sole rationale for the relationship, but he is also determined that the alliance for the good is also pleasant and useful to both parties.

Given that Aquinas includes the love of sinners and of enemies in the obligations of charity, it might look as if his topic was more altruistic and less self-centred than Aristotle's, in which we are not expected to feel any commitment to the underprivileged and outcasts in society. But Aquinas's goals are not in fact directed primarily at the benefit of the beloved neighbour or sinner; we do not, in Aquinas, love the beloved sinner for her own sake, but for the sake of God: our goals are determined not by the interests of the other but by the interests of God. God alone we love for his own sake. Thus there is a sense in which God alone can be loved altruistically,[64] and the apparently altruistic love of neighbours and enemies is not conceived for *their* sake—even if it is also not conceived for one's own sake, but first for the sake of God. On the other hand, it does, as in Aristotle, involve taking the ultimate well-being of the other as a goal in place of our own goals in determining a course of action. In this sense both Aristotle's co-operative alliance, and Aquinas's charity, are concerned with deciding *my* action on the basis of *someone else*'s perceived interests. The other is in this sense a 'second self'.

## 7. CONCLUSION

It is Aquinas who juxtaposes the Aristotelian text on co-operation with the Christian tradition of charity towards God and neighbour. We should, I would argue, rightly be shocked at this juxtaposition: it must make us sit up and think because in many ways Aristotle was clearly engaged in an enterprise far removed from that of Aquinas, and his ethics of co-operation among well-bred classical citizens does not correspond in any straightforward way to the ideals of unconditional devotion that are the hallmark of charity. But while we should be shocked that Aquinas should read Aristotle's text as a text about charity, we should at the same time recognize the benefit that derives from the fruitful juxtaposition of the two ideas. There is no reason to dismiss Aquinas's discussion as absurd. In fact it can alert us to the many ways in which the problems and issues are the same for Aquinas and the tradition of Christian charity as they were for Aristotle in analysing co-oper-

---

[64] I use 'altruistically' here to represent Aristotle's ἐκείνου ἕνεκα (1166a4). In this restricted sense altruism occurs only when the benefactor acts for the sake of the beneficiary personally, and not for the sake of a third party.

ation. What emerges most clearly is that the relevant issues are not primarily about affections or feelings towards others, but rather the active commitment to the well-being of the other. The key differences that remain are not only in the motivation by which one takes another's interests into account, but also the range of possible objects of such concern and the extent to which a positive reciprocal contribution to the relationship is required. While these differences are fundamental they are not the only features to notice, and the analysis of Aquinas's reading of Aristotle contributes to a constructive understanding of what is peculiar and what is common to the co-operative ethos of *philia* and the altruistic ethos of charity.

# 7

## *Philanthropia*, God's Love for Mankind in Origen

Origen is often compared with Plotinus and the Platonic tradition in general; and the comparison is not infrequently made specifically in respect of his treatment of love. This issue has become classic for two main reasons: first because Origen's *Commentary on the Song of Songs* concentrates on the love or desire that the soul has for God almost to the exclusion of any mention of God's love for humankind;[1] and secondly because in the introductory section of the same work Origen claims that terms related to *agape* and terms related to *eros* are interchangeable.[2] Since Anders Nygren made his classic distinction between these two motifs, and questioned the propriety of modelling the relationship between God and humanity on acquisitive love,[3] there has been reason to doubt whether Origen's use of the *eros* motif is helpful or legitimate as a contribution to a distinctively Christian understanding of love. According to Nygren such a model is an alien intrusion into Christianity from the Platonic tradition.

Thus the charge in this case against Origen would be that he is too much of a Platonist to be a good theologian. Some of the ways in which he might be defended against this charge have been explored in Chapter 3: we may argue that the stress on the soul's desire is an accident of the subject matter in the Song of Songs that Origen is commenting on, and does not in any case represent his estimate of the importance of such desire in theology when viewed systematically; and we may suggest that there are unexpected benefits from taking the text seriously and pressing the claim that *amor* and *caritas* (or *eros* and *agape*) are interchangeable.

---

[1] Such love is occasionally mentioned, for example in *ComCt*, prologue, 70; 1. 102; 2. 158.

[2] In the Latin translation (by Rufinus) in which the commentary is preserved the terms are *amari* and *diligi*, evidently translating ἐρᾶσθαι and ἀγαπᾶσθαι.

[3] See Anders Nygren, *Agape and Eros*, esp. p. 391. See also Ch. 3, above.

I shall not return to either of these lines of defence in this chapter; instead I want to turn to a third route of enquiry and ask whether it is really correct to say that Origen has very little to say about love that is directed from God towards humankind (or, incidentally, from human beings towards others less well endowed than themselves). I shall be arguing in this chapter that there is far more material on God's love for humanity than we might suppose and that error arises from looking for the term *agape*, since Origen rarely uses that term. Indeed, Origen does not use the term *eros* very much (nor, in the Latin translations, *caritas*, *dilectio*, or *amor*). We shall have more success if we examine the occasions on which God is said to show *philanthropia*, since these reveal that there are certain consistent features that characterize God's love in Origen.

Secondly I shall argue that while there is some background in Platonic and Stoic thought for ascribing *philanthropia* to God, among others, Origen does something markedly different from his philosophical predecessors. He uses the term primarily for the Incarnation and self-revelation of God. It is this aspect that explains why Plotinus cannot afford to attribute *philanthropia* to the supreme One, whose concern for the lower orders does not involve a self-sacrificing love in the way that Origen suggests.

### 1. SELF-SEEKING LOVE IN PLOTINUS

To establish the traditional problem we may first take a brief look at Plotinus. In two well-known passages, *Enneads* 3. 5 and 6. 7, Plotinus develops the idea that love (*eros*) is found where beauty and goodness is appreciated and desired by the soul: 'Now everyone recognizes that the emotional state for which we make this "Love" responsible rises in souls aspiring to be knit in the closest union with some beautiful object.'[4] Although in *Ennead* 3. 5 Plotinus stresses that love for the good and beautiful springs from a certain kinship between the soul and the beauty it desires, in the end it is lack or need that accounts for the desire. The Good itself, which is the ultimate object of the soul's longing, is the one thing that is

---

[4] Plotinus, *Ennead* 3. 5. 1 (translation by Stephen MacKenna).

utterly without need.[5] For the good there can be no higher object
that it needs or wants, and, being self-sufficient in this way, it cannot
reasonably be said to have erotic love. So after all the one thing that
the Good lacks is love.

On the other hand it would be wrong to suggest that the independence of the Good means it takes no responsibility for things
beneath. The Good is, indeed, responsible for the outflow of goodness and beauty on to the intellectual beings immediately below,
and it is only because of this dispensation from above that they are
beautiful and attractive to the soul.[6] This outflow of goodness from
the supreme Good down the hierarchy of beings is the explanation
of providence and the tendency of the world as a whole, and rational
beings in particular, towards goodness. Thus, in so far as we can
attribute to the Good some responsibility for the well-being of the
lower orders, to that extent it may be termed provident or concerned
for things outside. But this providence is at no cost to the One and
is no threat to its sufficiency, and we should probably hesitate to
call it 'love'. The One overflows with goodness and dispenses love
to others in providing desirable objects to love, but it is not itself a
lover.

## 2. SELF-SEEKING LOVE IN ORIGEN

Few of the features of Plotinus' analysis of love on the part of *souls*
are incompatible with Christian doctrine. That a soul's love for
God is inspired and given by the very God who is its object seems
fair enough. Few would deny that God is in some sense beautiful
and lovable. Self-seeking desire may not seem a proper attitude,
but a longing to follow Christ, and to be near him or to emulate
him, as closely as possible—these responses are not only acceptable
but encouraged. Thus the difficulties of adapting Plotinian love to
the Christian soul need not be great.

The problems become much more acute in the case of God,
however. We may be happy to start with a beautiful and transcendent God, inspiring devotion and love in rational souls. But if
his perfection means that he has no love for what is other, and if his

---

[5] *Ennead* 3. 5. 1.
[6] *Ennead* 6. 7. 21.

providence can help only the wise and the good, then the theory seems incompatible with fundamental doctrines of the Church. Thus if Origen is presenting a theory that essentially matches or anticipates that of Plotinus, we might feel that he has missed something essential in Christian doctrine. So is it the case that Origen has developed a theory that has no room for God's love?

The *Commentary on the Song of Songs*, as we have already observed, develops the theme of the desire of the beautiful bride (the soul or the Church) for the beautiful bridegroom (Christ) with the aim of achieving mystical unity with him. Although it may be an oversimplification to suggest that that is the only theme of the work,[7] yet there is sufficient material that will fit into that description to suggest that Origen is working with a model of Platonic love very similar to that found in Plotinus.[8] If Origen dwelt only on the love of the soul, or of the Church, *for* Christ, it might be difficult to resist the conclusion that for Origen, as for Plotinus, the transcendent desirability of God renders it impossible for him to engage in love, since that would imply weakness and lack. But that conclusion will not so easily follow if we can identify other passages where Origen *is* prepared to speak of God as lover.

3. GOD AS LOVER IN THE *COMMENTARY ON THE SONG OF SONGS*

It is apparent even within the *Commentary on the Song of Songs* itself that Origen is willing to speak of God as showing love towards humanity. We may take two of the clearer passages as examples.

(*a*) *Commentary on the Song of Songs*, 3. 189–90.[9] In this passage Origen is considering the soul's request 'ordinate in me caritatem'.

---

[7] This is an oversimplification since (*a*) the bride is beautiful only because absolved from uncomely sins (e.g. *ComCt*, 2. 113); (*b*) the bridegroom is lovable in part at least because of his Incarnation (1. 107) and obedience to death (2. 153) not for his transcendence alone; he does not appear beautiful to others (3. 174); (*c*) the experience to which he draws the bride is not merely for her satisfaction but for the education and improvement of her spiritual insight (3. 218 ff.; 4. 228 ff.).

[8] See, for example, *ComCt*, prologue, 74. 10–15. On the similarities between Origen and Plotinus in respect of love see H. Crouzel, 'Origène et Plotin', in Lothar Lies (ed.), *Origeniana Quarta* (Innsbruck, 1987), 430–5.

[9] This passage is a continuation of the passage on inordinate love discussed above in Ch. 3.

What does it mean to set love in order? Origen replies that different 'orders' of love are appropriate to different objects. Thus, although we are to love all mankind and all rational beings similarly and equally in virtue of the fact that they are human or rational (or both), nevertheless we may have a special and different love for some particular people. To illustrate this point Origen uses the example of God's love for humankind. God, after all, loves everything that is and hates none of the things he has made, but there are still distinctions in his love: his love for the Hebrews differs from his (undoubted) love for the Egyptians, and his love for Moses differs from his love for Aaron and again from his love for the other Israelites. Thus distinctions and differences do not prevent his love from being universal for everyone.

(b) *Commentary on the Song of Songs*, prologue, 70. Again the discussion starts from a question about the love that we are expected to show. This love treats everyone as a neighbour and is illustrated by the parable of the Good Samaritan. Origen also observes in passing that the Saviour became a neighbour to us in just this way (namely by deeds of love[10]) when he did not pass us by as we lay half dead from the wounds of robbers. The implication is that Christ loved us in the same way as he recommends us to love one another.

In neither of these two passages is the mention of God's love towards humankind important to the argument as a whole. In the prologue passage the main point of the discussion is to suggest that the first and primary object of love is God.[11] Similarly in the passage from book three love for God is considered first, and secondly love for neighbours. God's love for his creatures serves merely to illustrate the sense in which love may be equal and yet differentiated according to the object. It is not in either case central to the issue concerning the soul's love for God and for others.

It might seem, then, that Origen never stops to consider whether it is actually possible for God to love his creatures, since God's love is never the focus of direct attention or discussion in this commentary. An opponent might argue that the allusions to God's love for humanity are actually inconsistent with the Platonic structure of love envisaged in this work, and that they are therefore an

---

[10]  *ComCt*, prologue, 70. 26.
[11]  *ComCt*, prologue, 70. 29–32.

anomaly, a careless intrusion that Origen cannot consistently afford to admit. That criticism will not be adequately refuted by going outside the commentary to consider other works of Origen, since we should still need to show that the Song of Songs commentary was consistent with itself. Nevertheless it will be helpful to ascertain whether elsewhere and in other writings Origen is strongly committed to the view that God can be said to love humanity, and whether he indicates any means of reconciling that claim with the view that God is perfect and desirable as an object of love.

## 4. DOES GOD SHOW *AGAPE* OR *EROS* IN OTHER WORKS OF ORIGEN?

In the Song of Songs commentary Origen speaks of the love that is from God in terminology borrowed from the Johannine texts that he is citing.[12] Thus, although the purport of the passage as a whole is to argue that *agape* and *eros* (that is in the Latin translation, *caritas* and *amor*) amount to the same thing, it appears that if anything is explicitly attributed to God as a lover it is *agape* (*caritas*).[13]

The same goes for our other text from book three. God, we are told, 'amat omnia quae sunt', an allusion to a text in the Wisdom of Solomon (11: 24) where the Greek reads ἀγαπᾷς. Hence Origen may have written ἀγαπᾷ. In any case the overall concern of the passage is with *caritas* or *dilectio*, that is *agape*, and that is what is attributed to God.[14]

Our first route of enquiry would therefore naturally be to look for other passages in which Origen suggests that God has *agape* for his creatures. The search for such passages bears little fruit, however. *Caritas* is explicitly attributed to God in the sixth homily on Ezekiel,[15] where Origen argues that God is not impassible but undergoes human feelings; and in the commentary on Matthew we are told that Jesus had a love 'that doth not seek its own'.[16] In

---

[12] 1 John 4: 8 and 16; 1 John 4: 7. Origen, *ComCt*, prologue, 69–70.

[13] *ComCt*, prologue, 70.

[14] *ComCt*, 3. 190. 4; cf. 158. 4 ff.

[15] *HomEzek*, 6. 6 (40–52) (references are to Sources Chrétiennes, vol. 352).

[16] *ComMt*, 12. 41 (GCS40. 163. 30).

general, however, *agape* more often names the love that others have for God.[17]

On the other hand, it is even more rare to find *eros* or *amor* attributed to God. In the Song of Songs commentary God is called 'lover of souls' (*amator animarum*[18]), which is clearly an allusion to Wisdom 11: 26; but the Greek it translates is φιλόψυχος and makes no mention of *eros*. When the first homily on Ezekiel calls God a 'lover of men' (*amator hominum*[19]) it is unlikely that Origen's original used the term *erastes*; the Greek term was almost certainly *philanthropos*.

Thus it might appear that Origen only occasionally speaks as though God had either *agape* or *eros*, and that the occasions are too few and too isolated to establish any coherent picture of how this love could be accommodated into Origen's system. On the basis of this evidence we might conclude that Origen is not deeply committed to God as lover, and that his system is fundamentally the same as that of Plotinus.

Such a conclusion would be erroneous. Two features of the material we have just considered are worth pursuing: first the universal nature of the love for humanity mentioned in the Song of Songs commentary, a love which is distinctive for the fact that it 'takes every human being as neighbour',[20] regardless of worth or status; and secondly the degradation such love implies on the part of God, which appears in the Good Samaritan paradigm in terms of the fallen state of the victim and in the Saviour's descent 'from Jerusalem to Jericho'.[21]

These features recur frequently in other works of Origen, but not as features of the *agape* of God but of his *philanthropia*, his love for humankind. We have already identified one instance where the term *philanthropos* probably lies behind Jerome's Latin translation of the first homily on Ezekiel, but the term is relatively common in Origen. Looking at the major works preserved in Greek, I have found seventy-two examples where someone or something is said

---

[17] For example, *CCels*, 3. 81; *Exhortation to Martyrdom*, 2; 6; 37; *ComMt*, 12. 2; 12. 23; 15. 21; 17. 14; *PEuch*, 28. 3; *HomJr*, 5. 2; *PArch*, 2. 8. 3. Other examples where *agape* shows *agape*: *ComJn*, 32. 20; *FragmMt*, 388; 533.

[18] *ComCt*, 3. 190. 1.

[19] *HomEzek*, 1. 1 (319. 13); cf. 6. 10 (389. 4–5).

[20] *ComCt*, prologue, 70. 17–18.

[21] Prologue, 70. 21.

to be *philanthropos* or to have *philanthropia*.[22] Not all of these ascribe the quality to God, though a significant proportion do.[23] Of those that do refer to God, not all stress the features that I am suggesting are significant, namely the lack of prejudice and the humiliation or self-emptying, but again a fair proportion do. Thus I hope to support with a range of examples my contention that (*a*) what is called God's *philanthropia* is essentially the same as what is called 'love' in the Song of Songs commentary, and (*b*) that, for Origen, God's *philanthropia* is subtly different from the conventional virtue attributed by Stoics, Plato, and indeed Philo to their philanthropic gods, and rulers, precisely because in Origen the paradigm is given in the Incarnation, and the Incarnation involves humiliation on the part of a transcendent God stooping to solidarity with all classes of humanity.

### 5. *PHILANTHROPIA* AS AN ATTRIBUTE OF STOIC AND MIDDLE PLATONIST DIVINITIES

Clearly the first task is to outline the use of *philanthropia* in philosophy immediately before Origen. Much work has been done to assemble the material in this field already, by a distinguished succession of Classical and Byzantine scholars.[24] To avoid unnecessary duplication I shall not survey the texts again, but summarize

---

[22] It was necessary to concentrate on the works preserved in Greek because φιλανθρωπία regularly gets lost in Latin translation. Jerome's translation of the homily on Ezekiel (1. 1 and 6. 10) is a rare exception. φιλανθρωπία is sometimes translated *misericordia* (e.g. *ComMt*, 202. 22; 262. 29; 400. 8; 524. 24; 528. 23; the translator of this commentary may not be typical) and perhaps sometimes *clementia*; it does not appear to be translated *humanitas*, although Gellius (*Noctes Atticae*, 13. 7) implies that that was a common rendering. See H. Hunger, ''φιλανθρωπία. Eine griechische Wortprägung auf ihrem Wege von Aischylos zu Theodorus Metochites', AAWW (1963), 100, repr. in H. Hunger, *Byzantinische Grundlagungforschung*, Variorum Reprints (London, 1973), ch. 13.

[23] Forty-six examples refer to God or one of the Trinity. Twenty-five examples refer to human beings showing *philanthropia*, sometimes as an analogy for God (e.g. *CCels*, 3. 62. 6). One example (Celsus apud *CCels*, 8. 33. 6) refers to demons.

[24] For example: S. Lorenz, 'De Progressu notionis φιλανθρωπίας' (diss., Leipzig, 1914); S. Tromp de Ruiter, 'De vocis quae est φιλανθρωπία significatione atque usu', *Mnemosyne*, 59 (1932), 271–306; H. I. Bell, '*Philanthropia* in the Papyri of the Roman Period', *Coll. Latomus*, 2 (Brussels, 1949), 31–7; A. J. Festugière, 'Les Inscriptions d'Asoka et l'idéal du roi hellénistique' *Récherches de science réligieuse*, 39 (1951), 31–46; G. Downey, '*Philanthropia* in Religion and Statecraft in the Fourth

what seems to be the consensus and then generalize.

It is clear that *philanthropia* was a virtue regularly attributed to rulers in the Hellenistic period. This is linked with the mystique according to which kings were envisaged as images of the divine, if not in some sense divine themselves. Thus, whether we suppose that *philanthropia* was first a characteristic of the gods and then applied to humans in an analogous position of power,[25] or first a characteristic of civilized, humane, members of the classical polis, and subsequently a mark of rulers, both human and divine,[26] it is apparent that in Hellenistic times it was a virtue practised most evidently by those whose status set them above the recipients of the benefits they provided. There is a degree of condescension on the part of gods who deign to take thought for the well-being of mortals, as there is on the part of rulers who show clemency towards prisoners or captives, or who enact legislation providing for their less fortunate subjects.[27] But this condescension costs little to either the rulers or the gods: it is a condescension they can afford precisely because they are supreme, and which is proper to them because they are well-endowed, educated, and humane: so far from debasing them, these acts of beneficence reinforce the appearance of wealth and superiority, enhancing the divine status of the dispensers of providence.

The Stoics were quite clear that their god was *philanthropos*.[28] Indeed, a passage of Clement's argument that God is *philanthropos* is thought to derive from a Stoic proof of the same proposition;[29] but it is clear from that passage and from others on the same topic that for Stoic thinkers god's *philanthropia* was manifested in

Century after Christ', *Historia*, 4 (1955), 199–208; C. Spicq, 'La Philanthropie hellénistique, vertu divine et royale', *Studia Theologica*, 12 (1958), 169–91; J. Kabiersch, *Untersuchungen zum Begriff der Philanthropie bei dem Kaiser Julian* (Wiesbaden, 1960); H. I. Martin, 'The Concept of *Philanthropia* in Plutarch's Lives', *American Journal of Philology*, 82 (1961), 164–75; Hunger, '*Φιλανθρωπία*'; L. J. Daly, 'Themistius' Concept of *Philanthropia*', *Byzantion*, 45 (1975), 22–40; M. Zitnik '*Θεὸς φιλάνθρωπος* bei Johannes Chrysostomos', *Orientalia Christiana Periodica*, 41 (1975), 76–118.

[25] As is implied by Hunger, '*Φιλανθρωπία*', for example; cf. Aeschylus, *Prometheus*, 11. 28; Aristophanes, *Peace*, 390.

[26] As Spicq, 'La Philanthropie hellénistique', 169–73. Cf. Plutarch, *An seni resp. gerenda sit*, 796E; Martin, 'The Concept of *philanthropia*', 166–7.

[27] Cf. Spicq, 'La Philanthropie hellénistique', 181–2.

[28] Cicero, *De div.* 1. 82. 3; Cleanthes, *Hymn to Zeus*; Plutarch, *Comm. not* 1075E.

[29] Clement of Alexandria, *Paid.* 1. 8 (SC 70. 63. 1–2); *SVF* 2. 1116; Long and Sedley, 60. 1.

providence; god helps humankind and cares for them in providing and directing the natural environment to their advantage. Very much the same is true of the philanthropic attitudes of the gods in Plutarch; they work through providence in providing material benefits in the natural world.[30] Hence, although god is immanent in the material world for the Stoics, while for Middle Platonism the divine is transcendent, in neither case does *philanthropia* involve stepping down across a divide, not only because the Stoic god is, as it were, down already and is not threatened by associating with the world, whereas for the Platonist providence operates at a distance and need not imply messy involvement with matter; but more fundamentally because providence does not threaten the divine status of the provider: so far from requiring identification with the needs and weaknesses of mortals, it implies that god, unlike them, has no lack and can supply their needs without detriment to himself.[31] This contrasts with Origen's view, not only in that Origen envisages the divine stepping down from transcendence to immanence, but also in that God's act is not one of providence supplying human needs, but of taking the sins and weaknesses on himself, with a counter-providential concern not merely for the virtuous and deserving but also for the sinful and undeserving.[32]

## 6. PHILO

Before we turn to Origen we must stop to glance at Philo, not only because Philo is keen to attribute *philanthropia* to God in ways that are familiar from Stoicism, particularly in respect of providence,[33] but also because, in a particular passage that we shall have to look at, *De Cherubim* 99, he refers to a descent to earth on the part of God as arising out of *philanthropia*:

[30] For example, Plutarch, *De Pyth. Or.* 16. 402A.

[31] This is true not only of the Stoic and Middle Platonist examples, but also of Plato, *Laws*, 4. 713c5–e2, where Kronos, being φιλάνθρωπος, sets up good government for mankind.

[32] I say 'counter-providential' meaning that providence was usually thought to ensure that good fortune fell to those who deserved it and bad things befell the wicked. When the reverse was true it was generally a reason to doubt the existence of providence.

[33] For example, Philo, *De Virt.* 188; *De spec. leg.* 3. 36; *De opific. mundi*, 81. On this subject see Spicq, 'La Philanthropie hellénistique', 174–5.

Aiming to ensure that his sojourn will be most agreeable and come about with the dignity that befits it, when God the king of kings and ruler of all things, out of his clemency and philanthropy considers the creature worthy of visitation and comes down from the ends of heaven to the furthest reaches of the earth for the benefit of our race, what sort of dwelling place ought we to prepare for him?[34]

While it is clear that Philo is envisaging a direct intervention on God's part, rather than his continuing providence, it must be obvious that Herbert Hunger is wrong to say that Philo is referring to the Incarnation as an act of *philanthropia*.[35] There is, after all, nothing about incarnation here at all, and it is only with Christian hindsight that we are tempted to read back anything remotely analogous to Christian doctrine in this passage. Philo goes on to suggest that it is the virtuous soul that forms a fitting dwelling-place for the invisible God, since no corporeal temple would be good enough for God to set foot in.[36] Clearly Philo's God would not make himself a house of clay, but will rather make a visitation as a ruler makes his tour of inspection of a distant province, providing that he can be entertained with dignity, not in humility. There is no suggestion that God, the Father here, not the Logos, will adopt human nature; his assistance is the helping hand of a superior king, bringing 'laws and ordinances to sanctify and consecrate'.[37] Of course it is an act of condescension that he should visit these lowly parts at all, but the condescension does not extend to identification with the lowly. Thus, although Philo's use of *philanthropia* in this context may be an important background to Origen's use of the word in the context of the Incarnation, it lacks what I take to be the most important feature of Origen's usage, the sense that in being *philanthropos* God becomes *anthropos*.

[34] *De Cher.* 99.

[35] Hunger, '*Φιλανθρωπία*', 7. Doubtless Hunger's reading was prompted by Spicq's suggestion that Philo was writing with almost prophetic inspiration, Spicq, 'La Philanthropie hellénistique', 175.

[36] Philo, *De Cher.* 100.

[37] Philo, *De Cher.* 106.

## 7. CLEMENT OF ALEXANDRIA

Earlier in the passage from the *Paidagogus* that we used as evidence for the Stoics, Clement offers on his own behalf an argument against those who think that God is not good.[38] These people, he suggests, 'are ignoring the greatest example of God's *philanthropia*, that he became *anthropos* for our sake'. *Philanthropia* is responsible for God's identification with humanity, that is with *all* humanity, as Clement stresses again a few lines later: 'It is in this that the Lord the teacher is most excellent and unimpeachable, in that he feels for the nature of each and every human being, due to the super-abundance of his love for mankind.' Thus we find in this passage of Clement *both* of the features so prominent in Origen, namely solidarity with human nature in becoming *anthropos*, and the idea that every human person, in virtue of humanity alone, is the object of philanthropic love.[39]

We might be tempted to see Clement as a link between Philo and Origen, although Clement differs a little from Origen in that he envisages that the objects of love are worthy and lovable, mankind being the best of God's creation.[40] But my concern here is not to trace development or influence, but rather to illustrate and explore what is important in Origen's treatment of *philanthropia*, noting how its characteristic features, though anticipated in Clement, are incompatible with the invulnerable gods of Stoic or Platonic philosophy.[41]

## 8. ORIGEN

As we have seen, it was normal to attribute *philanthropia* to the pagan and philosophical gods because of their providence and the good gifts they supply. It is remarkable, therefore, that there are no

---

[38] Clement, *Paid.* 1. 8 (62. 1).

[39] We might suggest that both features reflect a stress on the ἄνθρωπος element of φιλάνθρωπος. Cf. Hunger, 'Φιλανθρωπία', 12; Spicq 'La Philanthropie hellénistique', 178.

[40] Clement, *Paid.* 1. 8 (63. 1).

[41] I am not saying that Clement is the first to say that God is φιλάνθρωπος, but that he anticipates the association of φιλανθρωπία with incarnation and the universal concern for all human nature *qua* human that we find in Origen.

comparable examples in Origen.[42] By contrast Origen's references to *philanthropia* fall largely into two categories: (1) Incarnation, the human life and death of Christ, and (2) revelation in the scripture and the teachings of Christ. A sense of Origen's overall project suggests that these two are strictly analogous: both scripture and the life of Christ are revelations of the Word, geared to providing the means of salvation for all mankind, whether simple or wise. Since the preliminary revelation in Old Testament scripture is completed in the coming of Christ, Origen perceives that the love for mankind is continuous between the one and the other, and is summed up in the taking of human nature by God the Word.

## (i) *Revelation*

I shall take one example of revelation as an act of *philanthropia*, *Contra Celsum* 7. 41.

[God who] through excessive *philanthropia* is able to give to the more intellectual a theology that is capable of uplifting the soul above the things of this world, and none the less descends even to the lowest level of the least well-endowed minds of uneducated men and the more simple-minded women and slaves and generally all those who have had no help from anyone but Jesus alone towards living a better life, as far as it was possible, with teachings about God that they could grasp.

This is one of many passages in the *Contra Celsum* in which Origen emphasizes Christianity's universal appeal, to the simple as well as the sophisticated.[43] In this passage such universality is a mark of *philanthropia*: it reveals the fact that God loves every human being for her humanity, not for her wisdom, virtue, or intellectual brilliance.[44] The intellectual revelation of theological doctrine, and the

---

[42] Apparent counter-examples: acts of providential intervention in specific cases, *ComJn*, 6. 36; *CCels*, 2. 78; indulgence in response to request *PEuch*, 29. 14. 7. The endowment of creation is never referred to *philanthropia*, though there may be some slight bias from the subject matter of the treatises that are preserved in Greek.

[43] See also *CCels*, 1. 9; 1. 27; 1. 64; 3. 50; 3. 54; 3. 75; 6. 1; 7. 59; 8. 50. The analogy with a doctor healing the sick occurs at 3. 62; 3. 74; 4. 15.

[44] This does not imply that women, slaves, and the like are naturally inferior. The analogy with the sick (*CCels*, 3. 74, SC 136. 166. 10) suggests that their weakness is accidental, not essential. *CCels*, 8. 50 is emphatic that they are equal members of society, and at *CCels*, 7. 44 Origen suggests that the simple have the best deal. Cf. *ComMt*, 15. 27.

concrete revelation of Christ's life on earth, are presented as two parts of the same project of illuminating the entire human race.

## (ii) *Incarnation*

Our main concern will be with the numerous passages that link God's love for mankind (*philanthropia*) with incarnation, self-emptying, sin and death. We can only look closely at a small selection that illustrate the points most clearly.

### (a) Incarnation

At *Contra Celsum* 4. 17 Origen distinguishes Christ's incarnation from the Platonic doctrine of routine descent of souls into mortal bodies in the cycle of reincarnation: 'He [Celsus] would have recognized one extraordinary descent, chosen out of abundant *philanthropia*, for the conversion of the "lost sheep of Israel", as Holy Scripture says in its mystical terminology . . .' Christ's incarnation stands out as distinct from Platonic reincarnation partly because it is unique and extraordinary, but mainly for its motivation. Unlike the Platonic soul, cast into bodily life as a punishment or imprisonment against its will, Christ's incarnation is chosen for a loving purpose, to redeem the lost sheep.[45]

### (b) Self-emptying and humiliation

Although Origen frequently presents the Incarnation as a form of teaching (a simpler substitute for book-learning) he does not gloss over the humiliation it involves on God's part. Humiliation serves not only as the means of accommodating God to the limits of human understanding,[46] and as an inconvenient necessity in the task of saving the lowly as well as the great,[47] but is also essential in the task of bearing the sins of all humanity, the task which ultimately requires the death of the 'lamb of God'. The kenosis is thus not only educationally desirable but also sacrificial.

---

[45] Cf. *ComJn*, 2. 31. The use of the word φιλανθρωπία of the Incarnation goes back to Titus 3: 4. Origen cites that text explicitly at *ComMt*, 15. 27; *HomJr*, 5. 1; *CCels*, 1. 64, and may have it in mind on several occasions when he uses φιλανθρωπία and χρηστότης together, e.g. *CCels*, 1. 67; 4. 15; 4. 26; 7. 44; *HomJr*, 1. 1; 4. 4. 11.

[46] Cf. *CCels*, 1. 9. 36; 2. 38. 23; 4. 15. 2.

[47] Cf. *ComMt*, 10. 1. 6; *CCels*, 3. 62. 6.

1. The best text to illustrate this theme is from the *Commentary on John*, 6. 57. 294:

It was a feature of the *philanthropia* of Jesus alone to eat and drink with sinners and tax-collectors, and to present his feet to the tears of the penitent woman, and to descend even to death on behalf of the ungodly, setting no high premium on his being in equality with God, and to empty himself, taking the form of a slave.

The context here concerns the fact that the angels would have been unwilling to tolerate the impurity and impropriety of associating with humanity in its unredeemed state before Jesus had done his cleansing work. Jesus is not such a snob as the angels: first, he does not mind associating with sinners and does not cling to his position of honour, and this is a mark of the universality and lack of prejudice that are characteristic of his love for mankind; but secondly the humiliation is itself the means of restoring humanity to a condition fit for God, and of overcoming death. Christ's death on behalf of the ungodly is part of the same move of self-emptying as having his feet washed with the penitent's tears, and is the means whereby his last enemy, death, is put under his feet, as Origen observes in the next chapter.[48]

2. Christ's 'stooping' to inferiority extends to his peripatetic manner of life; the fact that he visits every town and village illustrates his *philanthropia* that knows no prejudice:

We reproach the Jews because they attack Jesus's love for mankind, in that he did not despise any city, nor even any village of Judaea, in order that the kingdom of God might be preached everywhere: they criticize his wandering lifestyle as that of a vagabond or tramp lacking nobility of physique. But it is not lacking in nobility to endure such pains for the benefit of those who were unable to hear him in every place.[49]

*(c) Death and sin*

We have already seen that in the *Commentary on John* Origen links the self-emptying of Philippians 2: 6–7 with Christ's death.[50] The

[48] *ComJn*, 6. 57. 295–6. Kenosis is also associated with φιλανθρωπία in *CCels*, 4. 15 (see below) where Christ's purpose is analogous to a doctor healing the sick, *CCels*, 4. 15. 11–18.

[49] *CCels*, 2. 38. 23–29. Cf. *ComJn*, 13. 54. 369.

[50] *ComJn*, 6. 57. 294.

humiliation involved in that death is associated most notably with sin: Christ dies because he takes upon himself the sins of others. Origen twice refers that move to *philanthropia*.

### 1. *Commentary on John*, 2. 26. 166

No one should take it that we are disrespectful towards God's Christ when we say these things [sc. that he took upon himself the sins of others]; for by the same reasoning whereby the Father 'alone possesses immortality', whereas our Lord, through love for mankind, took death upon himself, the death on behalf of us, so also the Father alone satisfies the text 'in him is no darkness at all', while Christ, through his kindness to mankind, received on to himself the darknesses of ourselves, in order that by his power he should abolish our death and destroy the darkness in our soul.

Here *philanthropia* is the term used to explain why our Lord assumed death on our behalf, whereas his taking the darkness of our souls is a matter of τὴν πρὸς ἀνθρώπους εὐεργεσίαν. Clearly the two terms *philanthropia* and *euergesia* are saying much the same thing.[51] Origen is saying that both mortality and sin are assumed by Christ for the same reason (λόγῳ) and to the same end, that is to abolish death and sin. The motive is Christ's kindness or love for mankind. It is for this reason that it is no impiety to attribute sin, darkness, and death to Christ.

### 2. *Commentary on John*, 6. 53. 274

Indeed this lamb that is slain has become the expiatory oblation, according to certain mystical words, for the whole world; on behalf of that world, in accordance with the father's love, he accepted even slaughter, and bought the world with his blood from the one who had purchased us when we were sold for our sins.

---

[51] Both φιλάνθρωπος and εὐεργέτης are political terms familiar in Hellenistic motifs of kingship. Origen effectively inverts the conventional political images in applying these terms to the unkingly behaviour of Christ in taking death and sin upon himself.

Here *philanthropia* describes the attitude of the Father, but still
with reference to the redemption of the world and specifically to
the means of that redemption by the sacrifice of the blood of the
lamb. The lamb serves as the victim who takes upon himself the
sin and death of all humanity and it is in this sense that Origen can
say that the lamb is 'the man', the humanity of Christ.[52] Thus
*philanthropia* involves identification not with some perfect
humanity but with mankind in sin and death. Christ's role as victim
is an example of *philanthropia* because it is an act of becoming
*anthropos*.

I have used these examples to support my claim that Origen uses
the term *philanthropia* not to indicate the remote providence of
Stoic and Platonic gods, but rather a love that can only be expressed
in incarnation. The characteristic features of this love are that it
stoops to the level of humanity to the extent of assuming sin and
death, and that it shows no prejudice, respecting the fallen as well
as the great. Thus it appears that Origen does regularly ascribe to
God a love that involves total commitment to all humanity, in
accordance with the paradigm of the Good Samaritan in the Song
of Songs Commentary.

So far so good. We have two further questions to ask. First,
does this kind of *philanthropia* find a place in Neoplatonism? And,
secondly, can Origen accommodate it into his system without incon-
sistency?

---

[52] *ComJn*, 6. 53. 273. This has christological implications. In particular we can
see that Christ's pre-existent soul, being a prerequisite for his incarnation, is a
device that enables God's φιλανθρωπία to be both the distant condescension of
conventional kingship (since sin and death belong to 'the man') and an act of self-
sacrifice, since it enables the otherwise impassible God to become fully involved in
humanity. It explains also why the φιλανθρωπία characteristically expressed in the
Incarnation is only partly new, since God has been united to a perfect human *nous*,
and hence deeply involved in φιλανθρωπία, from time immemorial. What is added at
the Incarnation are the psychic and bodily aspects that enable the *nous/Logos* to feel
as fallen man feels, and to bear suffering, pain, and death. See Rowan Williams,
'Origen on the Soul of Jesus', in R. P. C. Hanson (ed.), *Origeniana Tertia* (Rome,
1985), 131–7.

## 9. NEOPLATONISM

Can the term *philanthropos* be used of the One, or of any member of the Neoplatonic hierarchy?[53] I propose to look at Plotinus and Porphyry.

### (i) *Plotinus*

Surveying the use of φιλανθρωπία in Plotinus is easy since it never occurs. I shall return subsequently to speculate on the reason.

### (ii) *Porphyry*

Porphyry uses the terms φιλανθρωπία and φιλάνθρωπος ten times in his extant works, but only once is the quality ascribed to the divine, and on that one occasion Porphyry disagrees with the view he presents. Why, asks Porphyry, at *Quaestiones Homericae ad Iliadem* 1. 50,[54] did the plague in *Iliad* 1 start among the dogs and mules? Some people, giving a 'rhetorical solution', say that the divine, being philanthropic, wanted to allow the Greeks a chance to repent.[55] This explanation, which Porphyry rejects, resembles comparable passages in Philo[56] and Origen[57] allegorizing Old Testament texts. Porphyry, unlike Philo and Origen, is not happy to ascribe philanthropic motives to God. It is tempting to speculate that by this time the idea smacked too much of Christianity for Porphyry's comfort. Elsewhere in his works *philanthropia* is practised only by

---

[53] Arguably we should ask not only about the occurrence of the words φιλανθρωπία and φιλάνθρωπος but also whether the same idea occurs under a different name. However I think it is probably obvious that nothing directly comparable to incarnation, or to the features I have been dwelling on, finds any place in Neoplatonism. What is now interesting is that even the word φιλάνθρωπος is no longer applied to the divine.

[54] This depends upon a reconstruction of Porphyry's QQ *Homericae* using evidence from the scholia. The wording cannot be wholly trusted.

[55] Porphyry favours a 'truer and philosophical' solution, on the basis that plagues arise out of the ground and hence affect the lower forms of life (dogs) first, and mules because they are essentially fragile.

[56] Compare Philo on God's purpose in the ten plagues, *De vita Mosis*, 1. 109–10; 134.

[57] Compare Origen on the captivity of Israel, *HomJr*, 1. 1 and 1. 3, where Origen calls God φιλάνθρωπος for providing the incentive to repentance.

humans towards humans or animals, but with no suggestion that they do so in imitation of a divine model.[58]

Thus it appears that Plotinian Neoplatonism specifically avoids attributing *philanthropia* to the divine, whereas Plato and Middle Platonists were content to do so. Yet Plotinus and Porphyry are not rejecting the providence of God nor the power of the divine to direct the world toward good. Like Origen they no longer use the term *philanthropia* for providence displayed in the natural order of the world. So, although the supreme Good is responsible for goodness in the world, it is never *philanthropos*. In linking the term to the Incarnation Origen may, I suggest, have contributed to its acquisition of associations that were unwelcome for Neoplatonism.

### 10. ORIGEN'S CONSISTENCY

Last, but not least important, is the question of Origen's consistency. If God is both object and subject of love, must he be both perfect and imperfect, perfect to be desirable and imperfect because himself engaged in desire?

We may leave aside for now the question of whether Origen does envisage that our love for God must depend on a lack.[59] God's love for mankind, his *philanthropia* as Origen presents it, by contrast, not only does not presuppose a prior weakness in God, but clearly crucially depends upon his stepping down from a position of prior strength to a position of weakness and emptiness. If we press the case we can derive an inverse symmetry between love for God, resulting in assimilation to God, and God's love for humanity, resulting in a sort of assimilation to mankind.

Something like our question was posed by Celsus, and Origen's reply appears at *Contra Celsum* 4. 15:

The one who descended to men subsisted 'in the form of God' and through *philanthropia* 'emptied himself' so that he could be accommodated by

---

[58] Porphyry, *De abst.* 1. 5. 4; 3. 20. 51; 3. 26. 48. *Ad Marcellam*, 5. 35. 13. *QQ Hom. ad Il.* 24. 15–16. *QQ Hom. ad Od.* 5. 118. 6; 7. 32. 8; 10. 329. 10; 13. 119. 48.

[59] This issue is problematic because it seems to imply that love ceases at the time the desire is fulfilled (see Gregory of Nyssa, *De an. et res.* 88–96). The issue is considered above, Ch. 1.

human beings. But it was not a change from good to bad for him, since he committed no sin; nor from beauty to ugliness, since he 'did not know sin'; nor did he come from good fortune to misfortune, but although he 'humbled himself', none the less he was blessed, even when he humbled himself for the benefit of our kind. But nor was there any change from best to worst for him; how could what is kind and philanthropic be 'worst'?

We might, in fact, want to quibble with Origen as to whether he need be so defensive in preserving the immutability of Christ in this passage; indeed elsewhere Origen is not afraid to make God passible.[60] But the most telling point is the last one: how could what is kind and philanthropic be 'worst'? To add *philanthropia* to God is to add a virtue, not a vice: it makes God more, not less, perfect.[61] Nevertheless, it is not a virtue that can be added to the One of Neoplatonism without seeming to compromise its transcendence and independence.

## 11. CONCLUSION

It has sometimes been suggested that God's relationship with humanity in Origen is modelled on fatherhood.[62] The fatherhood image does indeed fit into the Middle-Platonic conception of a provident deity rewarding the good and correcting the bad, but it clearly does not do justice to the distinction between providence and love. *Philanthropia*, as we have seen, is distinctive for the fact that it takes as its object those who have no filial ties, simply because they are human, not because they are sons. Thus, if we are treated as sons that is only because we have first been made sons by adoption in the first and greatest act of God's 'love for mankind', which was the incarnation of his own Son.

Thus, although there are numerous texts that presuppose that God acts towards us as a father towards his sons,[63] they do not explain the motivation by which God acts in this way. The question

---

[60] For example, *HomEzek*, 1. 4; 6. 6. Cf. *CCels*, 4. 18 on mutability in Christ's soul, again a matter of *philanthropia*. *ComMt*, 17. 17–20 is more hesitant.

[61] Compare *CCels*, 2. 38. 23–9.

[62] See, for example, Peter Nemeshegyi, *La Paternité de dieu chez Origène* (Paris, 1960).

[63] For example, *HomEzek*, 1. 1.

must go one further step back to recognize that God treats us as sons only because he first loved us as mere human beings with no claim on his love either of merit or descent.[64] This *philanthropia* differs from fatherly providence in that, so far from rewarding the good and chastising the wayward, it lays the sins of the wayward on the Son who is innocent.

[64] I would have said that we have no claims of kinship; but Origen is insistent, *PArch*, 4. 4. 10, that even after the Fall the image of God is not corrupted beyond recall, and that humanity retains a kinship, *consanguinitas* (perhaps = συγγένεια), with God. Restoration of the image depends on that residual affinity. Thus it would be incorrect to say that there is no kinship between God and humanity for Origen. But equally that does not detract much from the significance of transforming a minimal *consanguinitas* into filiation.

# 8

## Dionysius the Areopagite's *Divine Names* and the Meaning of 'God is Love'

It might arguably be fair to say that recent theology, that is particularly since World War II, has taken a special interest in love as an attribute of God. To some extent this has actually been a response to the events of World War II and the scale of the atrocities in the concentration camps; somehow the traditional doctrine of the impassibility of God seemed to make the problem of evil on such a scale hard to cope with: surely God, if he is a decent God at all, would not sit back and watch unmoved? Hence theologians on the defensive took to stressing God's interest and care for the suffering world, his involvement and presence in the parts apparently most god-forsaken, and his self-emptying love in doing so. This love has to carry the burden of explaining how it is that God is both good and caring while appearing either powerless or aloof.

There are three issues bound up in intimate connection: (i) the love of God and what counts as an example of loving response or action; (ii) the problem of evil; and (iii) the passibility or impassibility of God. The issues are not entirely new, but they arise in a new way because the demand that God should reveal himself as feeling for the victims of oppression (and not just sorrowing over the sins of the oppressors) leads to a conception of love as being manifested in suffering, grief, and subjectivity. It is nothing new to have much to say about the love of God: in the West Augustine or Aquinas might spring to mind more readily as a thinker steeped in the notion than any twentieth-century writer, while Origen and Gregory of Nyssa ensure that it is not absent from Eastern traditions either; but there remains something very different about twentieth-century talk of the love of God, that marks it out from both Eastern and Western traditional doctrines. On the other hand it might be fair to say that the recent theologians I have in mind come from the West.[1]

In this chapter I shall start by picking out the characteristic themes that can be illustrated from Process theology and from Moltmann (or rather one work of Moltmann, since I shall focus on *The Crucified God*; this should not be taken to imply that what I say here would apply to his later work). By juxtaposing these with the text from Dionysius that is the main subject of this chapter I hope to clarify the differences and explore why formulations that superficially have some resemblance lead to such different results.

## 2. GOD'S LOVE IN RECENT THOUGHT: TWO EXAMPLES

### (i) *Process theology*

It may seem predictable that I should use Process theology as an example of recent emphasis on God as one who loves. It makes a good straw man because here we can find explicit, or as near as we are likely to find it, the reassessment and adaptation of the divine names that Dionysius himself is concerned with. On the implications of rethinking the picture of God in Process terms Norman Pittenger has this to say: 'this means that the conventional list of divine attributes is in need of thorough revision, or at least careful reinterpretation.'[2] The attributes which Pittenger proposes to revise or reinterpret are the very ones that Dionysius interprets or reinterprets. Yet Dionysius' interpretations are largely what Pittenger might call the conventional ones, the ones Pittenger would gladly see modified if not abandoned. Perhaps this seems unsurprising. But the paradox is that for both Dionysius and Pittenger the interpretation centres on a unique role assigned to love. It is precisely because love is the most important feature of Pittenger's God that he wants to abandon the conventional interpretations. In the previous paragraph he had made that point: 'The distinctively

[1] Although there are 20th-century thinkers in the Eastern tradition who stress the love of God, the points made here cannot be taken to apply to them. For example, Sergei Bulgakov's account of the ecstasy of the Holy Spirit, and of kenosis, resembles Dionysius more than it resembles Moltmann.

[2] N. Pittinger, *The Lure of Divine Love* (New York and Edinburgh, 1979), 93.

Christian model ... can be stated very simply: God is the cosmic Lover ..... Above all God is Love, love-in-act, loving Action.'[3] 'God is love' is thus the central focus, but it is interpreted to mean that God is the Cosmic Lover, and it means that God's loving involvement with the world is the sum total of his being. It is this that requires the modification of attributes such as omnipotence, since omnipotence will be limited by God's total involvement with the world, his suffering love. On this view love is God's chief, or rather sole, characteristic and his sole activity. He depends on the world both for his being and for the sphere in which he acts.

## (ii) *Moltmann*

In *The Crucified God* J. Moltmann develops an interpretation of the claim that God is love in 1 John 4. Comparable with Pittenger's suggestion that this involves self-identification with the world and receptivity,[4] Moltmann stresses the unconditional nature of God's involvement, particularly with what is godless and forsaken.[5] Moltmann prefers to talk of God's grief, or more particularly the grief of the Father combined with the love of the Son, but the grief follows from the suffering love in which the Father is involved because of his pathos and his commitment to the world. The result is a stress on *kenosis*, God's self-emptying, but in Trinitarian terms this emerges as the delivering up and abandonment of the Son by the Father.[6] The Father's suffering-love involves him in such grief as to lead to a crisis, God's abandonment by God. It is called *kenosis*, but in the final analysis the Father's act is not strictly speaking *self-* emptying, since it is not himself that he empties: the Father appears to act out of desperation rather than gratuitous love (even though that desperation is brought on by an initially free and gratuitous love); he sacrifices the Son and it is the Son that 'suffers dying' while the Father 'suffers grief'.

In the forsakenness of the Son the Father also forsakes himself. In the surrender of the Son the Father also surrenders himself ... The Father

---

[3] Ibid.

[4] Ibid. 82.

[5] J. Moltmann, *The Crucified God*, 2nd edn., English translation, by R. A. Wilson and John Bowden, of *Der gekreuzigte Gott* (London, 1974), 247–8.

[6] Ibid. 241–7.

who abandons him and delivers him up suffers the death of the Son in the infinite grief of love.[7]

In this way Moltmann seeks to preserve relations within the Trinity. The Father continues, apparently, to love the Son while delivering him and abandoning him to the Cross, and hence the Father suffers too. But is his suffering and grief anything like a voluntary self-emptying? The grief is an on-going result of God's nature both before and after he delivers up the Son: it follows from his gratuitous love for the world which has weighed on his mind since the world began. In the Incarnation he does not make a new move of love but rather commits the ultimate deed of rejection and infanticide brought upon him by the dilemma of his infinite love for the world he created. All the suffering in human history is automatically the suffering of God because pathos and involvement with the world is the lot he has chosen. His love, then, and his humiliation and his grief and his self-emptying are not extraordinary acts of involvement with the world by a God who is ordinarily inclined to independence and self-sufficiency, but rather the typical, even unavoidable, actions of a God who neither would nor could, unless he changed his will, break out of the noose his love had got him into, because that love is himself.[8] His involvement with the world becomes a dependence and a weakness, a grief to him.

Of course we should be careful not to suggest that the love (or grief) that Moltmann's God has for the world is not free. Clearly God is under no compulsion from without, and he is entirely free to act in accordance with his nature and will, which is what constitutes God's freedom. In this sense his impassibility need not be threatened by the pathos and suffering he undergoes in relating to the world. His love may also be 'unmotivated' in the sense that it is freely given, demanding nothing in return. The contrast I am making is not between free love and compulsory love (indeed, compulsory love would seem to be an incoherent notion) nor between unmotivated and motivated love. Rather I am dis-

---

[7] Ibid. 243.

[8] On pp. 270–1 Moltmann argues that God's *pathos* is a free relationship, because 'creation, covenant and history of God spring from his freedom'. Thus God is not made subject to necessity imposed from without. On the other hand the pathos is not peculiar to the Incarnation. The thesis of *The Crucified God* is that it is in the event of Calvary that we perceive God's being as such; the vulnerability in evidence at Golgotha must be a vulnerability in the whole essence of God.

tinguishing between, on the one hand, the idea that God's ordinary love that he has for his creation entails humiliation and necessitates the Incarnation as a routine manifestation of that same love, and, on the other hand, the idea that the Incarnation was a separate decision, radically different from the love manifested in God's concern for his creation and not simply a logical consequence of it, because it was incarnation and not creation that involved humiliation. In other words it is a distinction between ordinary and extraordinary love.

One might be tempted to say that Moltmann's God is characterized by extraordinary love, because he is more loving than we might expect. When I speak of 'ordinary love' I do not mean to imply that it is dull, predictable, or ungenerous. God's love is ordinary not in relation to what we might expect a god to have but in relation to what God himself has in other contexts; thus on Moltmann's view, and on Pittenger's view, God ordinarily and universally has the suffering love that is manifested in total identification with all the sufferings of history, both as the zealous God of Israel, the provident creator, and the incarnate Christ on the cross. Alternatively we may suggest that God has both ordinary love and extraordinary love, and that the Incarnation is not simply another act of the same sort as creation and the providential regard for creation. To explore how this might be worked out and whether the result is satisfactory we can turn to Dionysius.

### 3. DIONYSIUS THE AREOPAGITE

I have chosen to look at the text in Dionysius the Areopagite's *Divine Names* not because it is typical, but rather because it looks as if it might be untypical; does it not look, after all, as though there is no real difference between the old and the new? Does not Dionysius say just what Moltmann and the others are saying now? I shall attempt to show that he does not.

The *Divine Names* is one of four treatises which, together with ten letters, form the corpus of Dionysius the Areopagite. The identity of the writer is unknown; he, or she, writes under the pen-name of the Dionysius mentioned in Acts 17: 34 as a convert of St Paul in Athens. 'But some men joined him and believed, among them Dionysius the Areopagite and a woman named Damaris, and others with them.'[9] In accordance with the identity he has adopted, Dionysius cites no authorities later than the New Testament and the Apostolic Fathers by name, and up to the fifteenth century it was generally assumed that he was who he said he was.[10] Nowadays, however, few would be happy to place the works earlier than the fifth century AD and we have no evidence that they were known before 532. The main reason for thinking that the writings could not have come from the pen of the original Areopagite of Acts, whoever he was, is that they are steeped in Neoplatonism. Short of suggesting that Plotinus and Proclus were followers of Dionysius the Areopagite we have little option but to conclude that Dionysius knew the work of Proclus and Plotinus. Dionysius himself frequently names someone called Hierotheus as his teacher; it is not clear whether this is part of the fiction of his pseudonym or whether it refers to a teacher of his own (fifth- or sixth-century) day. In general, internal and external evidence seems to point to a Syriac milieu for the Dionysian writings and probably also for the teacher called Hierotheus.

Dionysius is particularly concerned with apophatic theology, the way of negation and the general problem of how it is possible to speak about God. It is in this connection that he embarks upon his discussion of the *Divine Names*. These names include love, *eros*, and Dionysius' discussion of love is important not only because it is an extended discussion of what it means to call God 'love', which gives it scarcity value, but also because it is famous for two reasons in particular. One is that Dionysius discusses the difference, or as he sees it lack of difference, in meaning between the terms *eros* and *agape* when applied to the love of God (by, for, or from God). He argues against being fussy about terminology and in favour of using *eros* of God. For this he incurred the wrath of Anders Nygren.[11] The defence of the term *eros* occurs in chapter 4 of the Divine

---

[9] To be a member of the court of the Areopagus in the 1st century AD was essentially an honorific status, which would imply that Dionysius was a high-ranking citizen, had probably been archon, and was most likely well educated. Hence it is not inappropriate to attribute sophisticated philosophical treatises to him. Only the anachronistic content of the philosophy is improbable.

[10] Dionysius cites Ignatius at *DN* 709B and 'Clement the Philosopher' at *DN* 824D, in addition to names known from the New Testament. This would imply a 'dramatic date' of about 110 AD at the earliest. Dionysius would be rather elderly.

[11] Nygren, *Agape and Eros*.

Names, 708D–709D. This passage is not our immediate concern at present.

The other aspect of this passage that is notorious is that, despite being strongly coloured with Neoplatonism, it envisages not only that the lower orders of being in the hierarchy will love and yearn for the supreme one but also that the supreme one itself loves the lower orders of being, with an ecstatic love that is 'downward flowing'. The fact that the supreme one is not only *eromenos*, a beloved, but also *erastes*, a lover, is often hailed as new in Dionysius and highly significant. Here at last, Michele Schiavone suggests,[12] Neoplatonism bows to real Christianity: here we have God not as *amatus* only but also as the act of love towards all being; this is unknown to Aristotle, Plato, Iamblichus, and Proclus; its origin is solely in the Gospel message. Unlike pagan Neoplatonism, maintains Schiavone, Dionysius has given us a personal conception of God, the God of Holy Scripture not a metaphysical principle.

Rist goes less far in the extent of innovation he attributes to Dionysius; according to him the ingredients were all there in his Neoplatonic predecessors, and it is the combination of them that is Dionysius' real achievement. Proclus did envisage a love that descends, though within strictly defined limits; but Proclus' first principle is not *eros*. Dionysius has combined Plotinus' notion that the first principle is *eros* with Proclus' vision of a descending, as well as an ascending, love. That is Rist's view.[13]

Both Rist and Schiavone assume that Dionysius has been led to modify his Neoplatonism and introduce the loving God because of his Christianity and his concern to adapt his theory to the themes of scripture.[14] In other words they imply that in Dionysius (1) the love that God has towards his creatures is intended to represent the love that is ascribed to God in Christian scriptures, (2) that it does correspond to the Gospel message in a recognizable way, and (3) that Dionysius was right to make these changes. By contrast I am proposing (1) that the love attributed to God by Dionysius in this passage is not motivated by Christian but by Neoplatonic

---

[12] Michele Schiavone, *Neoplatonismo e cristianesimo nello Pseudo-Dionigi* (Milan, 1963), 86–7.

[13] J. M. Rist, 'Eros and Agape in Pseudo-Dionysius', *Vigiliae Christianae*, 20 (1966), 235–43; 235 and 239–40.

[14] See also the similar approach in C. A. Bernard, SJ, 'La Doctrine mystique de Denys l'Areopagite', *Gregorianum*, 68 (1987), 523–66; 548, 550; also Nygren, *Agape and Eros*, 583.

considerations, (2) that it does not correspond to the kenotic love ascribed to God in the New Testament in connection with the Incarnation and Atonement, and (3) that Dionysius was right.

In chapter 4 of the *Divine Names* Dionysius discusses first the name 'Good': God is the good, or goodness itself;[15] secondly 'beauty' or the beautiful;[16] and thirdly 'love'.[17] It is instructive to see that the account of these names is to some extent parallel. In each case Dionysius starts with the notion that the One (Goodness and Beauty) is the cause of those qualities in all other things. God is the Good primarily in the sense that all good things receive their goodness from him, are made good by him.[18] The good is the source of their being and of all order and intelligence and immortality among the ranks of creation since all these things are good. Hence it is that creation flows from his superabundant goodness.

The same goes for beauty. God is beauty because he is the source of beauty in all things.[19] What follows first and foremost from the fact that God is beauty and goodness is that his creation, the things that relate to him, partaking of his goodness and yearning for it, are themselves good and beautiful. And hence it is that love is treated in the same way:[20] love is the power that causes various things to love each other, and the cause of all forms of love, both of inferiors for their superiors, of equals for equals and of superiors for their inferiors, all these God causes or inspires in respect of being love.[21]

Nevertheless, the causal sense in which God is goodness, beauty, and love is not the only sense. Dionysius is too much of a Platonist to allow that his principle of goodness and beauty should itself be devoid of goodness and beauty. Hence he is committed to self-predication: the Good is itself good and Beauty is itself beautiful.[22]

[15] *DN* 693B–697B.
[16] *DN* 701C–708A.
[17] *DN* 708A–713D.
[18] *DN* 693B.
[19] *DN* 701C.
[20] *DN* 712C, 709C–D.
[21] *DN* 708A, 709D, 712A. On the causal meaning of terms such as αὐτοαγαθότης and αὐτοκάλλος see *DN* 11. 6 (953D–956B).
[22] Dionysius appears to deny self-predication in *DN* 654CD, but only in the sense that we are not to suppose that God *has* the qualities in exactly the same way as things that 'participate' have them. This (*a*) fits Dionysius' apophatic approach that resists straightforward assertions about the divine attributes, and (*b*) guards against the Third Man argument that would infer that God has the properties because he participates in something higher.

This is not much discussed in connection with the name 'good', perhaps because of an ambiguity in the account of the Good that makes it seem obvious that Goodness itself must be good; all things, we are told in 4. 1–4, have their being because of the Good which extends its goodness to all existent things[23] and throws its rays of goodness on to all things so that they live and have being. Perhaps this means only that it gives them the goodness that they derive from it, but in providing such goodness it can hardly fail to be, itself, good. Thus we understand that in bestowing being and goodness on other things the Good is itself good, is characterized by the same quality that it causes.

When we get to beauty Dionysius gives us a full discussion of the difference between beauty (*kallos*) and beautiful (*kalon*) and an argument for why the Beauty itself must be beautiful. Self-predication is made explicit.[24] In general, he says, we distinguish between beautiful and beauty, since the beautiful thing is what participates in beauty, and its beauty is its participation in that cause that makes things beautiful. But in the case of the transcendent beauty, we call it beauty (*kallos*) because it gives beauty to other things, but we also call it the beautiful (*to kalon*) because it is itself all-beautiful and super-beautiful, in an absolute and not a relative way. The account of how beauty is beautiful is closely reminiscent of passages of Plato in which he proposes that forms possess their characteristics in a non-relative way.[25]

Thus when we come to 'love' we are prepared for *eros*, as cause of *eros* in others, to be self-predicating too. Just as the Good itself is also good, and beauty itself is also beautiful, so also Love itself, the one who instils love in others, will also be loving. The basis for this claim, which Dionysius recognizes is a bold one[26] is not scripture but the logic of his Platonism. The system works like this: we could not explain how God could be love in the sense of the source or cause of love unless he were himself good and beautiful; it is because he is beautiful that he is desirable and lovable, that he is beloved, *eraston* and *agapeton*.[27] Self-predication of beauty and goodness is the basis for supposing that love is a name for God at

---

[23] *DN* 693B.
[24] *DN* 701C–D.
[25] e.g. *Republic*, 475d–80a; *Phaedo*, 74b–75a; *Hippias Major*, 288b–289d.
[26] *DN* 708A, 712A.
[27] *DN* 708A.

all, since he would not be lovable if he were lacking in goodness and beauty.[28] But by the same sort of reasoning God must be himself active in love to explain how he can be beauty and goodness in an efficient sense: to be the cause of beauty in other things God must have other things that can partake of his beauty and goodness and being. The existence of things outside God in which God is interested and about which he cares (is zealous[29] ) is best explained, according to the *Divine Names*, by the notion that God himself is characterized by that ecstatic love, the love that steps outside itself to live in, and for, the beloved. Beauty, goodness, and love are all tied up together in the one who creates in order to give his life, goodness, and beauty to the things he has made. Just as Paul, with ecstatic love for Christ, could say, 'It is no longer I who live, but Christ who lives in me'[30] so it would follow that the ecstatic God would be able to say, 'It is no longer I who live, but my creation lives in me.' The whole creation is the object of the divine creative love and providence that gives it being and keeps it in being.[31]

Two expressions of the love that God has towards what is outside himself are mentioned in *Divine Names* chapter 4: one is the fact that God is inclined (timelessly) to externalize himself and generate, the fact that he did not remain alone, and the other is his continuing providential care for things. In the first sense love logically pre-exists in the Good prior to (not temporally but logically) the generation of the Son and before creation. It seems clear that we are to take the passage about love as an explanation of the Trinity as well as about creation. 'For the beneficent love of things, pre-existing superabundantly in the Good, did not allow him to remain without offspring, barren by himself, but roused him to practical action in accordance with his superabundance that is generative of all

---

[28] This takes for granted a Platonic explanation of love as desire for what is good and fine. Contrast recent suggestions that love can only be directed at what is weak: e.g. the debate between Mora, 'Thank God for Evil', Lowe, 'No Love for God', and Mackinnon, 'Evil and the Vulnerability of God', which concludes that God can be lovable only in being vulnerable.

[29] *DN* 712A.

[30] Ibid.; Gal. 2: 20.

[31] In *CH* 177C, Dionysius suggests that goodness is the explanation for God creating things and that it was through goodness that he called them into communion with himself. In *DN* the latter function belongs to beauty. *CH* seems simply less precise, referring everything to goodness, while *DN* distinguishes the activities in order to show that ecstatic love is necessary for God's work of self-giving to get going at all.

things'.[32] The Trinitarian life of God and the fact that he is a creative God by nature are thus explained by ecstatic love. But it is also used to explain why he does not, like some gnostic deity, cut himself off from the World he has created—produce it and then forget it. Because of his love he lives for the world by taking a provident interest in it, making, perfecting, maintaining, and converting everything towards himself.[33] He does this from a position of inestimable superiority; this is the supreme example of that providential regard that superiors have towards inferiors which is one of the three types of love that Dionysius lists as the work of *eros*. This love involves no vulnerability, no shame, no humiliation, and no self-emptying: it proceeds from a superabundant fullness that has enough and to spare, can retain its position of absolute pre-eminence and yet take thought for things below, that can step outside itself and yet remain within itself undiminished.[34] This is not kenotic love and it has nothing to do with the Incarnation or the Cross. God remains intact.

Scholars have sometimes remarked on Dionysius' failure to mention the Incarnation when he talks of God's love. Explaining this omission, Rist suggests that Dionysius' interest is 'Cosmic Theology' here, and that he is following Proclus and the Neoplatonists' concerns. In other words, Rist implies that the Incarnation would have fitted in to the same account had Dionysius been concerned with that issue;[35] Bernard even suggests that in stressing the unity of *eros* and *agape* Dionysius is including the Incarnation as a manifestation of the same love.[36] But these apologies clearly will not do. Dionysius is interested in the Incarnation elsewhere;[37] its absence from this passage cannot be explained as an accident of context but is surely instructive.

For the clue to why the Incarnation cannot be included as an example of God's ecstatic love we might look at what is said about God's goodness. Dionysius, following Platonic tradition, draws an analogy between the Good and the Sun.[38]

---

[32] *DN* 708B.
[33] Ibid.
[34] *DN* 712B.
[35] Rist, 'Eros and Agape in Pseudo-Dionysius', 235, 243.
[36] Bernard 'La Doctrine mystique', 548.
[37] e.g. *DN* 648A–649A; *CH* 181BC.
[38] *DN* 693B.

And just as the sun in our realm, without making any deliberation and without making any choice, simply in virtue of its very being lights up all things that have the potential to partake of its light according to their particular measure, so in the same way the Good (which is above the sun as the transcendent archetype is in its very subsistence above the faint image) sends forth the rays of its entire goodness to all things that are, in an analogous manner.

So God creates and cares for the goodness of his creation as the sun lights the world, not deliberately, not because it chooses to, but just because that is the sort of thing it is. The sun is bright: it cannot help lighting up anything in a position to be lit; God is good: he cannot help providing for things that have the capacity to partake of his goodness; God is loving: he cannot help bestowing his love on all his creatures. Of course we are not to infer that these effects are contrary to the will of God any more than we should suppose that the sun is reluctant to warm the world. Dionysius does not say that God creates unwillingly, but simply that he neither deliberates nor chooses; he will not need to deliberate over an activity that is wholly in accordance with his nature and will.[39] Thus we are not invited to suppose that the need to create or externalize himself causes God any discomfort or grief; nor, indeed, does the on-going loving relationship that he has with creation, his providential regard for the well-being of things: this is simply a continuation of his goodness and ecstasy and cannot be a source of grief. Unlike Moltmann's God, who is crippled with grief by his involvement with a world he is unable to help, Dionysius' God is never inadequate. He pours forth goodness with such abundance that there is always more than enough, all that the world is capable of taking on board. His self-giving is the joyous ecstasy of living for the good of the beloved.[40]

That applies to God's creative love and to love within the Trinity, but it will not do for the Incarnation, which is, after all, the key feature of Christianity. It is for this reason that I argued that Dionysius' account of God's providential love for the lower orders of creation was not a concession to the Christian message, but

[39] This need not imply that individual actions are not chosen from a range of possible ones. What is not chosen is the type of action: God is not faced with a choice to be or not to be, to be good or not to be good, to create or not to create.

[40] *DN* 712A–B.

derived from the Neoplatonism of his system. Nevertheless this would not be entirely fair, since I also want to suggest that Dionysius' notion that God's essential nature includes an overflowing ecstatic love for what is outside itself is a proper prerequisite for a correct understanding of how *kenosis* works.

The Incarnation for Dionysius is not something automatic that follows from the Divine nature and involves no conflict with it; on the contrary it is a special event. It is undertaken on behalf of humanity in particular, not simply the whole creation,[41] and hence it cannot flow straightforwardly from that universal providence that the Good God has towards all creation. It is an act of choice,[42] not the inevitable consequence of God's loving nature; indeed, it required a deliberate choice on Christ's part not to abandon the human form he had taken upon himself,[43] and clearly there was a real option, and perhaps inclination, for him to do so. And finally it was an act of *kenosis*, a stepping down from God's normal over-flowing nature into an emptiness that was not his own, and it is in this that shame and humiliation are to be found: 'Christ emerged from the hiddenness of his divinity to take on human shape ... he came down to us from his own natural unity to our own fragmented level'.[44] This is in some sense to transgress the boundaries that God in his nature as justice and providence is concerned to preserve.[45] Although Dionysius urges that this did not mean the total loss of 'his own real condition',[46] nevertheless it is clear to him that this self-humiliation does not and could not follow logically from the transcendent nature he describes when he analyses the meaning of *eros*. The Incarnation is not said to be due to *eros*, nor *agape*, which Dionysius argued was the same thing. The Incarnation is always said to be due to *philanthropia*, and this is clearly not simply explained as the involuntary result of God's nature as the provident

---

[41] καθ' ἡμᾶς, *DN* 648A. For stress on the concern for humanity see *EH* 441AB.

[42] ταχθείσης τε καὶ αἱρεθείσης, *CH* 181C; cf. διαδέχεται, *EH* 440C.

[43] *CH* 181C.

[44] *EH* 444C (trans. Luibheid). Cf. *DN* 592A: φιλάνθρωπον δὲ διαφερόντως, ὅτι τοῖς καθ' ἡμᾶς πρὸς ἀλήθειαν ὁλικῶς ἐν μιᾷ τῶν αὐτῆς ὑποστάσεων ἐκοινώνησεν, ἀνακαλουμένη πρὸς ἑαυτὴν καὶ ἀνατιθεῖσα τὴν ἀνθρωπίνην ἐσχατιάν, ἐξ ἧς ἀρρήτως ὁ ἁπλοῦς 'Ιησοῦς συνετέθη, καὶ παράτασιν εἴληφε χρονικὴν ὁ ἀΐδιος, καὶ εἴσω τῆς καθ' ἡμᾶς ἐγεγόνει φύσεως, ὁ πάσης τῆς κατὰ πᾶσαν φύσιν τάξεως ὑπερουσίως ἐκβεβηκὼς μετὰ τῆς ἀμεταβόλου καὶ ἀσυγχύτου τῶν οἰκείων ἱδρύσεως. The feminine subject of this passage is the deity (θεαρχία).

[45] *DN* 889C–897C.

[46] *EH* 441B.

creator. Rather it is love beyond the call of duty, more than just providence, not involuntary but chosen at some expense, and chosen not for the sake of fulfilling his nature (as ecstatic love was) but to empty his nature for the sake of humanity. In other words kenotic love is not ecstatic love.

Kenotic love is the mark of the distinctively Christian message, as Dionysius observes.[47] But Dionysius quite rightly does not suggest that that is what he has described in his account of God as the principle of *eros*. On the contrary, that is used to explain only three types of love, ours for God, his for all things outside himself, and that of equals within or outside the Trinity.[48] It is not used to describe that peculiar kenotic love for humanity in particular that is manifested in the Incarnation and the events of Christ's life and death.[49]

So does the Cosmic Love described in 708A to 713D have any place in the Christian understanding of God? The answer must surely be yes. What Dionysius has described is the fullness of which kenosis can be the emptying; it is basically unhelpful to say that Christ reveals a God who is essentially self-emptying, since that offers us no notion of what it is that he can empty himself of. We cannot have a God whose sole nature is kenosis since when he empties himself there will be nothing but emptying of emptying; we cannot have a God whose sole activity is to break down barriers, since he will not then be breaking any barriers by doing so. Dionysius' God is not one who must empty himself to be true to his nature. On the contrary, the Incarnation is the act of self-sacrifice that goes beyond what is demanded and beyond what his creative love would lead us to expect; that love would keep him inviolate.

It is one thing to say that we need to know what it would mean for God to be full and another to say why Dionysius' account is appropriate. Two points need to be stressed: (1) the fact that the causal sense of God's goodness, love, and beauty is the primary one and (2) that we have a sense in which God can be loving and self-

---

[47] *DN* 648A.

[48] Rist, 'Eros and Agape in Pseudo-Dionysius', 241 suggests that the mention of love among equals refers particularly to the Trinity.

[49] Dionysius stresses the Incarnation as a whole, rather than just the Cross and death of Jesus. References to the passion and death of Christ are rare. However we are told that Christ 'was obedient to the arrangements of the Father' (*CH* 181C). Christ's death is prominent in explaining the symbolism of baptism, *EH* 404A–C.

giving without humiliation. A third point worthy of more detailed discussion than we can afford here is the question of the internal relationships within the Trinity which are a necessary background for understanding the Incarnation.[50] The first point preserves God's influence and gives him the capacity for independence; he is not in danger of becoming simply a sentimental old man who does nothing but worry about his offspring. Rather he starts from a position of power: without himself getting emotionally involved he could still be causally responsible for the being, goodness, and beauty in the world. As the supremely desirable object of love he can remain detached and yet make the world go round. Thus we are not in danger of finding that our God is nothing but a cosmic lover who cannot be lovable.

On the second point, Dionysius' account of this ecstatic love, which follows from his acceptance of self-predication, avoids the danger that we should be left with an image of God as, in his own nature, simply a remote and powerful manipulator. Rather God distributes his goodness and beauty not for his own ends but because he lives outside himself, in and for the objects of his love. Thus we are not committed to what might seem to follow from less attractive versions of kenosis—the idea that the self of which God empties himself is a dominating, omnipotent, ruthless, and revengeful God. Dionysius allows that he is good, provident, and loving, without thereby making his self-sacrifice an inevitable and meaningless conclusion. By nature he is involved in ecstatic love, a love which manifests the superabundant fullness of his goodness and beauty. By an additional move he chooses the kenotic *philanthropia* that involves humiliation and vulnerability, a breakdown of the hierarchy of dependence that his zealous concern for creation sought to preserve. Thus God's essential nature remains *both* loving and caring, *and* free of humiliation, and the full force of the humiliation undertaken in the Incarnation can be appreciated. God as we

---

[50] The Incarnation is God's own *self*-emptying because Father and Son are one in love; they are the overflowing of unity into trinity in ecstatic love. If the Father did not love the Son the Incarnation would manifest no love on the Father's part. But if the love that generates the Son were the same love that sent him to his death, namely an overriding love for the world at any cost, then even the generation of the Son would already look like an act of premeditated cruelty: he would be generated purely for the purpose of sending him to his death. Dionysius, by separating the two motives, can allow that God loves the Son regardless of his intention to redeem mankind.

know him in weakness and humiliation on the Cross, not only need not be God in his own nature, but cannot be, if we are to understand kenosis and give any meaning to the resurrection.

# 9

# Bonds of Love: Augustine, Dionysius, and Aquinas

It is sometimes said that Augustine, in the *De Trinitate*, identified the Holy Spirit as the bond of love (*nexus*, or *vinculum, amoris*) between Father and Son.[1] Strictly speaking this is clearly incorrect, since Augustine does not use either *vinculum* or *nexus amoris*. He consistently enumerates three elements, lover, beloved, and love,[2] and the Holy Spirit is occasionally identified as the third of these, love,[3] but love is not said to be a bond. Augustine does not identify the Holy Spirit as a 'bond of love' in so many words.

Nor indeed does Anselm, who takes up the idea of the Spirit as Love in chapters 49–57 of the *Monologion*, but does not elaborate on what love is.[4] Peter Lombard, likewise, follows Augustine for the most part.[5] But Aquinas has much to say about what love is, and though he also uses Augustine as his basis he differs from his predecessors in introducing the notion of bond into the analysis of love. *Nexus amoris* and *vinculum* occur occasionally[6] and *nexus Patris*

---

[1] The phrase 'bond of love', *nexus amoris* or *vinculum amoris*, is used to describe Augustine's theory by e.g. L. Hodgson, *The Doctrine of the Trinity* (London, 1943), 68, 110, 226; K. E. Kirk, in A. E. J. Rawlinson (ed.), *Essays on the Trinity and the Incarnation* (London, 1928), 224; F. W. Green, in the same volume, 298, where the phrase is apparently attributed to W. Sanday (who does not use it); L. Dewar, *The Holy Spirit and Modern Thought* (London, 1959), 120; A. I. C. Heron, *The Holy Spirit* (London, 1983), 89; R. P. C. Hanson, 'The Filioque Clause', in *Studies in Christian Antiquity* (Edinburgh, 1985), 290–1, where the phrase is attributed to Karl Barth (who does not use it).

[2] e.g. *De Trinitate*, 8. 10. 14 (*PL* 42. 960); 9. 2. 2 (961–2); 15. 6. 10 (1064); cf. 6. 5. 7 (*PL* 42. 928).

[3] *Amor, caritas*, or *dilectio*. Especially *De Trinitate*, 9. 12. 17 (*PL* 42. 970); 15. 17. 27–19. 37 (1080–7). The terms *caritas* and *dilectio* are interchangeable (*De Trin.* 15. 18. 32). *Caritas* is a species of *amor* (*Enarr. in Ps.* 31. 2. 5).

[4] The spirit is said to be a *communio* of Father and Son (*Monolog.* 57, p. 69). Love is identified as the substance of the *summus spiritus* (*Monolog.* 53, p. 66).

[5] e.g. Peter Lombard, *Sent.* I, dist. 10–14 and 17; but in I. 31. 6 he claims that the Holy Spirit is said to be *connexio*.

[6] *Nexus amoris, In I Sent.* 31. 3. 1; *Super Ev. Ioann.* 1. 2. *Vinculum, In I Sent.* 10. 1. 3; 31. 3. 2; 32. 1. 1.

*et filii* is a common phrase;[7] and the claim that love is a bond is attributed to Augustine's *De Trinitate*, inaccurate though this attribution is.[8] However, St Thomas notices that there are problems with applying this to the Spirit, and the definition of love as a bond is introduced as a difficulty.[9] In Quaestio 37 of the first part of the *Summa Theologica* the third objection to love as a proper name for the Spirit is that Love has to be a *nexus* or *medium*, according to Dionysius the Areopagite.[10] St Thomas recognizes that this fits ill with the Holy Spirit as an entity that proceeds. His reply is odd, since having distinguished between the love produced[11] by the principle who loves, on the one hand, and the relationship between lover and beloved on the other hand, he still concludes that the Holy Spirit is the love of Father and Son in both senses, as a mere medium and connection and also as a 'person' proceeding from them. We are left to conclude that the Spirit is a *nexus* and not a *nexus*.

Aquinas perhaps reached this conclusion through thinking that both Augustine and Dionysius the Areopagite had claimed that love, and hence the Holy Spirit, was a bond between the things it joined. But was Aquinas right to think that? In the remainder of this chapter I propose to look first in some detail at the passage of Dionysius to which Aquinas alludes, then more briefly at what Augustine was saying, and finally to consider how helpful it is to think of the notion of a bond of love in the context of the Trinity.

I. DIONYSIUS, *DIVINE NAMES* 4

Let us understand by the term 'eros' a certain unifying and combining force. This applies whether we might be speaking of divine love, angelic love, intellectual love, the love of souls or love in nature ...[12]

---

[7] e.g. *In I Sent.* 10. 1. 3; *Summa Theol*, 1a, 37. 1; 39. 8; 1a 2ae, 1. 8; 3a, 3. 5.

[8] *Summa Theol*, 1a 2ae, 26. 2; cf. also 28. 1. But elsewhere Aquinas refers to Dionysius rather than Augustine, e.g. *Summa Theol*, 1a, 37. 1; *In I Sent.* 10. 1. 3.

[9] *Summa Theol*, 1a, 37. 1; *In I Sent.* 10. 1. 3.

[10] The reference is evidently to *DN* 4. 12 (709C) and 4. 15 (713B); see below.

[11] 'Spirated', *Summa Theol*, 1a, 27. 4.

[12] *DN*, 4. 15, 713A.

These are the words which the writer of the *Divine Names* attributes to his own teacher; he is quoting from a text that he calls the *Erotic Hymns* of blessed Hierotheus.[13] Dionysius himself had said something rather similar, using much of the same vocabulary, three sections earlier in his treatise at chapter 4. 12, 709C:

To those who understand the divine scriptures aright, it is with the same force that the term 'agape' and the term 'eros' are applied on the part of the sacred writers in accordance with the divine revelations. And this is for a force that is one-making and binding, and one that is peculiarly sustaining in the beautiful and good ...

These two passages, making reference to love as 'a force that unites and combines', appear to be the texts to which Aquinas refers, when he appeals to the authority of Dionysius in connection with discussions of love. St Thomas quotes, or alludes to, one or other of these two passages about the unifying force of love on at least seventeen occasions in his major works. But while St Thomas seems to make no distinction between the two passages in Dionysius, a closer look at the point Dionysius is making may suggest that he was not merely repeating himself.

On most of the occasions on which St Thomas cites Dionysius on the unifying force of love it is unclear which of the two passages in chapter 4 of the *Divine Names* he has in mind. Indeed, it seems unlikely that Aquinas is concerned to make any distinction between the two, since what he has picked up from Dionysius is a brief formula that serves to define love, a formula consisting of the claim that love is a *vis unitiva* or, sometimes, *virtus unitiva*: 'a force that unites'.[14] On the other hand, on some occasions Thomas adds a third element to the formula, claiming that love is *virtus unitiva et concretiva*, 'a force that unites and compacts'.[15]

First of all we can set aside any distinction between *vis* and *virtus*. St Thomas seems to use the two terms interchangeably. In his own exposition of the *Divine Names* he uses the term *virtus* to translate

[13] Ἱεροθέου τοῦ ἁγιωτάτου ἐκ τῶν ἐρωτικῶν ὕμνων. It has been suggested that the title 'erotic hymns' refers to a commentary on the Song of Songs; see Ceslai Pera, OP, commentary on Aquinas's expositio of this passage (Turin and Rome, 1950), 153. The identity of Hierotheus is unknown apart from the references in Dionysius.

[14] *Quaest. Disp. de carit.* 9. 7; *De spe*, 1. 11; *Summa CG* 1. 91. 758; *Summa Theol*, 1a, 37. 1. 3; 1a 2ae, 26. 2. 1a, 2m; 28. 1. sc.; 2a 2ae, 25. 4c; 29. 3. 3m.

[15] *Summa Theol*, 1a, 60. 3. 2a; 1a, 20. 1. 3a; 1a 2ae, 25. 2. 2a.

δύναμις in both occurrences of the phrase, but evidently he was also familiar with other translations that had used the term *vis*. There seems no reason to pin any importance to which of these terms he uses on each occasion, and neither indicates that he is referring to one or the other passage in particular.

It is also true that we cannot infer from the addition of *concretiva* which of the two passages in the *Divine Names* is being cited. *Concretiva* translates συγκρατική (combining) in Hierotheus' text at 713A, where love is said to be a unifying and combining force. But the same term συγκρατική (sustaining) occurs in Dionysius' own phrase at 709D, and is similarly translated by Thomas, in his *expositio* of this passage, as *concretiva*. In the latter case συγκρατική is the third characteristic attributed to love, whereas in Hierotheus' text it was the second, as it appears in Aquinas's formula;[16] but either text would be sufficient for St Thomas to derive the simple formula *virtus unitiva et concretiva*. It seems plain that St Thomas takes *both* passages to be putting forward the same analysis of love, an analysis that can be briefly summed up in the definition 'a force that unifies and compacts'.

Dionysius uses the same kind of language in two passages, one in his own name and one in the name of Hierotheus. Aquinas seems to treat them as saying much the same thing. But is Dionysius actually doing the same thing in both places? Do the two passages say the same? Since the second passage purports to quote another writer it is, of course, conceivable that it makes the same point as the earlier passage, and serves as an authority in support of the same view. On the other hand that is not the only possibility. Dionysius does say that Hierotheus' work bears on the same topic,[17] but it need not follow that all that he himself was saying was supposed to be merely repeating what Hierotheus had said. Some have wondered whether Hierotheus is anyone other than Dionysius himself, given the similarity of his thought and expressions; but the similarity of the vocabulary should not lead us to overlook the differences, or to suppose that they are talking about the same issue.

---

[16] The second adjective used at 709D is συνδετική (binding); it is not explicitly included in Aquinas's formula, but appears to be in his mind since he cites the formula as evidence that love is a kind of bond, *Summa Theol*, 1a 2ae, 26. 2; 28. 1.

[17] *DN* 713A.

## (i) *The passage from 'Hierotheus', 713A–B*

Let us understand by the term 'eros' a certain unifying and combining force. This applies whether we might be speaking of divine love, angelic love, intellectual love, the love of souls or love in nature. It motivates the higher things to providence for the inferior, and again the things of the same status to communal relationship, and at the furthest extremes the subordinate things towards conversion to the better and superior.

In the first place the passage purporting to come from the work of Hierotheus explicitly provides an account of love that is to apply to all kinds of love, whether divine or among angels or in any other section of the hierarchy. What is love in any of these cases? What we mean by love, the author suggests, is the same in all these cases, since it refers to a force that unites and combines things.

Hierotheus seems to be seeking a definition of love that applies across the board in all cases. Having given us a list of five kinds of love—divine, angelic, intellectual, love at the level of souls, and natural love—he then includes a list of the effects that the force of love may have. These effects include not only love between members at the same level of the hierarchy—love between those of equal rank—but also the upward response of lower orders to the higher and the downward-looking care of higher orders for the lower. It appears that he lists these three directions that the force of love may take as a corrective, lest his initial list of types of love implied that love was only between those at the same rank in the (Neoplatonic or Christian) hierarchy. Angels may have angelic love for angelic objects; intellects may have intellectual love for intellectual objects; but could an angel have a love for an intellectual object? Hierotheus seems to say yes, that it is the *same* force for unity and combination that operates between the members of different ranks when they turn in devotion to what is higher or to what is lower in a spirit of providential concern.

We have, in the passage attributed to Hierotheus, a purely general definition of love. There is no reference in this context to any passages from scripture, and although the definition is clearly intended to include love of a divine kind it does not say anything specific about that. Indeed, if we ask whether Hierotheus had a view on whether God has a particular kind of love for any particular objects, we should be unable to answer it from this passage. Hierotheus seems concerned to affirm that wherever love occurs it is a force of a unifying kind; he does not claim that it necessarily occurs in all the cases or between all the ranks, but where it does occur it will have the unifying effect. When he observes that the providential concern of higher ranks for lower ranks is an example of the effect of love, he does not specify which of the higher ranks show this concern, nor for which objects, nor in what circumstances. We might suppose that he thought that God sometimes showed care for some of his creatures, but we are not told when or why.

The same is not true of the two subsequent passages apparently quoted from later in the same work of Hierotheus.[18] Here the author claims to have explained what the various kinds of love are that do occur in the world, and seeks to gather them into a coherent system, ultimately with reference to the transcendent cause of all love. He concludes that there is a single self-moving force for unity that reaches out from the good to the very last rungs in the Platonic hierarchy and back. There is little to determine whether Hierotheus' Platonism is 'Christianized', but in these passages at least he seems to have made no reference to scriptural texts.

The first extract from Hierotheus at 713B, claiming that all love is understood as a force that unifies and combines, seems to be an observation of the most general sort. It matches exactly the use made of it by St Thomas, when he cites the phrase as a universal definition of love in all kinds of contexts concerned with love, whether human or divine. It makes a point about the definition of love, but contributes no further analysis of when or where the phenomenon occurs.

(ii) *The passage in Dionysius' own name, 709C–D*

To those who understand the divine scriptures aright, it is with the same force that the term 'agape' and the term 'eros' are applied on the part of the sacred writers in accordance with the divine revelations. And this is for a force that is one-making and binding, and one that is peculiarly sustaining in the beautiful and good, one that was formerly established

[18] 713B–D.

thanks to the beautiful and good, and given forth from the beautiful and
good thanks to the beautiful and good, a force that holds together things
that are of the same rank in accordance with their communal relationship,
a force that motivates the principal things to their providential regard for
the subordinate, a force that establishes the inferior in their conversion
towards higher things.

I want to suggest that this passage at 709C–D is doing something
rather different from the passage from Hierotheus at 713A–B. It
is, I suggest, developing and using the same terminology as the
quotation from Hierotheus, but using it to say something about
how and why love, of a certain sort at least, must be attributed to
God and must be derivative from God. In this passage, it seems,
he is not merely alluding to a common definition of love, but is
explaining the connection between unity in love when properly
understood, and the unity of 'the beautiful and good', which is
itself inescapably both object of love and involved in love.

Dionysius, unlike Hierotheus, has started out with some texts
from scripture to explain, and begins with an explicit concern with
the scriptural vocabulary for love. Given that some theologians are
prepared to speak of *eros* while scripture itself rarely uses the term
and speaks more often of 'charity', are we to suppose that one term
rather than the other is more proper for the divine? There are three
questions before us in *Divine Names* 4. 12:

1. Is one term, rather than another, correct for the love of God?
2. Regardless of the terms used, can it be right to suppose that
   God has erotic love?
3. If we claim that scripture does attribute erotic love to God,
   what justifies that as theologically or philosophically appropriate?

The three questions are very closely related, and Dionysius deals
with them in order in 4. 12. In the course of his discussion he
attempts to distinguish genuine erotic love from something else
that we normally think of as charity, and also to distinguish genuine
erotic love of the sort approved by God from certain kinds of
partiality and divided loves of a bodily sort that we tend to think of
in erotic terms.

Answering the first question, concerning the correctness of one
term rather than another, Dionysius concludes that it is incorrect

to make a fundamental distinction between *eros* and *agape* with regard to the divine. This is not to say that he wishes to eliminate the distinction altogether in any context. His point concerns what is appropriate with regard to the divine and to the usage of theologians and the writers of scripture. Observing that they use the two terms interchangeably is not necessarily to say that the two terms have the same sense in any context. It is important to notice that Dionysius does not say, as Hierotheus does at 713A, that his present analysis of love applies to all kinds of love at all levels of the hierarchy.

Does Dionysius think that all charity amounts to erotic love? In 4. 11 he had explained how two different expressions might be used to convey the same idea, or to refer to the same thing, to show that a verbal difference need not entail a difference of reference. The examples suggest that we should not infer that the two terms, which refer to the same thing, are used with exactly the same sense. We may, for example, refer to the number four either by the word 'four' or by the expression 'two twos'. We need not suppose that the two phrases are indistinguishable in meaning. So *eros* and *agape* may sometimes, that is in the case of the love that the scriptures speak of, refer to the same kind of love. But Dionysius does not deny that people take the terms as having different connotations, presumably because in other contexts besides that of the divine love they may mean different things.[19]

Dionysius recognizes, then, that *eros* and *agape* can have different implications, and mean different things in different contexts; but he wants to claim that the other usages, outside the divine context, are in some sense a mistake. They are a mistake because the divided and bodily love which people call '*eros*' is not real love; it is not even a true likeness of the genuine love; it bears some almost accidental relation to love itself.[20] So if the terms *eros* and *agape* carry different meanings in our ordinary talk of particular love, that is not their proper meaning, because it does not speak of what is genuinely called 'love', the thing to which the words primarily

[19] See, for example, 709B–C where people are said to think of an inadequate bodily form of love as *eros*, and scripture's avoidance of the term is to exclude such connotations. Clearly in that context '*eros*', rather than *agape*, serves to name this inferior kind of love, and hence the two terms carry over distinct meanings even where, in divine love, they both refer to the superior kind of love.

[20] 709B–C.

refer, which is a love that most of us are unable to comprehend.[21] Dionysius, as a Platonist, links the primary meanings of terms to the genuine and perfect form, even where that is inaccessible to those who generally use the language in question.

The words for love, then, have a proper use and a transferred use; the proper use is for the unified divine love; the transferred use occurs in our language about partial and divided love at the particular and bodily level. It is only in the latter context that the two words refer to different kinds of love, while in their proper use they name the same divine love, although by a kind of contagion they may imply some of the connotations of the transferred usage. There is no fundamental distinction between two kinds of love at the divine level. Genuine love is the love that flows from the beautiful and good, and at that level both terms are used to mean the same thing by the writers of scripture.

This means that there is a significant difference between what Dionysius says here at 709B–C and his later quotation from Hierotheus at 713A–B. There Hierotheus says that his definition of love as a unifying force applies to whatever kind of love we care to mention. But Dionysius speaks only of a special context in which *eros* is used by the writers of scripture, and used in a way that is interchangeable with *agape*. Then it carries a rather different meaning from some other occasions where it speaks of a love at a lower level. So Dionysius asks what force the term carries in that special divine context; the writers use the term, he suggests, to refer to a force that is peculiarly associated with unity.[22]

It seems, then, that the term *eros* is not always used of the force for absolute unity that it occasionally and properly names in the scriptures. Earthly-minded thinkers understand it in a different way because they normally use it to name a different kind of love that is partial and divisive. So Dionysius' definition of love at 709C–D—'and this is for a force that is one-making and binding, and one that is peculiarly sustaining in the beautiful and good ...'—gives the meaning of the terms for divine love in Holy Scripture, but not the meaning of the term *eros* in any other context, whereas Hierotheus, and later Aquinas, sought a definition of 'love' for any context.

[21] 709B–C.
[22] 709C–D.

Dionysius' explanation of the meaning of the term *'eros'* in the sacred writers also provides the answers to the other two questions tackled in this section of the chapter. Should we say that genuine erotic love is a divine attribute? And if so why is it philosophically correct to do so? It is not merely scriptural authority that guides what is correct language about God. It is satisfactory to use the term *eros* because its meaning is appropriate and justified by the philosophical implications. The reason why love is proper to God is because divine love is an impulse to a kind of unity beyond the comprehension of our ordinary loves. It is this link with absolute unity that must make love, for the Platonist, no accidental attribute of God but an essential feature, since Dionysius' God is the One of Platonic philosophy, or 'the beautiful and good' that is the object of all desire and the source of all that is.

So for Dionysius it is not true, as apparently it is for Hierotheus, that any example of love is a kind of force that seeks to unite and combine two things of any kind. Dionysius thinks that that is the case for genuine love, but that genuine love is 'one-making' precisely because it is properly located in the One. It makes things one because it is the One at work outside itself; and that will not be true of love that does not originate in the unity of the beautiful and good, so that the love that we speak of when we use *eros* of earthly love will not necessarily be an example of a force for unity in so far as that love may be far from reflecting the divine love that is properly called *eros*. Dionysius proceeds to specify that the source of such love lies in the beautiful and good, 709D, and lists a number of examples where this love may occur between the ranks of the hierarchies. But his observation is not a general one about a definition of the word 'love'. It is a specific answer to the question about the meaning of the term in scripture, that shows why it is right to say that God must be involved in erotic relations, and why *eros* will have a particular meaning in that context. If that is what *eros* means in that context it will be undeniable that it is an appropriate attribute for God.[23]

---

[23] See further Ch. 8 on Dionysius' Platonist reasons for attributing outward-flowing love to God, in addition to the upward-tending desire of others for God.

(iii) *The notion of a 'bond'*

If this interpretation is right, it is the second passage of Dionysius, the passage in which he purports to cite Hierotheus, that best fits the use that Aquinas makes of the reference to unity. St Thomas derives from this passage a general definition of love as something that brings things together and unites them. For Dionysius that is true of the proper love that springs from God; Hierotheus, like Aquinas, offers that as a general account of anything we call *eros*. But Aquinas derives from Dionysius not only the claim that love is a 'unifying force' but also the authority for claiming that love is a 'bond'.

Even if we are right to suggest that Aquinas has in mind the second of the two passages in chapter 4 of the *Divine Names* it is not obvious why Aquinas should take Dionysius to be speaking of a 'bond'. The phrase he quotes speaks of a 'unifying force',[24] but it remains unclear why we should take Dionysius' 'unifying force' to be a bond. Dionysius uses the word *dunamis*;[25] St Thomas, as we have seen, translates it *virtus* in his commentary on the *Divine Names*, and sometimes *vis*, sometimes *virtus*, in his other works.[26] Nothing in the text of the *Divine Names* requires that it be taken to mean 'bond'; it is said to be a 'binding power' as well as a unifying and combining power,[27] but we might still take this to be the cause of any bonds rather than the bond itself.

To find the basis of St Thomas's interpretation we can turn to his own commentary on the passage at *Divine Names* 713B. There he argues that the phrase 'unifying and combining power' is merely a circumlocution for the simple 'unification' (*unitio*). 'Power' here cannot signify an act or passion since love is not an act or passion; hence we are not to take 'unifying power' as meaning power to produce unification or bonds, but as itself the unification or bond that joins the objects. Hence we are to read Dionysius' phrase '*virtus unitiva*' as if it read '*unitio*' and our surprise at this phrase being support for the notion that love is a bond may be resolved.

---

[24] *Summa Theol*, 1a, 37. 1. He also refers to the phrase on fifteen other occasions.
[25] 713B: ἑνωτικήν τινα καὶ συγκρατικὴν ... δύναμιν.
[26] *Vis unitiva* in *Quaest. Disp. de carit.* 9. 7a; *De spe*, 1. 11a; *Summa Theol*, 1a, 20. 1; 37. 1; 1a 2ae, 25. 2; 2a 2ae, 29. 3. *Virtus unitiva* in *Summa CG* 1. 91. 758; *Summa Theol*, 1a, 60. 3; 1a 2ae, 26. 2; 28. 1; 2a 2ae, 25. 4.
[27] συνδετισῆς, 709C.

Nevertheless it is not evident that St Thomas is correct to interpret Dionysius thus. As regards the text there is little to tell in favour of a different view, since Dionysius is quoting Hierotheus and it is hard to reconstruct what he might have had in mind. The phrase that mentions the 'unifying force' is, in any case, not prominent in the passage in the way it becomes significant in Aquinas. All the same it seems possible that St Thomas is conflating cause and effect. He says that a binding force can be either a process bringing about bonds between two things or the bond itself that joins them. I take it that he means that we could think of my act of tying the rope round your wrists as a binding force that causes your wrists to be bound together; that would be a process that causes a bond. Alternatively we could say that the rope that is tied round your wrists is a binding force that holds your wrists together. In that case we are thinking of the bond itself as a 'binding force'. In the first case, then, it is the process that I engage in as I wind the rope around that constitutes the force. But love, Aquinas claims, is not a process like that, so that kind of account of how love provides a unifying force will not do. Given the initial dilemma, we are now left with only one option, that the 'unifying force' is the bond itself. That conclusion plainly depends upon his initial claim that there are only two ways in which something can form a binding force, but arguably there could be a third option that allows that a binding force might be neither the bond itself, nor the *process* by which such a bond is created, but the cause or tendency which leads to the formation of such bonds.

Take for example someone who is fond of cats. Because of her fondness for members of the feline species she has a tendency to cultivate the acquaintance of cats whenever she has the opportunity, as a result of which she may form certain bonds or relationships with certain individual cats. It may happen, however, that from time to time she has no opportunity to indulge her fondness because she knows no friendly cats to form a relation with. Now, it is clear that she is still fond of cats even when there is no bond with any particular cat. So the fondness for cats is not identical with the bond of relationship. Nor is it identical with the process by which she forms such bonds, for that will involve stroking, petting, feeding perhaps, or allowing it to sit on her lap; none of these processes will be going on when she has no cat to communicate with. Yet her love of cats may yet remain, and perhaps grieve over the absence of the opportunity to express itself. It seems clear, then, that the love is the cause which leads her to engage in the processes of forming an attachment, and to form the bonds of attachment. In this sense, then, love is something other than either the process or the bond.

The same account seems to be required for God's love of mankind. The bonds of God's love will be formed with individuals so that the love which God has for mankind in general will not be any one bond. That would imply that he loved only one human being, or else that he had no general love for mankind, but only individual relationships. But it seems we need to claim that he has a general love that makes him inclined to engage in such relationships with individuals. On the other hand, we cannot say this is simply a sum of all the individual relationships, since we also need to hold that his love makes him consistently inclined to enter into more bonds of love, just as the cat-lover will consistently seek acquaintance with any available cat. Thus it seems we should need to challenge the idea that love is either the process of forming bonds, or the bond itself. In these cases at any rate we have a third option, the inclination to engage in such bonding. There seems no reason not to describe that aspect as a 'unifying force' or a 'binding force'.

Aquinas, of course, was invoking the Dionysian formula in a discussion of the Trinity, and in that case we might think the position is less clear. Since the Father only has one Son to love, and hence only one bond to form, it is not obvious that we need to suggest a general tendency to form such bonds; indeed, perhaps that might seem impossible if there could not be more than one such object of love. Perhaps it is only where we can envisage a number of objects all similar in the relevant respect, for which we would feel a similar inclination to form attachments, that we can speak of a general love such as a love for cats, or for humankind. If I love my mother, on the other hand, that will not be a love that springs from my general love of mothers; on the contrary it will be a unique bond, and would involve no inclination to form similar bonds with others. Nevertheless we might still, I suggest, wish to distinguish between the cause of that bond, the love that I, like others, feel towards a mother figure even if we do not have a mother to love, and the bond itself that I form with the mother I am lucky enough to know. In the case of God the Father, his beloved Son is not transient or subject to loss, so that we cannot, as we can with human love, envisage an occasion when his love remains, but its object is removed and there can be no bond. But this should not lead us to suppose that we cannot make the conceptual distinction between God's love for his Son, and the bond or relationship that is initiated by that love or force for union.[28]

## 2. AUGUSTINE, *DE TRINITATE*, 8. 10. 14

Aquinas suggests that Augustine called love a union or bond (*unio vel nexus*) in *De Trinitate* 8.[29] If we examine the definition of love at *De Trinitate* 8. 10. 14 it appears that again St Thomas has brought some interpretation to bear upon the text.

Love, says Augustine, is 'a certain life linking two individuals or seeking to link them, namely the lover and the beloved'. No doubt Aquinas has picked up the term *copulans*, which I am translating 'linking' and taken it as the work of a bond. He explains Augustine's disjunction 'either linking or seeking to link' as referring to two sorts of union:[30] 'linking' (*copulans*) refers to the emotional bond or union between lover and beloved, which is essential to love; 'seeking to link' (*copulare appetens*) refers to the real union which love desires to bring about, the goal towards which it works. Thus on Aquinas's theory of love an emotional bond (at least) between two individuals is the *sine qua non* of love, and (apparently in virtue of being *sine qua non*) in fact constitutes love itself, while the real union of lover and beloved is another goal sought by love.

Such a reading is by no means impossible. But there is another way to make sense of what Augustine was saying. We might take the term 'link' in both 'linking' and 'seeking to link' as referring to the *same* type of relationship, the emotional bond. Thus there would be two kinds of love: a love that included an actual relationship with another individual, where the love in question 'links' the lover to the beloved, or alternatively a love that only seeks a relationship

[28] We might ask what would happen if we envisage the Father, *per impossibile*, at a time before the generation of the Son 'desiring to beget' because of his love. Then we should have to suggest that his love was logically prior to the Son and distinct from the bond that could be formed with the individual Son once begotten.

[29] *Summa Theol*, 1a 2ae, 26. 2 and cf. 28. 1. Neither *unio* nor *nexus* is actually used of love in the *De Trinitate*.

[30] *Summa Theol*, 1a 2ae, 28. 1.

with a beloved individual, in which case the love in question 'seeks to link' the lover with the beloved. Augustine would be assuming that love could exist even where there is no actual link between lover and the individual beloved but only the desire for such a link. Aquinas excluded this when he made an emotional bond a necessary condition of love.

If we return to our fondness for cats, it seems that we can explain it in Augustine's terms. The cat-lover may have a relationship or bond with some individual cat, or perhaps bonds with more than one individual cat; but she may also have a desire to meet and become acquainted with another cat of which she knows but who is as yet too shy to come near, or she may hope to meet some other cat, as yet unknown, one day, no matter whose or where. It seems true to say that her love links her to some cats and also seeks to link her to other cats, so that in this case we may make sense of Augustine's claim that love is something that 'links' or 'seeks to link' us to others. Augustine's disjunctive (*vel*) would allow that we still have love even when we have only the seeking a relationship and no actual tie with an individual. I still have a love of cats even when I have no cat of my own and am still unable to make the acquaintance of the cat I seek to meet. According to Aquinas, it would be impossible to explain that desire, without any actual bond, as a genuine case of love.

For Augustine, I am suggesting, it is possible to describe as love some kind of tendency that causes us to enter into loving relationships; for Aquinas that is impossible; what Aquinas has built in is a requirement that looks like mutuality, in that to have a genuine case of love there must be a bond with an individual. But this need not mean that there is mutual love. To love is to love somebody. It is conceivable that one might love somebody who did not respond or did not even know. Have we then got a link, in Augustine's sense? It seems so, since a link is some kind of relationship, and one plainly has a relationship, though not a mutual one, with the unresponsive beloved. But Aquinas has offered us a distinction between that link, one's emotional attachment to the beloved, on the one hand, and the stronger link of union which one seeks to achieve with the beloved, and which will presumably only be possible in a mutual relationship. So we can distinguish three degrees of attachment, first the desire to form a relationship with another, secondly the emotional attachment to another individual, thirdly the union which we seek to achieve with the beloved. According to Aquinas, love is the second of these, and hence is a bond, and it seeks to bring about the third, which is union. Alternatively we can take Augustine to mean that love is the cause of both the first and the second kinds of attachment, that it causes our desire to form relationships and hence also causes such bonds as we have with others. In this sense we may be loving, or have love, regardless of whether our desire to form a relationship with a beloved is fulfilled or not.

Augustine and Aquinas were dealing with relationships within the Trinity, and it remains unclear how we should decide whether the bonds or relationships are essential to love within the Trinity; but this much is clear already, that the kind of love which causes bonds of affection should be distinguished from the individual bonds that result. Aquinas, it seems, fails to allow that the inclination to form loving relationships is love; hence he takes over the phrases in Augustine and Dionysius that imply that love is a kind of force that brings about union and bonding, and infers that love is the bond that results from such a force, rather than the cause of that bond.

### 3. LOVE AND BONDS OF LOVE IN THE TRINITY

Whether or not Aquinas correctly represents Augustine and Dionysius the Areopagite, it remains to consider whether love is a helpful notion when applied to the Trinity. The classic claim is that the Holy Spirit is a 'bond of love', but if this formula depends upon the notion that love is a bond, we may be able to rescue some of Augustine's insights while questioning whether the notion of a 'bond' will do the work we need. Perhaps Augustine did not mean to say that the Spirit was a 'bond of love'.[31] If, instead, the Spirit can serve as the cause of relations, within the Trinity and beyond it, most of the difficulties can be eliminated. Hence it is worth recognizing that the grounds for taking Augustine to refer to a 'bond of love' lie exclusively in Aquinas's powerful but perhaps misleading interpretation.

---

[31] The definition at *De Trinitate* 8. 10. 14 is not specifically applied to the Spirit.

We can consider one issue now: how many Spirits must we posit? If, as Aquinas suggests, love is the bond uniting lover to beloved, such a bond will be formed if God the Father loves God the Son. But if God the Son loves God the Father there will be another bond between lover and beloved in which the Son is lover and the Father beloved. It is hard to see how we could define the two bonds as the same, given that love need not be mutual so that there is a relationship of love between the two as soon as one has an emotional tie with the other. Then it seems that a lover has a bond with the beloved; but if there are two distinct lovers each will have a bond with the other. To have two bonds between Father and Son would seem to leave us with two distinct Spirits, the two bonds that unite them.[32]

One way to avoid this would be to suppose that Aquinas does think in terms of a bond being a bond of mutual love, and that there is one single bond that links those whose love is reciprocal. In that case there will be only one bond in so far as the Father and Son each enters a mutual relation with the other and forms a single bond. For Aquinas there is no causal explanation of the love in the Trinity in the suggestion that the Spirit is bond of love; rather the mutual love of Father and Son jointly produces the bond that is the Spirit.

If, on the other hand, love is not the individual bond, but the cause of such bonds, there is nothing to prevent one love giving rise to a number of different bonds or relationships. Nevertheless, this too may seem problematic; while it is reasonable to suppose that a love that proceeds from the Father can cause bonds between the Father as lover and the object he loves, it is less clear that the Father's love can cause bonds in which the Son is lover. The Father's love will explain his inclination to involve himself in relations with those he loves. It will not explain why anyone else is inclined to love. This difficulty arises if we take as our model the love of ordinary individuals; but, as Augustine explained, the model for God's love of his Son must be not love between independent individuals but self-love.[33] If the persons of the Trinity are not substantially independent it may make sense to say that the love

---

[32] On this issue see Augustine, *De Trinitate*, 6. 5. 7 (*PL* 42. 927–8).

[33] We should not, of course, reject this analysis of God's love on the grounds that self-love is, in our experience, bad. Its badness derives from the fact that it is not love of God. Cf. *De doctrina Chr.* 1. 22. 21.

originated by the Father also directly explains the bonds of affection into which the Son enters as lover.

Two things govern Aquinas's interpretation of Augustine on love; one is his Aristotelian approach which is reluctant to see love hypostasized as external to the relationship between lover and beloved; the second is his dogmatic acceptance of the procession of the Spirit from the Son as well as from the Father, and the Spirit's place as logically third in the Trinity. Of course Augustine was also moved to make the Spirit derivative, at least from the Father and in some sense from the Son too,[34] but his open-mindedness about what precisely was meant by procession means that he is less inclined to allow procession to govern his analysis of love in the Trinity, but rather the reverse.

[34] *De Trinitate*, 15. 17. 29; *CMax. Ar.* II. 14. 1.

# CONCLUSION

The chapters in this book are in many respects independent studies united by the fact that they focus on questions about love. They do not cover all that might be said on the subject, nor do they tell a single story through the chronological span of seventeen centuries or more to which the various texts, that I have selected to discuss, belong. But they are not, in fact, independent studies, and if they do not tell a chronological story that is because I have deliberately tried to tell a story about love that can be told best by ignoring the questions of who learnt what from whom; it can be told best by asking instead who loved whom and for what, regardless of when, or how, or what they loved. Indeed, the question 'for what?' is the one I have tried to ask and then reject as the question that leads us astray. The studies in this book are all, in their various ways, directed to showing that 'for love' is sufficient answer to the question 'why?', and that the answer 'for love' in itself supplies a motive, so that seeking some further explanation or motive for love is inevitably a confusion.

There are two main claims that I have tried to defend. One is that the correct way to understand the ancient tradition concerning *eros* is to see love as inexplicable, in the way suggested by the motif of Eros the god of love with his arrows. In other words we are not to seek the reason why anyone loves another by looking for some quality that is admirable or desirable in the other, but rather to see love as occurring regardless of whether there are desirable features in the beloved. The second claim follows from this, namely that where desire or admiration of fine qualities occurs and is associated with love, it would be a mistake to suggest that the desire or appreciation was itself love, or was the motive that inspired us to love. Rather it makes more sense to see desire, and appreciation of what is good, occurring as a result of love, as the expression of the love that enables us to see such qualities as good and desirable.

What I want to suggest, then, is that love is an attitude that is acquired with no motive or purpose, but that it is an attitude that changes our whole outlook and response to the object or person whom we love. It is no accident, of course, that love often coincides with a sense of longing or of desire, or a yearning to realize what is best in the beloved and in ourselves. But it need not follow that love *is* the desire, nor that the desire could occur without the love that enables it to arise, and leads us to appreciate what is fine and to devote ourselves to the causes and the people that we love. The difference is, I am suggesting, that we would not see those objects as worthy of our devotion if we did not see them under the influence of love. In love they present themselves under an aspect that draws us to them and enables us to see the truth and what is worthy of our devotion.

It might be said that sometimes, in cases of infatuation, we see in unworthy objects qualities that are not there. Hence love, it might be said, if it changes our outlook, may change it to a self-deceiving attitude which responds with devotion to a set of imagined qualities. How then can we say that love is a motive that leads us to see what is fine and to aspire to the truth? Perhaps we should need to distinguish such infatuation from the kind of love that is concerned with truth. Indeed, self-deception seems to involve not a response to the other person as she really is, but an imaginative construction of a person to be the object of devotion. In that case we should not say that love had formed and moulded our response, since it would not be a response. Thus, while we might say that love explains why we respond to what is best, and why we can see it as attractive only with the eyes of love, we should not say that everything that we see as attractive or desirable is seen under the aspect provided by love. We may desire something when we deceive ourselves. We may devote ourselves selflessly to a cause that has no worthy purpose.

Nevertheless we may still say that when we do see the beloved, and respond, with the attitude that is genuinely loving, we shall expect that response to combine the selfless devotion to all that is good and truly worthy in the beloved with the longing to bring whatever falls short to the fullness of beauty, whether in ourselves or in the beloved. There is, then, an element of true appreciation of the individual, both for her good qualities and weaknesses, but seen always in the attitude that seeks to bring out what is most lovely. This explains the presence of both desire and aspiration to improvement in the tradition of *eros*.

What I have described in this account of love as a motive or explanation for our response to the beloved, is intended to reconstruct the Platonic account of love as aspiration in the *Symposium*. But it is also intended to be an account of how I would myself describe the role of love in altering our perceptions of individuals and of the world; and it is intended to be an account of how we might see love as essential in explaining the very possibility of a response to God or his response to us. Only with an attitude of love, I would suggest, could we respond to God, or he to us, as we really are; without *eros* we should not recognize him or see him as worthy of our devotion, just as he, without love, could not see in us anything to merit his attention.

# APPENDIX

# Anders Nygren and Gregory Vlastos

This book addresses questions about the nature and explanation of love, and how that love figures, when properly understood, in the relationship between individuals, and between the individual and god, in ancient thought and in Christian theology. Two writers have been particularly influential in building up a popular prejudice against Plato, and against the 'Platonic love' that is essential to true philosophy for Plato. One of these is Anders Nygren, whose claims about the difference between Platonic *eros* and Christian *agape* have become widely and uncritically accepted in much popular Christian teaching. It is impossible to challenge Nygren's thesis except by starting from a wholly different starting point, and building up a positive picture of love as a motive in Christian devotion. That picture is, in effect, what the whole of this book seeks to create. It does not do a piecemeal job of attacking Nygren's account of the story, but it tells a story of its own from the same ancient and early Christian texts as he was reading.

Gregory Vlastos has been influential with a different readership. His article called 'The individual as object of love in Plato'[1] reflects some of the same concerns as Nygren, and although Vlastos disagrees with Nygren's one-sided and inadequate understanding of what the Greeks could regard as love,[2] he does not actually break loose from the dichotomy that he inherits from Nygren. His objection to Nygren is that Nygren fails to see that Greek thinkers, other than Plato, were aware of a non-egoistic kind of affection that matches Nygren's notion of *agape*. Because Nygren fails to take account of other strands of Greek thought, Vlastos suggests, he is able to develop an attack on the Ancient Greek way of love as a whole. But for Vlastos some charges are still justified against *Plato*, though not simply for taking love to be an egoistic tendency, as Nygren's challenge had stressed, but also for his failure to value the individual, seeing in love only an admiration of the qualities that an individual instantiates, and not the individual as a person in her own right.

Despite my respect for Vlastos's approach and his insight into the importance of the individual beloved, I find myself in profound disagreement with his article; the studies I am presenting in this book are

---

[1] Gregory Vlastos, 'The Individual as Object of Love in Plato', in G. Vlastos *Platonic Studies* (2nd edn., Princeton, NJ, 1981), 1–34.

[2] Ibid. 6 and n. 13.

directed as much to a revision of his understanding of the ancient views on love as to a challenge to Nygren's supposed contrast between the classical and the Christian.

Vlastos's article has five main parts and two appendices. I have little to say on the central sections which suggest that Plato's neglect of the individual as a proper object of love is linked to his political communism, which requires a devotion to the general values of the state rather than the particular good of any individual within it. This is because I take the *Republic*, which is the text that Vlastos is discussing in these sections, as an analogy for the individual soul, as indeed Plato constructs it. Hence the doctrine of the *Republic* is one of valuing the concerns of the individual as a whole and enabling a person to develop the strengths of all parts of her soul in a well-ordered life. This is a work that argues for a holistic understanding of the individual, and revises the purely intellectual care for the soul advocated, apparently, in dialogues such as the *Phaedo*, where the appetites are identified with the body and to be repressed altogether. But while the *Republic* has much to say about our internal relations with our own selves, it has nothing to say about our relations with other individuals. Of course the analogy with the state suggests an analysis of how a city could, ideally, promote its collective good. But that is not to say that such a state would be desirable, nor that such collective good *should* override the good of an individual. It merely serves to illustrate how, if you treat something that is a collection of parts as a unity with unified interests and purposes, as of course a person might be, and a state *qua* state tries to be, then the interests of the parts, in so far as they conflict with the interests of the whole, will need to be modified or denied. Otherwise the well-being of the whole person, or the state as a whole, may suffer. Thus Plato's analogy points out the importance of seeing the individual as a whole person, with appetites and emotions as well as intellect, and so far from denying a concern for individuals, it rather presupposes just such a concern. Of course this cannot prevent there being a conflict, as there still must be today, between the interests of individuals in a state and the interests of a state viewed as a collective unity.

The first part of Vlastos's article uses Aristotle's account of *philia* to show that some Greeks, apart from Plato, were well aware of affection of a generous sort, directed to persons as persons. He takes Aristotle's talk of *philein* to be about 'loving'. Indeed, he objects to the traditional translation 'friendship' as being too weak, and failing to capture the depth of affection implied in Aristotle's notion of *philia*. Vlastos's main ground for this contention is that Aristotle includes among his examples of *philia* the relationship between mother and child.[3] Vlastos takes this to be 'maternal affection'; but Aristotle is referring to the way in which mothers behave,

---

[3] Ibid. 3–4 and n. 3. Cf. Aristotle, *NE* 1166a2–6.

trying to do the best for their children and caring for their well-being. Whereas Vlastos takes this example to indicate that Aristotle's discussion must be about *affection*, I have argued the reverse in Chapter 6 above. The mother–child relation is just one of a number of examples that Aristotle takes, some of which seem to involve affection. But it seems clear that Aristotle's interest is in the way we work for another person's interests, sometimes regardless of our own. That this may be connected with affection, that affection may account for why we do it in some circumstances is, of course, undeniable. I do not want to suggest that the mother does not act so out of affection for her child, nor that Aristotle was unaware of that factor, but I do want to suggest that that was not his concern or interest in mentioning the mother as an example.

Aristotle's discussion is not *about* affection, though it does mention it occasionally. Does this alter Vlastos's point? Of course it is correct to suggest that Aristotle may have been aware of self-denying affection and love, and hence that we can say that the Greeks knew of such a thing. But it does not show that Aristotle discussed it, or thought it tremendously significant. I have suggested that the partners engaged in Aristotle's perfect form of friendship also may feel some affection and love for each other. But there too the fact that they love each other is not Aristotle's primary concern. So Vlastos is, of course, right, that Aristotle and others recognized the possibility of such love.

That is, I believe, true of Plato too. Vlastos wishes to suggest that Plato had no place for such affection, while Aristotle recognized affection and gave it an important place in ethics. My disagreement over Plato arises from the reading of the *Lysis*, on which I am at odds with Vlastos, but not because I disagree with him over the question of whether it 'is a vehicle of Platonic doctrine' in the sense in which he asks that question.[4] He answers that question 'no' on the grounds that the *Lysis* does not concern itself with the Theory of Forms and middle-period Platonic ontology. I share the view that there is no reason to read the Forms, or ontological questions of any sort, into the *Lysis*. What I disagree with is the manner in which one should read an aporetic dialogue. If Socrates gets an interlocutor to tie himself in knots and admit that, in the end, he does not know what he means, how far can we take Socrates' criticisms to convey what Plato holds to be true doctrine? Socrates persuades his companions to change their views by showing that there is a contradiction between two views that they previously took themselves to hold. If Socrates shows Hippothales that he holds *both* that his parents love him, *and* that love is motivated by self-interest, a motive which is not available in the case of parental love, then Hippothales must abandon one or both of these claims. It does not follow

---

[4] 'Is the *Lysis* a Vehicle of Platonic Doctrine', Appendix 1 to 'The Individual as Object of Love in Plato', in Vlastos, *Platonic Studies*, 35–7.

that Socrates held either claim to be true, since he may show the conflict between them without assenting to either. Nor is it apparent which of the two theses Hippothales must abandon. It is as likely, or more likely, that Socrates is encouraging him to revise his account of love rather than reject the claim that his parents love him. And even if *Socrates* suggests that one of those views is what he himself holds, it need not follow that *Plato* allows us to go away with that view still intact by the end of the dialogue. On my reading of the *Lysis*, which I have outlined in Chapter 3, the point of the dialogue is not, as Vlastos suggests, to put forward an analysis of love as motivated by desire, but rather to show that such an analysis is impossible and leads to an impasse. The regress that shows that no individual could be the ultimate object of our love is, on this analysis, part of the *reductio ad absurdum*, which shows that we cannot actually find an object to love, so long as we adhere to an analysis of love as desire for what is good. Hence, on my interpretation, Plato is arguing for the same kind of analysis as I am suggesting, that is that it is mistaken to see love as motivated by desire: rather it is the motive that inspires us to see individuals as beautiful and to care about them as objects of our devotion. The absurd conclusions of the *Lysis* follow precisely because Socrates was allowing his interlocutor to suppose that there must be a motive, whether self-interested or otherwise, for us to love any object. The point of the dialogue is not to accept that premiss but to show that it will not do.

This is the reason why I do not share Vlastos's view that Plato's discussions of love allow no place for affection for an individual. But even supposing that Vlastos were right that the *Lysis* rejects the standard examples of affection, it still follows that Plato knew of such examples and was aware that we should normally describe such relationships as love. It is because parental love seems an obvious example that it occurs in the *Lysis* as a difficulty for Hippothales. It follows that neither Aristotle nor Plato ignores such affection; if I am right about Aristotle he merely notices it in passing, and does not make it important in his ethics. I see no reason to think that Aristotle is more sympathetic to the kind of love that has regard to the individual beloved as she really is than Plato is. On the contrary I think that the correct reading of the *Lysis* shows that Plato is more open to this understanding of love than Aristotle appears to be.

In any case, however, it seems to me mistaken to interpret Plato as adhering to a view of love in which it is susceptible to explanation, in terms of self-interested motives. I have tried to show in my chapters on Plato how the suggestion that we appreciate the goodness and beauty of the beloved, which clearly is there in Plato, can be seen as a consequence of our falling in love with the individual, and that it is in virtue of our seeing the beloved with the eyes of the lover that we see her as beautiful and an object of devotion. Thus it is not that desire for the qualities she reveals explains our love, but that our love explains our appreciation of what we see in the individual. We learn to value beauty and truth by learning to love the individual. Without love, for Plato, we should never aspire to wisdom. It cannot be that the desire comes first, nor will the love of the individual ever be redundant. It is what explains our whole commitment to goodness and the endeavour for perfection.

Vlastos concludes with an appendix on sex in Platonic love. I have not been concerned in this book with sexuality or the physical aspects of any relationship. Many others have written on the subject of sexual relations in the ancient world, and I have nothing to add on that subject.

# BIBLIOGRAPHY

ALEXANDER, NEIL, *The Epistles of John* (London, 1962).

ALLEN, R. E. 'A Note on the Elenchus of Agathon: *Symposium* 199c–201c', *The Monist*, 50 (1966), 460–3.

ANNAS, JULIA, 'Plato and Aristotle on Friendship and Altruism', *Mind*, 86 (1977), 532–54.

ARMSTRONG, A. H. 'Platonic Eros and Christian Agape', *Downside Review*, 79 (1960), 105–121.

—— (ed.), *Classical Mediterranean Spirituality* (London, 1986).

BARKER, PETER, and GOLDSTEIN, BERNARD R., 'The Rôle of Comets in the Copernican Revolution', *Studies in History and Philosophy of Science*, 19 (1988), 299–319.

BARNES, J., SCHOFIELD, M., and SORABJI, R., *Articles on Aristotle*, vol. 3. (London, 1979).

BARR, JAMES, *Holy Scripture: Canon, Authority, Criticism* (Oxford, 1983).

—— 'Words for Love in Biblical Greek', in L. D. Hurst and N. T. Wright (eds.), *The Glory of Christ in the New Testament* (Oxford, 1987), 3–18.

BEIERWALTES, WERNER, 'The Love of Beauty and the Love of God', in A. H. Armstrong (ed.), *Classical Mediterranean Spirituality* (London, 1986), 293–313.

BELL H. I., '*Philanthropia* in the Papyri of the Roman Period', *Coll. Latomus*, 2 (Brussels, 1949), 31–7.

BERNARD, C. A., SJ, 'La Doctrine mystique de Denys l'Areopagite', *Gregorianum*, 68 (1987), 523–66.

BLUMENTHAL, H. J., and MARKUS, R. A. (eds.) *Neoplatonism and Early Christian Thought: essays in honour of A. H. Armstrong* (London, 1981).

BOLOTIN, DAVID, *Plato's Dialogue on Friendship* (Ithaca, NY and London, 1979).

BOMAN, T. G., *Hebrew Thought compared with Greek*, translation by J. L. Moreau of *Das hebräische Denken im vergleich mit dem Griechischen*, 1952 (London, 1960).

BONNER, GERALD, 'Augustine's Attitude to Women and Amicitia', in Cornelius Mayer and Karl Heinz Chelius (eds.), *Homo Spiritalis, Cassiciacum*, 38 (Würzburg Augustinus-Verlag, 1987), 259–75.

BOWDEN, J., *Jesus: The Unanswered Questions* (London 1988).

BROWN, RAYMOND E., *The Epistles of St John*, The Anchor Bible (New York, 1982).

BRÜMMER, VINCENT *The Model of Love* (Cambridge, 1993).

BURNABY, JOHN, *Amor Dei* (London, 1938).

BURY, R. G. (ed.), *The Symposium* (1909; 2nd edn. Cambridge, 1932).

CLARK, S. R. L., *From Athens to Jerusalem: The Love of wisdom and the Love of God* (Oxford, 1984).

—— *The Mysteries of Religion* (Oxford, 1986).

COHEN, DAVID, 'Law, Society and Homosexuality in Classical Athens', *Past and Present*, 117 (1987), 3–21.

COOPER, JOHN M., 'Aristotle on Friendship', in A. E. Rorty (ed.), *Essays on Aristotle's Ethics* (Berkeley, Calif., 1980), 301–40.

CROMBIE, I. M., *An Examination of Plato's Doctrines*, vols. 1 and 2 (London, 1962–3).

CROUSE, ROBERT D., 'In aenigmate Trinitas', *Dionysius*, 11 (1987) 53–62.

CROUZEL, HENRI, 'Origène et Plotin' in Lothar Lies (ed.), *Origeniana Quarta* (Innsbruck 1987), 430–5.

—— *Origen*, English translation by A. S. Warrall (Edinburgh, 1989).

DALY, L. J., 'Themistius' Concept of *Philanthropia*', *Byzantion*, 45 (1975), 22–40.

DALY, R. (ed.), *Origeniana Quinta* (Louvain, 1992).

D'ARCY, M. C., *The Mind and Heart of Love* (London, 1945; 2nd edn. London, 1954).

DE RIVERA, J. *A Structural Theory of the Emotions*, Psychological Issues, X, no. 4, monograph 40 (New York, 1977).

DE ROUGEMONT, D., *Passion and Society*, trans. M. Belgian (London, 1962).

DEWAR, L., *The Holy Spirit and Modern Thought* (London, 1959).

DILLON, J., '*Ennead* III. 5: Plotinus' Exegesis of the *Symposium* Myth', *ΑΓΩΝ* 3 (1969), 24–44.

—— 'A Platonist Ars Amatoria', forthcoming in *Classical Quarterly*.

DODD, C. H., *The Bible and the Greeks* (London, 1935).

—— *The Johannine Epistles*, Moffatt New Testament Commentary (London, 1946).

DODDS, MICHAEL J., OP, *The Unchanging God of Love*, Studia Fribourgensia (Fribourg, 1986).

DOIGNON, J., 'Saint Augustin et sa culture philosophique face au problème du bonheur', *Freiburger Zeitschrift für Philosophie und Théologie*, 34 (1987), 339–59.

DOVER, K. J., *Greek Homosexuality* (London, 1978).

—— Plato: *Symposium* (Cambridge, 1980).

DOWNEY, G., '*Philanthropia* in Religion and Statecraft in the Fourth Century after Christ', *Historia*, 4 (1955), 199–208.

DÜRING, I., and OWEN, G. E. L. (eds.), *Aristotle and Plato in the Mid Fourth Century* (Göteborg, 1960).

EDWARDS, M., 'Ammonius, Teacher of Origen', *Journal of Ecclesiastical History*, 44 (1993), 169–81.

FERRARI, G. R. F., *Listening to the Cicadas: A Study of Plato's Phaedrus* (Cambridge, 1987).

FESTUGIÈRE, A. J. 'Les Inscriptions d'Asoka et l'idéal du roi hellénistique', *Récherches de science réligieuse*, 39 (1951), 31–46.

FOUCAULT, MICHEL, *The Use of Pleasure, vol. 2 of The History of Sexuality*, trans. Robert Hurley (Harmondsworth, 1987).

—— *The Care of the Self, vol. 3 of The History of Sexuality*, trans. Robert Hurley (Harmondsworth, 1990).

FURNISH, V. P. *The Love Command in the New Testament* (London 1973).

GOULD, J., *Platonic Love* (London, 1963).

HALPERIN, DAVID M., 'Plato and Erotic Reciprocity', *Classical Antiquity*, 5 (1986), 60–80.

—— *One Hundred Years of Homosexuality and Other Essays on Greek Love* (New York, 1990).

——, WINKLER, JOHN J., and ZEITLIN, FROMA I. (eds.), *Before Sexuality: The Construction of Erotic Experience in the Ancient Greek World* (Princeton, NJ 1989).

HANFLING, OSWALD, 'Loving My Neighbour, Loving Myself', *Philosophy*, 68 (1993), 145–57.

HANSON, R. P. C., 'The Filioque Clause', in *Studies in Christian Antiquity* (Edinburgh, 1985), 279–97.

—— *Studies in Christian Antiquity* (Edinburgh, 1985).

—— (ed.), *Origeniana Tertia* (Rome, 1985).

HAZO, R. G., *The Idea of Love* (New York, 1967).

HERON, A. I. C., *The Holy Spirit* (London, 1983).

HODGSON, L., *The Doctrine of the Trinity* (London, 1943).

HONDERICH, Ted (ed.), *Philosophy through its Past* (Harmondsworth, 1984).

HUNGER, H., 'φιλανθρωπία. Eine griechische Wortprägung auf ihrem Wege von Aischylos zu Theodorus Metochites', Anzeiger der (K) Akademie der Wissenschaften in Wien (1963) 100, repr. in H. Hunger, *Byzantinische Grundlagungforschung* (London, 1973), ch. 13.

—— *Byzantinische Grundlagungforschung*, Variorum Reprints (London, 1973).

HURST, L. D., and WRIGHT, N. T. (eds.), *The Glory of Christ in the New Testament* (Oxford, 1987).

JOLY, R., *Le Vocabulaire chrétien de l'amour: est-il original?* (Brussels, 1968).

KABIERSCH, J., *Untersuchungen zum Begriff der Philanthropie bei dem Kaiser Julian* (Wiesbaden, 1960).

KEGLEY, CHARLES W., (ed.), *The Philosophy and Theology of Anders Nygren* (Illinois, 1970).

KOSMAN, A., 'Platonic Love', in W. H. Werkmeister (ed.), *Facets of Plato's Philosophy* (Amsterdam, 1976), 53–69.

KRAUT, RICHARD, *Aristotle on the Human Good* (Princeton, NJ 1989).

LEVI, A., 'Sulla demonologia Platonica', *Athenaeum*, 24 (1946), 119–28.

LEWIS, C. S., *The Four Loves* (London, 1960).

LIES, LOTHAR (ed.), *Origeniana Quarta* (Innsbruck, 1987).

LIVINGSTONE, E. (ed.), *Studia Patristica*, Proceedings of the Tenth International Conference on Patristic Studies, vol. XXII (Louvain, 1990).

LLOYD, A. C., 'The Principle that the Cause is Greater than its Effect', *Phronesis*, 21 (1976), 146–56.

LLOYD, G. E. R., *Polarity and Analogy* (Cambridge, 1966).

LONG, A. A., and SEDLEY, D. N., *The Hellenistic Philosophers*, vol. 1 and 2 (Cambridge, 1987).

LORENZ, S., 'De Progressu notionis φιλανθρωπίας' (diss., Leipzig, 1914).

LOVELOCK, J. E., *Gaia: A New Look at Life on Earth* (Oxford, 1979; repr. 1987).

LOWE, SUSAN, 'No Love for God', *Philosophy*, 60 (1985), 263.

MCCABE, HERBERT, *Law, Love and Language* (1968; 2nd edn. London, 1979).

MACKENZIE, M. M., 'Impasse and Explanation: From the *Lysis* to the *Phaedo*', *Archiv für Geschichte der Philosophie*, 70 (1988), 15–45.

MACKINNON, DONALD, 'Evil and the Vulnerability of God', *Philosophy*, 62 (1987), 102.

MAKIN, STEPHEN, 'An Ancient Principle about Causation', *Proceedings of the Aristotelian Society*, 91 (1990–1), 135–52.

MARCEL, R., *Marsile Ficin: Commentaire sur le Banquet de Platon* (Paris, 1956).

MARKUS, R. A., 'The Dialectic of Eros in Plato's *Symposium*', *Downside Review*, 73 (1954–5) 219–30.

MARTIN, H. I., 'The Concept of *Philanthropia* in Plutarch's Lives', *American Journal of Philology*, 82 (1961), 164–75.

MILES, MARGARET R., *The Image and Practice of Holiness* (London, 1989).

MOLTMANN, J., *The Crucified God*, 2nd edn., English translation, by R. A. Wilson and John Bowden, of *Der gekreuzigte Gott* (London, 1974).

MOORE, A. W., *The Infinite* (London, 1990).

MORA, FREYA, 'Thank God for Evil', *Philosophy*, 58 (1983), 399–41.

NEMESHEGYI, PETER, *La Paternité de dieu chez Origène* (Paris, 1960).

NUSSBAUM, MARTHA, *The Fragility of Goodness: Luck and Ethics in Greek Tragedy and Philosophy* (Cambridge, 1986).

NYGREN, ANDERS, *Agape and Eros*, English translation by Philip S. Watson of *Den kristna kärlekstanken*, 1930, (Chicago, 1953).

O'CONNELL, ROBERT J., SJ, '*Eros* and *Philia* in Plato's Moral Cosmos', in H. J. Blumenthal and R. A. Markus (eds.), *Neoplatonism and Early Christian Thought* (London, 1981).

OSBORNE, CATHERINE, 'Topography in the *Timaeus*', *Proceedings of the Cambridge Philological Society*, 34 (1988), 104–14.

—— 'The *nexus amoris* in Augustine's Trinity', in E. Livingstone (ed.), *Studia Patristica*, Proceedings of the Tenth International Conference on Patristic Studies, vol. XXII (Louvain, 1990) 309–14.

—— '*Nexus amoris* en el *De Trinitate*', *Augustinus*, 36 (1991), 205–12 (Spanish translation by José Oroz of the preceding article).

—— 'Neoplatonism and the Love of God in Origen', in R. Daly (ed.), *Origeniana Quinta* (Louvain, 1992), 270–83.

OUTKA, GENE, *Agape: An Ethical Analysis* (New Haven, Conn., 1976).

OWEN, G. E. L., 'Logic and Metaphysics in Some Earlier Works of Aristotle', in I. Düring and G. E. L. Owen (eds.), *Aristotle and Plato in the Mid Fourth Century* (Göteborg, 1960), 163–90. Reprinted in J. Barnes, M. Schofield, R. Sorabji (eds.), *Articles on Aristotle*, vol. 3 (London, 1979), 13–32, and in G. E. L. Owen, *Logic, Science and Dialectic* (London, 1986), 180–99.

—— *Logic, Science and Dialectic* (London, 1986).

PIETRAS, H., *L'amore in Origene* (Rome, 1988).

PITTENGER, NORMAN, *The Lure of Divine Love* (New York and Edinburgh, 1979).

PRICE, A. W., *Love and Friendship in Plato and Aristotle* (Oxford, 1989).

RAWLINSON, A. E. J. (ed.), *Essays on the Trinity and the Incarnation* (London, 1928).

RIST, J. M., *Eros and Psyche: Studies in Plato, Plotinus and Origen*, Phoenix supplementary vol. 6 (Toronto, 1964).

—— 'Eros and Agape in Pseudo-Dionysius', *Vigiliae Christianae*, 20 (1966), 235–43.

—— 'Some Interpretations of Agape and Eros', in Charles W. Kegley (ed.), *The Philosophy and Theology of Anders Nygren* (Illinois, 1970). Reprinted in J. M. Rist, *Platonism and its Christian Heritage* (London, 1985).

—— *Platonism and its Christian Heritage*, Variorum reprints (London, 1985).

ROBIN, L. *La théorie platonicienne de l'amour* (1933; 2nd edn. Paris, 1964).

RORTY, A. E. (ed.), *Essays on Aristotle's Ethics* (Berkeley, Calif., 1980).

ROSEN, STANLEY, *Plato's Symposium* (New Haven, Conn., 1968).

ROSS, W. D., *Aristotle's Metaphysics* (a revised text and commentary), 2 vols. (Oxford, 1924).

SANDERS, E. P., *Paul and Palestinian Judaism* (London, 1977).

SANTAS, GERASIMOS, *Plato and Freud: Two Theories of Love* (Oxford, 1988).

SCHIAVONE, MICHELE, *Neoplatonismo e cristianesimo nello Pseudo-Dionigi* (Milan, 1963).

SCOTT, ALAN, *Origen and the Life of the Stars* (Oxford, 1991).

SOBEL, ALAN, 'Love is not Beautiful: *Symposium* 200e–201c', *Apeiron*, 19 (1985), 43–52.

SORABJI, R., *Time, Creation and the Continuum* (London, 1983).

—— *Matter, Space and Motion* (London, 1988).

—— (ed.)., *Philoponus and the Rejection of Aristotelian Science* (London, 1987).

—— (ed.) *Aristotle Transformed* (London, 1990).

SPICQ, C., OP, *Agapè, prolegomènes à une étude de théologie néo-testamentaire* (Louvain 1955).

—— 'La Philanthropie hellénistique, vertu divine et royale', *Studia Theologica*, 12 (1958), 169–91.

—— *Agapè dans le nouveau testament*, 3 vols. (Paris, 1958–9).

TARELLI, C. C., ''ΑΓΑΠΗ' *Journal of Theological Studies*, NS 1 (1950), 64–7.

THOMAS AQUINAS, *In librum de divinis nominibus expositio*, ed. Ceslai Pera, OP (Turin and Rome, 1950).

TILLICH, PAUL JOHANNES O., *Love, Power and Justice* (London, 1954).

TRIGG, JOSEPH WILSON, *Origen* (Atlanta, 1983, and London, 1985).

TROMP DE RUITER, S., 'De vocis quae est φιλανθρωπία significatione atque usu', *Mnemosyne*, 59 (1932), 271–306.

VAN DE VATE, D., *Romantic Love* (University Park, Pa., 1981).

VLASTOS, GREGORY, *Platonic Studies* (1973; 2nd edn. Princeton, NJ, 1981).

—— 'The Individual as Object of Love in Plato', in G. Vlastos, *Platonic Studies* (2nd edn., Princeton, NJ, 1981), 1–34; repr. in Ted Honderich (ed.), *Philosophy through its Past* (Harmondsworth, 1984).

—— 'Is the *Lysis* a Vehicle of Platonic Doctrine?' (Appendix 1 to 'The Individual as Object of Love in Plato'), in G. Vlastos, *Platonic Studies* (2nd edn.,Princeton,NJ, 1981), 35–7.

WARDY, R., *The Chain of Change* (Cambridge, 1990).

WATSON, FRANCIS, *Paul, Judaism and the Gentiles* (Cambridge, 1986).

WERKMEISTER, W. H. (ed.), *Facets of Plato's Philosophy* (Amsterdam, 1976).

WEST, S., 'A Further Note on ΑΓΑΠΗ in P. Oxy. 1380', *Journal of Theological Studies*, 20 (1969), 228–30.

WHITING, JENNIFER E., 'Impersonal Friends', *The Monist*, 74 (1991), 3–29.

WILLIAMS, BERNARD, *Descartes: The Project of Pure Enquiry* (London, 1978).

WILLIAMS, ROWAN, 'Origen on the Soul of Jesus' in R. P. C. Hanson (ed.), *Origeniana Tertia* (Rome, 1985), 131–7.

WINKLER, JOHN J., *The Constraints of Desire: The Anthropology of Sex and Gender in Ancient Greece* (New York, 1990).

WITTGENSTEIN, L., *Philosophical Grammar*, ed. Rush Rhees, trans. A. Kenny (Oxford, 1974).

——*Lectures on the Foundations of Mathematics*, from the notes of R. G. Bosanquet, Norman Malcolm, Rush Rhees, and Yorick Smythies, ed. Cora Diamond (Hassocks, 1976; 2nd edn., Chicago, 1989).

ZITNIK, M., 'Θεὸς φιλάνθρωπος bei Johannes Chrysostomos', *Orientalia Christiana Periodica*, 41 (1975) 76–118.

# INDEX LOCORUM

# INDEX